POLITICS AND PRODUCTION IN THE EARLY NINETEENTH CENTURY

CLIVE BEHAGG

Routledge
Taylor & Francis Group
LONDON AND NEW YORK

First published in 1990 by Routledge

This edition first published in 2026
by Routledge
4 Park Square, Milton Park, Abingdon, Oxon OX14 4RN

and by Routledge
605 Third Avenue, New York, NY 10158

Routledge is an imprint of the Taylor & Francis Group, an informa business

British Library Cataloguing in Publication Data
A catalogue record for this book is available from the British Library

ISBN: 978-1-032-97576-4 (Set)
ISBN: 978-1-041-13110-6 (Volume 24) (hbk)
ISBN: 978-1-041-13118-2 (Volume 24) (pbk)
ISBN: 978-1-003-66811-4 (Volume 24) (ebk)

DOI: 10.4324/9781003668114

Publisher's Note
The publisher has gone to great lengths to ensure the quality of this reprint but points out that some imperfections in the original copies may be apparent.

Disclaimer
The publisher has made every effort to trace copyright holders and would welcome correspondence from those they have been unable to trace.

POLITICS AND PRODUCTION IN THE EARLY NINETEENTH CENTURY

CLIVE BEHAGG

ROUTLEDGE
LONDON AND NEW YORK

First published 1990
by Routledge
11 New Fetter Lane, London EC4P 4EE

Simultaneously published in the USA and Canada
by Routledge
a division of Routledge, Chapman and Hall, Inc.
29 West 35th Street, New York, NY 10001

Printed in Great Britain by
TJ Press (Padstow) Ltd, Padstow, Cornwall

British Library Cataloguing in Publication Data

Behagg, Clive
Politics and production in the early nineteenth century.
1. Great Britain. Small firms history. Social aspects
I. Title
306.36
ISBN 0-415-01916-8

Library of Congress Cataloging-in-Publication Data

Behagg, Clive
Politics and production in the early nineteenth century / Clive Behagg
p. cm.
Includes index.
ISBN 0-415-01916-8
1. Small business - Great Britain - Birmingham - History - 19th century. 2. Industrial relations - Great Britain - Birmingham - History - 19th century. 3. Artisans - Great Britain - Birmingham - Political activity - History - 19th century. 4. Representative government and representation - Great Britain - Birmingham - History - 19th century. I. Title.
HD2346.G72B574 1989
338.6'42'0942496090034 - dc20 89-34005

TO FREDA AND FREDERICK BEHAGG

Contents

Acknowledgements

This book is an extensively revised version of a Ph.D. thesis accepted by the University of Birmingham in 1982; its writing has taken a number of years and there are many people to thank. As my postgraduate supervisor, Dorothy Thompson provided constant encouragement and careful advice, for which I owe a special debt of gratitude. A special thanks also goes to my friend and colleague Andrew Foster, who undertook to read and comment on the thesis as it neared its final draft. Richard Price encouraged me to publish and acted as editor throughout the process of revision. His scholarly comments on all aspects of the book in draft were enormously helpful. I also benefited greatly from discussions with Geoffrey Crossick, who read and commented on the thesis. He also provided the opportunity to present my findings to the European Round Table on the Petite Bourgeoisie at the Universities of Bremen and Paris-Nanterre in 1980 and 1984. In working through the ideas in the first three chapters Patrick Joyce was also very helpful. A number of institutions were kind enough to provide a forum for the discussion of my work via seminars or guest lecture formats; I must therefore thank colleagues at the Universities of Birmingham, Warwick, Sussex, and Essex, Portsmouth Polytechnic, Middlesex Polytechnic, History Workshop, and the Society for the Study of Labour History, particularly Hugh Macleod, Adrian Randall, Bob Bushaway, Mick Reed, and John Rule. I mention these individuals only to express my gratitude for their time and the energy of their response to those parts of my work that they have seen. The errors are mine alone.

Research took me to twenty libraries and record offices and I am indebted to the librarians, archivists, and their staff, whose assistance was so important in establishing an empirical base for this study. Priscilla Williams made her Attwood collection available, and the Computer Centre at Birmingham University helped a good deal in the process of evaluating the probate material. The library at the West Sussex Institute of Higher Education provided excellent support throughout and the Institute's Research Committee provided an important grant of funds. Angela Bell typed the manuscript with considerable quantities of skill and good humour.

Final thanks go to Christine Behagg for her love and support during the writing. I have been threatening to publish this book for a long time. Its completion was delayed for three reasons and their names are Molly, Dylan, and Daisy. Their appearance between 1984 and 1987 created the marvellous domestic chaos that lies behind this book and any sense of perspective that now informs its author.

Introduction

This book charts the emergence of two radical political ideals from the experience of the workplace in the early nineteenth century. One of these, forged in a working-class image, contained within it a concept of participatory democracy, which drew strength from the attempts of the workforce to control its changing working environment, and found its fullest expression in the unsuccessful Chartist movement. The other, a middle-class concept of representation, formed part of a far broader rhetoric of justification offered by those who were actively involved in reorganizing production, and who were concerned to extend their authority into other spheres.

The locational focus is the town of Birmingham, but the book's claim to a wider significance is derived from its thematic focus on the profound changes in the socio-economic position of the small workshop in the early stages of industrialization. Birmingham was, thus, partly chosen because by the middle of the nineteenth century it retained a predominance of the smaller unit of production within its industrial structure. In this respect it was by no means unique. As long ago as 1932 Sir John Clapham pointed out that by the mid-nineteenth century the small workshop operating without benefit of steam mechanization was a more typical form of production than the factory. The latter, however, as the most dramatic manifestation of the industrializing process, has absorbed a good deal of the attention of subsequent social and economic historians and it has become necessary in recent years for us to be reminded of Clapham's point.[1]

The continuing prevalence of the smaller unit of production related, in some instances, to the retardation of a spreading factory system. The tragic case of the handloom weavers who fought replacement by the factory by lowering their own standard of life to truly painful levels, is well known. But there was nothing transitional, or even marginal, about the small producer *per se*. The workshop was to play a vital and continuing function as industrial capitalism advanced. It was, however, this function that was changing as the small firm moved from a central role in the productive process to one that was subsidiary to, and in support of, larger units of production within the broader economy. Thus, what was painful to workshop owners and their workforce in this period was not so much the problem of eclipse and absorption by the factory, but rather their transformation.[2]

It is the response evoked within this sector that is really of interest here, as an apparently traditional mode of economic organization confronted newer forms of production. Historians of European social movements have long acknowledged the role of the artisanal sector in the emergence of radical movements.[3] For England this work has found a powerful resonance particularly in the writing of Edward Thompson, Iorwerth Prothero, and John Rule.[4] In fact, taking the English, French, and German cases together there is a wide-ranging body of research work demonstrating the militancy of workers in the small-scale sector of the economy during the early stages of industrialization.[5]

Nevertheless, the temptation for English historians to relate the workers' sense of class to the size of the unit of production has proved irresistible. Whether the object of study be the London tailors, the Lancashire handloom weavers, the Northampton shoemakers, the Sheffield cutlers, the Birmingham metal-workers, or even the Oldham spinners, those who would attempt to argue that the 1830s and 1840s witnessed the emergence of an unprecedented class awareness have faced the counter-claim that in each of these areas the persistence of the small firm served to fragment and distort the workers' response to industrial capitalism.[6]

Thus the artisan has been seen, in one model, as the custodian of a growing working-class consciousness, reflecting an awareness of capitalism as both system and process, and responding to a hostile establishment through a continuum of agitation within which workplace militancy and radical politics were critical elements. In this context, it is argued, traditional hierarchies between workers in the workplace did not disappear but rather became less important than the awareness of a more fundamental social division.[7] Paradoxically, the same burgeoning of workplace militancy during the 1830s and 1840s, upon which much of this argument rests, has been cited precisely to cast doubt upon the existence of any substantial working-class consciousness in this period. This analysis has been ruthlessly compartmentalist, making a firm distinction between industrial agitation against the employer and 'political' agitation against the state.[8] The argument is that workplace protest in the early stages of industrialization was strongly sectional in its nature, reinforcing both the separation of the skilled and unskilled within the workforce and also the divisions between different occupational groups within the skilled sector itself.[9] This point has, at least implicitly, been emphasized by a wealth of trade union historiography, which, by dint of a concern to draw out strands of activity in certain trades has tended to highlight the distance between them.[10] Sectional policies pursued by early unions, it is further argued, served to insulate a large proportion of artisans from mass-based political movements.[11] In some ways the lynchpin of this analysis is the role of the small-scale employer of labour. Many employers, in these industries, appear to have accepted and even participated in early union activity.[12] Thus, the attempt by Prothero to examine the class-conscious outlook and political involvement of the London artisans during the Chartist period has been criticized by Musson on the grounds that the author ignores 'the number and importance of the ''upper'' trades both old and new, who were inclined to class collaboration', and also that he 'minimises the sectional characteristics of the lower trades'.[13]

Such a view of workplace protest during early industrialization tacitly and erroneously assumes the perpetuation of 'pre-industrial' modes in an 'industrial' context. It has, however, become a commonplace of trade union history since the Webbs' 'classic' statement on work relations in the workshop:

> Their occasional disputes with their employers resembled rather family differences than conflicts between social classes. They exhibit more tendency to 'stand in' with their masters against the community or to back them against rivals and interlopers than to join their fellow workers in an attack on the capitalist class. In short we have industrial society still divided vertically

trade by trade, instead of horizontally between employers and wage earners.[14]

In this idealized view of the eighteenth-century workplace the articulation of class consciousness was circumscribed by a traditional concept of the 'trade', accepted by both masters and men, within which each side fulfilled recognized obligations. Such an emphasis on the continuous development of workplace organizations, from the previous century, it is argued here, is helpful only inasmuch as it draws our attention firmly to the traditions of mutuality and the context of custom through which the early nineteenth-century workforce sought justification for their actions.[15] The work of W.H. Sewell on the workplace in France, for example, demonstrates convincingly that language, tradition, and even organization, transposed from one context to another, can assume different meanings and functions within the relevance of the new context.[16] The continuing presence of the small unit of production is, of course, a crucial link between a fully industrialized, factory-centred, economy and the system of decentralized production which preceded it. But the workplace of the 1830s and the 1840s was very different from that of the 1750s or even the 1790s. In this new context 'custom' and 'tradition' became flexible terms. They could, of course, be used to describe or encode agreements or methods of work that were of actual longevity.[17] But the crucial role of such a vocabulary in the 1830s and 1840s, a period of intense pressure toward workplace reorganization, was as part of a broader mode of justification by which the worker shifted the debate on what was happening in the workplace from the context of market considerations, by which the employer inevitably held *carte blanche* to institute whatever changes made his business more competitive, to ground held rather more firmly by the workforce. Legitimation based on custom placed the workforce in contact with an apparently tangible past, and it did not take new trades very long to construct 'traditions' which justified the work patterns to which they wished to adhere.

This book concentrates particularly on the second quarter of the nineteenth century, a period which saw an increase in the pace of British industrialization. Most trades appear to have registered an acceleration in the tempo of competition alongside declining prices and profit margins. Often this was associated with increased mechanization, in a complex causal relationship.[18] The work of Maxine Berg has emphasized that this was also a period when political economy was reformulated into a practical science of class domination aiming at 'greater capitalist control of the production process'.[19] Technology was simply one element in a broad spectrum of innovation designed to increase output and lower costs. Thus, contracting in the building trades, sweating in the tailoring trades, deskilling in the shoe trade, and mechanization in a host of others, all acted to reduce the power of labour to control or influence the work process. The activities of organized labour in this period were neither highly formalized nor continuous in a structural sense. But there is enough evidence to demonstrate a critical conflict for control, across a wide spectrum of trades and areas, from the 1820s onwards and with a dramatic escalation in the 1830s and 1840s.[20]

This question of autonomy was perhaps the major issue of the early industrial workplace, as workers in a large and increasing number of trades were compelled, by the attempts at reorganization that confronted them, to define what they conceived to be the 'legitimate pursuit of trade'.[21] There was little conflict in the way this definition was formulated, between the 'traditional' analysis of work and the new socialist critique of the 1830s. Significantly John Gast, James Morrison, and John Doherty, men at the forefront of trade union conflict in the period, were also leading lights in the early co-operative movement. In some ways there was little that was new in a theory of value which stressed the centrality of labour. The artisan's twin claims to the control of work and independence from charity derived directly from a recognition of his or her own importance in the chain of production. What emerged in the 1830s was an ideology that transcended sectionalism by evolving a language that was infinitely adaptable to the intricacies of infringement in very different trades, yet which, by its very nature, provided a comparative measure for all trades. Thus the work experience was being universalized in terms that went beyond occupational barriers while still reinforcing specific workplace practices in individual trades.

Where did the employer of labour in the workshop stand in all of this? Certainly in the early period of radicalism, described so vividly by Edward Thompson, masters and men could be found expressing their grievances jointly. Small masters, for example, were often leading members of trade-based organizations.[22] When Nassau Senior reported on combinations to Home Secretary Melbourne in 1832 he found it necessary to recommend 'the infliction of very severe pecuniary penalties upon any masters encouraging combinations to the annoyance of other masters'.[23] The following year the *Pioneer* called upon the members of trade societies to 'Declare to existing masters that you are willing to admit them to your union if they choose to enter themselves as workmen'.[24] Yet, paradoxically, as a number of studies have recently emphasized, the commitment of the small-scale employer of labour to economic liberalism was also a vital element in the process of restabilization following the Chartist challenge.[25] This aspect of the English experience was by no means unique. Dick Geary points out that in France, although masters and men mounted the barricades together in 1789, 1830, and the early days of 1848, they soon 'confronted one another over questions of wages, working conditions and the ownership of property'.[26]

The first two chapters of this book address this apparent ambiguity in the social consciousness of the small producer.[27] It is argued here that a central element in the reorganization of work within the industrializing process in its early stages was the transformation of the small-scale employer from artisan-type small master to *petit bourgeois* small manufacturer, a mirror image of the large-scale manufacturer. This transformation was crucial to the issue of tension and conflict in the workshop, but its importance has been obscured by two factors. First, the desire of historians to see the actors in the drama as passive reflections of economic structures. Thus, the argument has run, the workshop was the scene of a closely structured relationship between masters and men *because* it was a small unit of production, while the factory, as a larger and more impersonal unit, gave rise to social polarity and conflict. The work of Volkov on the prolonged antipathy between the German master-artisans and their journeymen suggests that there should be more to it than that. There was nothing *inherently* cohesive about the small unit of production.[28] Blackbourn argues that small-scale employers in nineteenth-century Germany were part of an 'awkward class which experienced difficult relations with both labour and large-scale capital'.[29] For France in the same period Haupt has suggested that in 'small craft businesses', relations between masters and journeymen were not 'characterised by that trust attributed to them by writers in search of harmony and consensus'.[30] The second factor is perhaps more pragmatic but it has been no less important. The recurrent desire of historians to use the bland occupational data available in census material and pollbooks for quantitative surveys has exacerbated problems of definition within the small-producer sector of the economy. The need to explore critical differences in social consciousness within occupational groups has thus been subordinated to the functional need to seek what Vincent calls an 'objective economic homogeneity' to suit specific purposes.[31]

However close he may have been to the artisan–small master in terms of objective economic criteria (size of firm, working capital, and workforce), the distinctive social identity of the *petit bourgeois* producer evolved as an explicit rejection of the values to which the artisan related. We may expect to find the small producer acting the part of either the artisan or the manufacturer (though rarely both). In this way the small-scale unit of production could be the scene of a closely structured relationship between employer and employee as the small master played the artisan role. The exaggerated respect paid publicly to masters who accepted terms put forward by the trades suggests a central concept of the 'honourable master' engaged in the 'legitimate pursuit of trade'. Such a course of action affirmed the small master's membership of the working community. Alternatively, the workshop could be the scene of fierce class conflict of the kind more familiar to us in the context of the factory, as the small manufacturer attempted to survive in a competitive economic universe by adopting the same techniques as his larger counterpart: mechanization, dilution of labour, increased workloads, or lower prices. A case could be made for the severity of the struggle between employer and employee being far greater in the workshop than in the large factory, since the shifting economic context served to emphasize the client status of the small producers in their reliance upon the credit and marketing facilities of either the larger firm or the merchant capitalist. The imperatives to reorganize work and thus enhance employer control could therefore be greater in the smaller unit of production where profit margins were slimmer and market viability more tenuous. Certainly the shop that operated 'under the price' or violated trade 'privileges' was as likely to be the target of the organizing workforce as the factory that did the same.

Hence the erection of barriers of differential experience and consciousness between largely non-mechanical craft workers and skilled workers within the factory may be seriously misleading for this early period of industrialization. In many cases the independent artisan producer clearly sought refuge *within* the factory. The continuance of sub-contracting in most large firms in the period can be seen as an attempt by the artisan to retain the viability of the smaller unit of production by the simple device of moving it, *en bloc*, into the manufactory. Here prices could be negotiated and daily, weekly, and annual work rhythms operated as if the component work units were still fragmented in a decentralized workshop pattern. In this respect the artisans eventually found themselves to be small masters in form rather than substance. The factory increasingly imposed restrictions whilst also involving the disadvantages of payment to rent bench space and power, or perhaps even the deduction of discount on the prices of goods 'sold' to the manufacturer by the small work unit within the large firm. We can identify the gradual emergence of the wage labourer from about the mid-century onwards. In the earlier period, however, the relationship between employer and employee was by no means a simple exchange of wages for labour-time. While work-groups produced goods and 'sold' them to employers in large or small concerns it was the product and not labour-time that was apparently exchanged. This underpinned the notion of the worker as an independent producer and this profoundly influenced the relationship with the employer.[32]

In the early stages of industrial growth, the workforce in both shop and factory attempted to reinforce their autonomy over work by stressing the separate and distinct nature of their culture and their community. In order to reorganize work such that it answered the needs of capital, rather than labour, the manufacturer had to penetrate the collective culture of the workplace. Faced with attempts in both large and small units of production to introduce different work structures, giving control of the labour process to capital, the workforce expressed its community solidarities via a range of formal and informal modes of organization. It defined the territory of the workplace as its own and claimed the right to organize the nature and pace of production. Chapter 3 explores the ways in which political idioms resonated through these forms of organization as projections of the social order. Chartism was to articulate the same ethos of representation through an active participation in political systems.

As far as the small-scale employer of labour was concerned the options were polarizing dramatically in the second quarter of the century. Economic pressures pushed such individuals to reorganize production; the role of the small firm was increasingly to service the needs of the larger firm and in order to do this it needed to organize itself on a similar basis. The small producer was thus being forced into a far greater, and economically more oppressive, dependence upon large capital than had ever previously been the case. He was locked into this pattern of dependency by an economic cycle which revolved on a weekly or bi-weekly basis. Short-term credit and slim profit margins made sales imperative and severely circumscribed the opportunities which a free market economy allegedly offered.

This was also a crucial moment culturally and politically. For both the working community and economic liberalism laid claims to the small producer as the symbolic embodiment of their value systems. For the working community the small master represented the viable alternative of independent production *within* the community. The choice between this and wage labour involved a mobility for the individual that was more economic than social. Of course, in comparison to the 'free for all' of economic liberalism, the adoption of artisan values could be a harsh taskmaster for the small producer. They involved, inevitably, accepting restrictions on apprenticeship, labour dilution, and certain types of machinery, as well as a rigid adherence to negotiated prices. This could threaten a small firm's market viability or place an absolute limit on expansion. Nevertheless it remained the option of the small producer to act within the working community in the traditional way. Producers' co-operatives, which were a recurring feature of early industrialization (and which are discussed in more detail in Chapter 2), represented an attempt to guarantee one corner of the market to this form of production. The small masters' problems were derived almost entirely from an increasing reliance upon the credit and marketing facilities of large capital. Within the co-operative venture the producer and the consumer were placed in direct contact, thus by-passing the small masters' dependence on the capitalist. In Britain, Robert Owen felt certain that the larger manufacturers would actually support such a venture financially;

a mistaken view which reflected his own lack of class perspective.

Nevertheless, between 1825 and 1850 trade-based protest activity (in the multiplicity of forms it took), Owenism, and finally Chartism, provided a vigorous critique of what was still, at this time, an immature capitalist system. For the large-scale manufacturer the attempt to breach craft control of both the content and pace of the work process necessarily involved undermining the artisan's role as an independent producer. Systematic work discipline involved a rejection, or at least a reformulation, of the community values upon which these movements were based. Thus the existence of a substantial sector of the economy which related to such a scale of values, and which lived them out in work routines and relationships outside the factory, only served to weaken the impact of work discipline within the factory itself.

The process of undermining the workers' alternative of small-scale production, however, involved some niceties of definition. The attack on the small master could not be confused with an attack on small producers as such. They had already been reserved a special place in the mythology of economic liberalism and, in this role, performed a vital function in promulgating the fantasy of an open society. 'All the manufacturers I have ever known began the world with very little capitals', Matthew Boulton explained to a select committee in 1799.[33] He would have done well to exclude himself from such an observation, of course, having inherited a thriving, large-scale business from his father and thus also been in a position to marry a woman with a dowry of some £28,000.[34] But such statements were reiterated like a creed through the nineteenth century. Samuel Timmins had, like Boulton, inherited a large firm from his father but nevertheless felt qualified to expound, in 1866, on the organic growth of the factory in his area:

> The history of every trade and every manufactory is really that of rapid growth. Beginning as a small master, often working in his own house, with his wife and children to help him the Birmingham workman has become a master, his trade has extended, his buildings have increased. He has used his house as a workshop, has annexed another, has built upon the garden or the yard and consequently a large number of the manufactories are most irregular in style. Whenever the business has

overgrown its early home and it is necessary to remove or rebuild, a better class of building is invariably adopted.[35]

Research into a number of trades in a number of areas suggests that such an analysis has more place in middle-class rhetoric than as a plausible explanation for the growth of the firm in the major industries. In textiles, for example, it is quite clear that the individuals who established factories were, broadly speaking, those who had co-ordinated the related processes during the outwork or domestic stage of development. The factory represented a shift from a circulating to a fixed capital commitment and was only rarely an organic growth outwards from the workshop of the small master.[36] Work by Gatrell, which emphasizes the importance of smaller firms in the Lancashire area, asserts that even these lay beyond the reach of the traditional mechanisms of upward mobility.[37] It will, of course, take more than empirical research to divest capitalism of the 'self-made man',[38] but nevertheless, the move from 'rags to riches' which this suggested was something very different to the traditional movement between worker and small master that had characterized small-scale production for so long. The reality of a limited mobility at the heart of the decentralized workshop structure,[39] was now to be usurped by a largely mythical social mobility which attested to the possibility of a meteoric rise to large-scale manufacturer status by the exercise of basic human qualities.

Thus in a period of intense structural economic change small-scale production in its artisan image perpetuated a system of values antithetical to the new social order. But in a different frame of reference, one within which the entrepreneur underwent the prescribed metamorphosis from caterpillar small producer to butterfly industrialist, the small unit of production was the cornerstone of an elaborate justification for the anomalies of capitalism. As a result of this, while certain forms of small-scale production were constantly lauded as examples of entrepreneurial spirit and individual endeavour, others were consistently pilloried. By the middle of the nineteenth century the small master had become a scapegoat. Increasingly equated with the 'garret-master', the responsibility for declining prices, wages, and quality was indiscriminately laid upon his shoulders.

Chapters 4 and 5 argue that the social, economic, and political facets of this justification for individualism are not separable. Just as the factory was portrayed as having grown from the small workshop and the factory owner or merchant as a working man made good, so the employer claimed the right to represent the employee by virtue of his economic dominance of the 'productive class'. The *Manchester Guardian* put it this way in March 1830, whilst supporting the limited democracy of the proposed parliamentary reform measures:

> As the mass of the middle classes never can have any interests adverse to the happiness and prosperity of those below them in society, the rights of the humblest order would be quite safe from violation under the protection of representatives chosen from a constituency in which that mass had a preponderance.[40]

Any defence of bourgeois democracy, in a local and a national context, necessarily hinged on reconstituting the unity of the classes, at least rhetorically, at the point of production. In 1841 in Birmingham, the mayor, P.H. Muntz, spoke out against the emergence of class divisions within the workplace in exactly these terms:

> With respect to the masters and workmen, he must say there never was a graver delusion than to try to persuade the latter that the interest of the former was quite separate and distinct from theirs. How such a deceit could have succeeded in Birmingham he knew not. Half the masters in Birmingham had been working men.[41]

Muntz, later to serve as MP for the town, was a second-generation industrialist who had inherited a large rolling mill and a mercantile firm from his wealthy father.[42] His optimistic notions of social mobility were not the result of personal experience. Rhetorically, however, he appealed to a traditional workplace relationship between masters and men in small-scale industry which had been one of the first casualties of industrialization, thanks to the actions of firms like his own. Once divested of the social and cultural obligations which its artisan version placed upon the employer this relationship could be called upon to underpin a supposed consensus within the workplace.

Just how convincing this linguistic construction was to a workforce for whom the destruction of the traditional relationship between employer and employee was a painful reality, is a matter for conjecture. The sleight of hand involved, however, has fooled more than one historian and it is, above all, for this reason that the focus of this book is the town of Birmingham. For the historiography of industrialization has long regarded Birmingham as the classic centre of small-scale production, displaying in its social relations a degree of social cohesion less common in areas where the factory acted to polarize the classes more sharply. George Allen, in an otherwise masterly study of the area's economic growth, gave a powerful impetus to such a view when he described relations at the point of production in a passage which clearly echoed Muntz's point: 'Most of the owners of the workshop or small factory, moreover, originally had been workmen themselves and this was a powerful factor operating against labour unrest.'[43] It is argued here that such an analysis confuses the process of social and economic change with the language of justification offered at the time by those who activated the process. The employer argued that he stood at the head of a working community, the various strata of which stood to gain equally from a flourishing economy. This much was a common element of the political economy: a harmony of interests enjoyed by 'free agents' exercising their essential economic freedom.[44] Once accepted that both masters and men stood to gain from a flourishing economy, one in the form of profit, the other in the form of wages and cheap consumer goods, then every form of economic rationalization adopted by the entrepreneur in the workplace could be justified on an 'end-versus-means' basis. The community of interests by which both employer and employee could be seen to benefit from a high profit economy could be used by the manufacturer as a *carte blanche* for almost any development, within his enterprise, that he felt might raise the level of profitability. This was later to be the very basis of the large-scale employer's posture as the 'new paternalist'.[45] But here it was a crucial element in underpinning work reorganization in both large- and small-scale industry during the early stages of industrialization.

For Birmingham, however, a static view of workshop relations, and their projection into larger units of production, has provided the basis for an interpretation of important political movements. Asa Briggs, following George Allen closely, saw in the continued predominance of the workshop within the town's economic structure the explanation of a degree of unity between working-class and middle-class radicals in the Birmingham Political Union (BPU) of the 1830s. The analysis focused on the workshop closeness between masters and men forged by a combination of close physical proximity in the workplace, the indispensability of skilled labour to small-scale production, the absence of large-scale capital investment, and the acknowledged possibility of upward social mobility from employee to employer status. This, Briggs suggested, created a degree of social cohesion which manifested itself in the local political context.[46]

This model, a pioneering attempt to relate economic, social, and political structures, became rather stretched in its uncritical application by other historians. Trygve Tholfsen used the analysis to explain the nature of the Chartist movement in the town (as, to be fair, did Briggs himself in his introduction to *Chartist Studies* in 1959).[47] Tholfsen also saw the small workshop–social cohesion model as a way of explaining the emergence of the Liberal Party in the town in the 1860s and 1870s.[48] In the opposite chronological direction more recent work by John Money has, retrospectively, laid the eighteenth-century groundwork for the Briggs–Tholfsen analysis of local radicalism.[49] The work of Alan Fox on the relative lack of trade unionism in the town reinforced the structural basis of the model.[50]

This interpretation has been applied to a variety of towns with similar industrial structures. Thus the model evolved for Birmingham has played its part in the analysis of social movements in Sheffield, London, and more recently (and perhaps less legitimately), Oldham.[51] In this way it has become an accepted means of qualifying any hypothesis concerning the growth of class relations in British industry before 1850. Rowe's work on London uses it to counter Prothero on artisan radicalism: 'It would seem more likely, however, that as in Birmingham the economic makeup of London's trading community facilitated a certain amount of co-operation between employers and employees.' It is a short step from this statement to the overall view that: 'The very word "class" is perhaps too rigid (and anomalously at the same time too vague) a definitive tool with which to judge some historical movement.'[52] Above all, the model has been used to fix class consciousness to the factory. D.S. Gadian, for example, assumes that he may undermine John Foster's hypothesis, on the presence of working-class consciousness in Oldham in the same period, simply by pointing out that the average size of firm in that town was substantially smaller than Foster thought it to be. Dr Gadian pursues this loophole relentlessly: 'the prevalence of small scale industry in Oldham', he argues, 'did much to enable masters and men to harmonise and unite in some common remedy as was possible in Birmingham'.[53]

Research into relations at the point of production during early industrialization has been consistently circumscribed by the Allen–Briggs–Tholfsen–Fox model of social cohesion in Birmingham. Yet recent research on the town fits uneasily into the pattern. R.B. Rose, for example, has suggested that by the close of the Napoleonic Wars in 1815 a working class with a political consciousness was beginning to emerge in the town.[54] Michael Frost, in a study of the education of working-class children in Birmingham, has drawn attention to a previously neglected interface between the classes. The extension of provided schooling, in its variety of forms, was a response, he suggests, to the breakdown of authority. Interest and investment in education for working-class children was always more forthcoming at times of social upheaval, particularly the 1790s, 1815–20, and 1827–33.[55] Hooper's analysis of the town in the 1850s and 1860s emphasizes the importance of local trade unions, whilst Bramwell's research in the same period explores the clear spatial segregation of the classes in Birmingham through an analysis of local community structures and values.[56]

Yet the simplicity of the orthodox interpretation has never been confronted or challenged directly and it continues to thrive. Douglas Reid's recent work on Birmingham affirms the notions of a workplace consensus between employers and the upper strata of the working class. Looking at the phenomenon of the works outing, popular with employers after 1850, Reid concludes that this is 'clear evidence that many artisans shared the aims and outlook of their employers'.[57] Yet to read the social relations of production through the medium of the gypsy party is to constrain the debate within a context defined by the employer. Bramwell, for example, has argued that the idea that the period witnessed the emergence of an upper echelon of 'temperance artisans' is 'largely illusory'.[58] The illusion was the creation of a liberal press anxious to justify the values of mid-Victorian individualism by welding them on to the working class. Of course, the old dictum that 'you don't have to believe everything you read in the papers' also applies to historians.

Clearly the critical period of social and economic development prior to 1850 requires a reassessment. The difficulties which this involves have been compounded by the powerful emphasis of English historiography on the emergence of the liberal state. Birmingham's history has been presented as a monument to the triumphant progress of the radical urban bourgeoisie. Thomas Attwood's Political Union, the most important extra-parliamentary influence on the passing of the Reform Act, was followed closely by the successful agitation for a Charter of Incorporation. The election of a liberal town council in 1838 initiated a protracted battle with local vested interests which took thirty-five years to resolve and culminated in the 'municipal socialism' of Joseph Chamberlain's Birmingham. Thus the political history of the town represents, in microcosm, the seemingly inexorable advance of English democracy, in a gradualist fashion, behind its middle-class vanguard.

In short, it is the mainstream of English historiography that has engulfed any historian attempting to penetrate the complex social relationships which actually underlay these developments, and it has proved impossible to swim against the tide of middle-class rhetoric. In Birmingham during the 1830s, in the face of rapid change in the workplace, this rhetoric reiterated the unity of the classes to an extent not found elsewhere. But the difference was essentially one of degree rather than type, and the crucial element here was Attwood and his followers. His currency formulae may have been idiosyncratic but the social language in which they were couched was familiar enough. He argued simply that productive capital should be represented politically by productive capitalists. As far as he and his middle-class radical supporters were concerned this was the sole aim of the Reform Act. The failure of the 1832 measure to realize this aim encouraged them on to further agitation in the early stages of Chartism (and the second phase of the BPU). But they never at any stage wanted anything more than that the economic authority of the middle class be reflected politically.

A close study of the BPU in the 1830s indicates clearly the existence of two very distinct concepts of political form. First, there was an appeal for a direct and active democracy by which the working community claimed participation at all levels of the political system, and second, the middle-class claim for a representative democracy with themselves the representatives. Each of these concepts reflected the struggle for authority within the workplace, and each was a function of those values and beliefs by which each side justified its actions. As concepts of political representation they were mutually exclusive and related to antithetical views of the social order. The alliance of classes within the BPU was always extremely volatile. It came into existence because of the working-class need for backing from men of property, and the middle-class need for the numerical strength of the working class. There was little more to it than that since the two classes were, at all times, making separate cases. The alliance held reasonably firmly in 1832 because the intransigence of the aristocracy converted Attwood into the people's hero. It foundered in 1834 because it could not survive the contest for workplace authority inherent in a growing trade union and Owenite movement. In 1839 the middle-class radicals, after a brief flirtation with the principle of universal suffrage, turned on the Chartists with appalling ferocity. The Bull Ring disturbances, detailed in the last chapter of this book, were rather more than the flare-up at a time of social and economic stress that they have often been seen to be. They constituted a conflict between two very specific concepts of democratic form, which reflected, in themselves, a deeper clash of values and belief.

The major methodological problems of a study of this kind lie primarily in the contextual analysis of terminology and language. For example, the willingness with which the anti-Poor-Law campaigners, the Short Time Committees, the Owenites, and the Chartists (at least in the early years of Chartism) acted in concert with middle-class radicals has often been equated with a hybrid and non-specific form of political consciousness most easily identifiable with middle-class radical ideals.[59] From this the argument necessarily follows that the working class failed to develop a distinct political standpoint,[60] and that political radicalism and trade unionism were incompatible forms, each detracting from the effectiveness of the other.[61] Thus, a political rhetoric, directed against the aristocracy, and actually shared at important points with the middle class, appears incompatible with an economic critique of capitalism.[62]

Yet we cannot understand the language of the debate unless we are able to rebuild the context from which it derived meaning. In the small workshop and the early factory the interface between labour and capital was a function not only of a conflict of interests (wages versus profits) but also the clash of values and belief, by which each side justified their actions in defence of autonomy. Yet if conflict in the workplace was a dialogue between these two value systems, in the process both sides often used common terms, though they ascribed different meanings to them. Both, for example, drew on three crucial concepts: social mobility, the workplace unity of interests, and respectability. For the artisan social mobility was generally that traditional mobility which reinforced his unity with the small master. In the employer's case the concept was more grandiose, providing proof that the new social and economic order was an open one, and justifying his own dominance of production. The artisan used the concept of a workplace unity of interests to reiterate an idealized past and to highlight the activities of 'illegal' masters. The manufacturer could draw on a similar concept to emphasize the impersonal nature of market forces against which the interests of the entire 'productive class' could be represented as being one. For the artisan 'respectable' behaviour defined the exact nature of the individual's obligation within the working community. For the manufacturer the term, when applied to his workforce, suggested an orderliness of behaviour that reinforced the nature of structural change in the workplace. The importance of context in such cases means that it is not enough for the historian to observe such terms in use. The meaning and value ascribed to them by the participants must also be understood.

Within the political response it should not surprise us to come upon a comparable ambiguity of language and meaning creating similar areas of congruence and divergence within radical rhetoric. Terms such as 'the People', 'representation', 'interests', or even 'constitution' are not separable from the social, economic, and cultural determinants of their use. If we are to heed Stedman-Jones's advice and see Chartism as a political movement we must also be aware of where its political language came from. It is hoped that by presenting, in Chapters 4 and 5, a narrative of local radical movements, utilizing the perspectives gained from an examination of the workplace in the same years, we may break through the opacity of the radical rhetoric and achieve a greater understanding of the relationships that actually lay behind it. For, however unsuccessful working-class organizations may have been in achieving their immediate aims, it is clear that the 'logic' of capitalism *was* being actively questioned, in this period, in Birmingham and in a hundred other centres of industry.

1

Industrialization and the transformation of the small producer

The growth of the factory in the first half of the nineteenth century did not threaten the existence of the small workshop as such, but it did change its internal nature significantly. The first two chapters of this book present the hypothesis that in this period the small producer was being transformed from artisan small master to *petit-bourgeois* small manufacturer, a mirror-image of the large-scale manufacturer. This transformation can be related to economic factors in that the growth of larger units of production served to emphasize the client status of the smaller unit. It was, however, as much a cultural as an economic phenomenon, changing as it did the very basis upon which the productive process was pursued at every level. It will be argued in later chapters that not only were these changes at the heart of workplace conflict in this period, but they were also crucial to the appearance of a distinct political ideal that could be seen as specifically working class in nature.

METHODS AND PROBLEMS

At the outset it is as well to acknowledge two major methodological problems, common enough to histories of industrial development. First, it is impossible to 'freeze' Birmingham's industrial system at any point in the first half of the century, with any degree of empirical accuracy. Second, as has been discussed in the introduction, the language used by contemporaries to describe the way in which the structure actually operated may distort its essential nature, because those who observed its operations were themselves part of the structure they described.

Turning to the first of these problems, some figures are available for study; the size of the workforce in census years, the distribution of workers between occupations, and the age–sex ratio within occupations are all attainable. There is, however, no way of knowing, for example, how many large firms were in existence in any one year or what proportion of the workforce was engaged in workshop production as opposed to employment in factories. Even Robert Grainger's 1843 report to the Children's Employment Commission only provides a glimpse of some of the factories in the town. It does not constitute a comprehensive overview of the number of factories or the number of workers they employed.[1]

In his study of the area published in 1929, G.C. Allen suggested that, by 1850, Birmingham's industrial structure consisted of a few large factories and a multiplicity of smaller workshops, producing the small metalware for which the town was famous. The impact of industrialization had been, in his view, to increase the number of smaller units operating, rather than to substantially increase the size of the average unit of production.[2] John R. Immer, in a research thesis in 1954, made some modifications to this analysis by pointing out that Allen had underestimated the number of large factories in the town by the middle of the century.[3] This is an important qualification but it does not undermine Allen's claim that the workshop continued to be the typical unit of production, a view that is accepted in this book. This chapter concentrates on the task of establishing the existence of distinct sectors in the town's major occupational groups, reflecting, it is argued, the underlying pattern of large- and small-scale units of production in each of the major industries.

Probate documentation was selected to augment this procedure because it provides a means of correlating occupation with an indicator of wealth. In the proving of each individual will (or administration papers if the deceased was intestate) an estimate was made of the individual's personal estate or personalty. This valuation was always approximate as perhaps the example of William Astbury, jobbing-smith of Lancaster Street, will indicate. After his death, in 1825, his personal estate was sworn to be 'under £100'. A note at the foot of his will indicated the calculation upon which the figure was based:

Household furniture	£34 0 0d
Shop tools	£37 0 0d
	£71 0 0d

The elaborate inventories which characterized probate documentation in earlier periods had long ceased to be a feature by the nineteenth century, and the will itself only occasionally supplemented the wealth–occupation correlation.[4] In addition, a number of difficulties should be acknowledged before proceeding further. The question of debt at the time of death poses problems. The personalty of Samuel Galton, banker and one-time gun manufacturer, was confirmed to be 'under £150,000' by his son Samuel Tertius Galton in a letter to the family's solicitor in 1832.[5] However, the younger Galton added that his father's outstanding debts stood at around £2,000 and this clearly was to be subtracted from the personal estate. In another case it is by no means clear whether a debt owed by the manufacturing chemist James Alston to his brother was included in his estimated personalty of 'under £35,000'. In addition, though the estimate of personalty included leasehold property, it rarely included freehold property. Thus it might be possible (though in effect unlikely) for an individual to die with a relatively low personal estate, but massive holdings of freehold property.

The making of a will was by no means undertaken by the majority of individuals and the use of probate documentation has to be assessed in this light. For the purposes of this study all of the wills and administration papers proved for the parishes of Birmingham, Aston, and Edgbaston during the years 1820 to 1840 were studied, covering some 3,743 individuals in all. Taking the findings of the local branch of the Statistical Society with regard to annual deaths in the parish of Birmingham, the individuals whose estates were proved would appear to account for around 7–10 per cent of those dying each year. Taking into account the high level of infant mortality, this would appear a reasonably high total.[6]

Nevertheless, the proving of an estate was in itself something of a mark of status and was held by those who preached the gospel of self-help to the working class to be one of the limited range of goals to which the individual could legitimately aspire. In November 1825 the Revd Timothy East presented a lecture to the mechanics of Birmingham entitled 'In all labour there is profit', and he touched on exactly this point. He concluded a fairly intricate piece of arithmetic on the way a mechanic could divide a weekly income of 21s into rent, food, and clothing with the following encouragement:

> should he spend two days in indolence at 3s 6d and expend in that time 4s his loss would be 11s; but suppose that he continued his exertion through the week, he would be a gainer by 11s. Let him then give his wife and family 6s and take 5s to the Savings Bank. If this were pursued for 20 years, the mechanic would have saved sufficient to render it worth making his will, and his son, from the money thus saved, might become greater than his father – might take the station of a manufacturer where his parent had been a workman.[7]

The passage speaks volumes as to the difficulties of upward social mobility for the workman. It also indicates that those individuals who made wills were those who had, at least to some extent, achieved some degree of individual wealth. Thus the group probably excludes a large proportion of the workforce who were wage labourers. By the same token, however, this may present a reasonable method for assessing the range of wealth amongst independent producers.

One final qualifier ought to be cited. Since death often followed retirement for the individual, the occupation cited most often is that of 'Gentleman'. Of the 3,743 wills consulted, 420 gave this as their designated occupation. Little can be made of this unless the will itself gives some kind of insight into the individuals' previous occupation.

Probate documentation, like most quantifiable material the historian may draw on, involves a range of difficulties which may ultimately limit its usefulness. Arguably, however, quantification can only ever provide a basis from which to interpret the available literary evidence for any given period and this is the spirit in which the probates have been used in this study: as a tentative way of approaching the broader spectrum of evidence. What is of particular interest is the relationship between the capital intensive and the low unit capital enterprises, particularly the way the relationship changed in the first half of the century. Here the difficulties associated with the contemporary language of observation, the second of the two major methodological problems mentioned earlier, becomes apparent. In this case there is no paucity of contemporary descriptions of how the industrial machine operated either as a system or in the nature of its component parts. There is, however, the problem that such descriptions were *themselves* part of the wider context of social relations and the process of ideological reproduction. Take, for example, the volume of essays produced in 1866 for the British Association. Edited by Samuel Timmins, *The Resources, Products and Industrial History of Birmingham and the Midland Hardware District* consists of a series of essays on the operation of the area's major industries written by the area's major industrialists. Thus Joseph Chamberlain contributed an essay on the nature and history of the screw trade in the town, John P. Turner wrote on button-making, John Goodman on gun-making, and so forth. G.C. Allen's study of the area draws heavily on this source for the remarkable detail it gives on industrial structure. His reliance upon the volume for perspectives on the nature of relations within the hierarchy of economic authority in these trades is, however, more problematic. The collection of essays reports an industrial system largely free from conflict. Most contributors claim that trade unions have a minimal presence, that wage levels are high, and that the opportunities offered through the small-producer sector afford the workforce a high level of independence; all the points in fact familiar to us through the Allen–Briggs–Tholfsen line of descent.

The contributors themselves were, of course, rather more concerned with their present rather than the past or the future. At times the contributions move embarrassingly close to self-advertisement. John P. Turner, for example, writing on the button trade, finds space for a coy passing reference to his own firm: 'There are still many houses doing a fair amount of business in metal buttons. "Hammond, Turner and Sons" for best fancy and uniform buttons.'[8] Similarly William Ryland, in his report on the plated ware trades, finds that the only trade dispute he can recall occurred in 1824 when workmen in the rest of the trade struck work because the wages they were receiving were well below those being paid at the firm of 'Waterhouse and Ryland'.[9] Most of the contributors were large-scale manufacturers and, in writing, were involved as much in the process of justification as in the objective desire to inform the public of the technical details of their respective trades. Thus Joseph Chamberlain writing of the absorption of smaller screw-making firms by larger enterprises, concluded that this was almost entirely an 'unmixed good',[10] a view presumably not unconnected with his partnership in the town's largest screw factory.

What is betrayed in observations of this order is a tendency for the large-scale manufacturer to present his actions publicly as if they were driven by an economic inevitability that was universally accepted by capital and labour alike. Much of this book is concerned with challenges made to this assumption from within the contemporary context. Nevertheless, commentators, such as those drawn together by Timmins, generally sought to place themselves squarely in a mainstream liberal tradition of consent and consensus, and historians have frequently proved only too willing to perpetuate this idea by taking their remarks at face value.[11]

In 1852 Harriet Martineau visited a number of Birmingham's larger factories to gather information for what she called 'a full but picturesque account of manufacture and other productive processes'. The results of her researches appeared as a series of articles in *Household Words* under engaging titles such as 'A Day at the Works' and 'The Wonder of Screws'. But after visiting Chance's glass manufactory (of special interest since it produced the glass for the Crystal Palace), she was asked 'not to notice the circumstances of women being employed instead of men' in one particular process. As Follet Osler, himself a manufacturer (and later a contributor to the Timmins' volume), explained to Martineau, 'in London it may perhaps create some unpleasantness and there may be those who might suppose that women not being so strong as men might not do their work so well though this is really not the case'.[12] Such an example of deliberate deception should not be taken to suggest that most of this kind of evidence involves wholesale and conscious distortion on the part of those who produced it. Rather it serves to remind us that the manufacturer existed as part of a matrix of relationships with competitors and external authorities. This type of material (and it makes up a large part of the documentation upon which our perception of the industrializing process is based) contains a view of the immediate world which is necessarily incomplete in significant areas.

What is missing, above all, is the fabric of the relationship at the point of production. We will consider this further when we turn to the workplace itself more fully in Chapter 3; nevertheless, a single instance may illustrate many of the pitfalls for the historian in using such evidence. In 1841 Thomas Hawkes, co-proprietor of the Eagle Foundry in Birmingham, was interviewed by Factory Commissioner Grainger. He provided him with a detailed statement of his relationship with his workforce, which he saw fit to cite as a model of its kind to his fellow manufacturers:

> Finds that by this kind of conduct the mechanics become better workpeople, and attached to their employer. Many of the workmen have been here a long time. Of those men who are 40, at least half the number have been employed in the manufactory 20 years. Many of the lads and younger men are the sons of workmen on the premises. Witness found this manufactory in an admirable state as regards the workpeople employed when he became the principal 15 years ago, the former proprietors, Mr. Smith, Mr. Francis and Messrs. Dearman, having paid great attention to the happiness and welfare of the mechanics. Is decidedly of opinion that the best results would be obtained if such conduct was generally observed by employers. Generally speaking, the workpeople are grateful for such consideration, a feeling which leads them faithfully to discharge their duties.[13]

This statement tells us a good deal about how Hawkes saw himself and how he wished to be seen but little of how successful he was in promulgating this image. There is, for example, little of the mutual respect and attachment, which Hawkes saw to be central to his relationship with his workers, in a letter written only a few years later by G.J. Holyoake's mother. She was writing to George to explain why his brother was no longer employed at the Eagle Foundry: 'Horatio as left the froundy because he would not attend at 6 o clock in a morning to waite for 2 or 3 days work a week so Hawkes told him to go and he took him at is word.'[14] George Holyoake had worked at the Eagle Foundry himself in the 1830s and he remembered Hawkes well:

> William – the acting 'Master' as he was called – was mainly an unpleasant person. He was exacting and always spoke with harshness. I saw old men who were in such terror at his

> approach that they would strike their hands instead of the chisel they were using, and were afraid of dismissal or reduction of wages in consequence of the incapacity which he witnessed, and which his presence caused.[15]

Of course, it is not suggested here that the Holyoakes were rendering an 'objective' account of work relations whereas Hawkes himself was schemingly 'subjective'. Both views draw upon, and relate to, very distinct value systems which specified 'correct' behaviour in their own particular ways. Thus the way the manufacturer assessed himself and the way he might actually be seen by his workforce formed the texture of relationships at the point of production. But the creation of historical documentation is not an egalitarian process. In this case we are given a rare insight for a number of unusual reasons. A working woman, able to overcome the problems of illiteracy, communicated with her son and the private letter survived. Her son was one of a small number of working people who wrote an autobiography in this period.

In most cases we do not have working-class testimony to place directly alongside the generalizations of the manufacturer, always the first witness for the defence in the case of industrial expansion. The large-scale manufacturer invariably adopted a language to describe the industrial system, which anaesthetized the object of scrutiny so that the operations of the market took place without pain. Samuel Timmins was able to claim, in his general history of the town's economy: 'Birmingham is in fact – Sheffield perhaps only excepted – the town of all others where the social and personal freedom is extreme. The large number of small manufacturers are practically independent of the numerous factors and merchants they supply.'[16] His prose glided smoothly over one of the most critical relationships in the entire system of production, that between the small producers and the parties who marketed their goods and whose credit ensured their existence. As a large manufacturer commenting on the small manufacturer, Timmins understated the economic nexus which drew the two together in an unequal bond. The rest of this chapter is devoted to re-creating more fully the nature of this relationship and the manner of its changing through time. It claims no special detachment from the kinds of sources outlined above, for the historian is constrained to use whatever is available. But the attempt has been made in this and subsequent chapters to contextualize the language of observation, as it was being used at the time, by exploring fully those value systems whose conflict composed the context itself, and from which the language used derived its meaning and impact.

THE STRUCTURE OF INDUSTRY

By the middle of the nineteenth century the borough of Birmingham contained a workforce of 113,982 men, women, and children, distributed through a wide range of occupations, summarized in Table 1.1.[17] Over half of the working population were concerned with trade and industry, with by far the greater number (22.83 per cent) involved in the production of various forms of metalware. Gun-making still accounted for 3 per cent of the working population with the traditional wood trades (chair-making, coopering, etc.) and the building trades together accounting for around 9 per cent of the total.

Table 1.1 Occupational structure of Birmingham 1851

	% of working population
Retail	9.2
Drink	2.65
Clothing	8.26
Leather	5.22
Domestic servants	11.78
Wood trades	3.06
Metal trades	22.83
Building trades	5.87
Guns	3.02
Buttons	4.3
Jewellery	3.99
Agriculture	0.84
Labouring	4.06
Professional	3.19
Transport	2.2
Finance	0.66
Administrative	0.26
Others	8.61
	100.00

Visitors to Birmingham often argued that the diversity of the town's industrial products insulated its working population from the kinds of all-embracing depressions so markedly apparent in single-industry centres such as Manchester or Leeds. C.P. Villiers, the investigator for the Poor Law Commission in 1834, for example, considered the town to be above the effects of widespread depression:

> The different condition of the working classes at the same time is not unusual at Birmingham; general distress from trade here can hardly occur. The manufacturers are so various that the cause for depression in particular ones are seldom in operation together.[18]

The town's working population, however, saw things differently. This clash of perspective was summed up by Thomas Baker, a working man and chairman of the Unemployed Artisans' Committee. Addressing a public meeting in 1832, he explained that:

> It was no novel thing to be treated in this sort of way. The middle, and higher classes had long been trying to persuade them, the working classes, that their bellies were full, when they were alarmingly and feelingly convinced that they were empty (laughter and cheers). Or if they allowed that distress did exist, they were always very ready to attribute it to idleness and profligacy.[19]

Thus, in Baker's view, apparently innocent observations on the diversity of the industrial structure were simply part of a broader explanation of poverty in terms of the moral failure of the individual.

In practice most trades appear to have suffered a depressed state at the same time, and by and large at those times when the national economy underwent a downturn. There may have been a diversity of product in the town but the internal structure of most trades was remarkably similar. This point may be drawn out by looking at the results of the probate survey referred to earlier.

Table 1.2 summarizes the probate material, occupation correlated with size of estimated personal estate at death, in twelve of the most prominent trades in Birmingham, for the 457 individuals who gave their occupations as falling into these categories. They include relatively new, mechanized trades, such as steel-toymaking and wireworking, along with more traditional trades, such as tailoring and coopering. Two initial points should be made here. First, to observe the almost uniformly large estates

Table 1.2 Estimated personal estates at time of death (in £s), Birmingham 1820–40

	£s											Thousands of £s															
	20	50	100	200	300	450	500	600	700	800	900	1	1.5	2	3	4	5	6	7	8	9	10	12	14	16	18	20 & over
Cutler and filemaker		1	3	1	2	2						2	1		1	1	1										
Gilt-toymaker		1	3	3								1	2		1		2										
Jeweller	4	1	5		3	3		1				2	2		1	1				1			1				
Steel-toymaker	3	1	5	3		3				1			2	2	1	3	1		1								
Wireworker			8	1	1					1		1	1					1						1			1
Brassfounder	5	2	12	13	9	3		6		6			3		2		1			1				1	1		3
Small-metalware-maker*	6	5	28	17	17	12		7		7		6	6	5	6	5		4	1								1
Button-maker	2	2	4	7	3	4		8		4		1	6	3	2	2	1		2				2		1		2
Cooper	1		6	1	2	1																					
Woodturner	1	3	1	1	1	1		1										1				1					
Tailor	1	1	8	6	1	5		1					1	4		2					1						1
Merchant or factor					3	1				1		3	1	4	2	4		5	3	2	2	3	3	1	1	1	8

*Consists of 42 different trades from awlmaker to watch-chain-maker
Total number of estates: 457

amongst the merchants and factors. Of the forty-eight individuals in this category who left wills or administration papers, only five died leaving personal estates of less than £1,000. At the other end of the scale they rise as high as £70,000. It was the merchant and the factor who provided credit and market facilities for many of the smaller producers and thus their presence was woven into the fabric of almost every trade. Second, and in many ways more surprisingly, the table indicates a very distinctive pattern of personal wealth within every trade. Each occupational grouping displays two major clusterings of estates, one up to the £600 mark and one from £1,000 upwards with only 19 of the total of 445 estates falling in the middle ground between £600 and £1,000. This, it could tentatively be suggested, is the distinctive area of differentiation between the small-scale producer (below £600, though most are below £450) and the large-scale producer (above £1,000). Above all, it is the repetition of this distinctive dual clustering of estates at the two ends of the spectrum of wealth, through each of the trades, that is of interest.

Rather than an even graduation of wealth, therefore, a fairly dramatic break appears in the table between the small firms and the larger firms. A closer examination of some of the individual trades appears to confirm this initial impression. Table 1.3 gives a breakdown of the eighty-two individuals involved with all aspects of button-making who had their wills proven in the period. Most of the estates here fall at or below £450, particularly in those trades, such as stamping or burnishing, which dealt with a subsidiary single process in the production of a button. The larger estates beginning at around £1,000 range as high as £30,000.

Table 1.4 repeats the pattern, this time for the more traditional industry relating to the production of leather goods. In this case the larger estates, with one exception, fall between £1,000 and £7,000 so that here the upper range is more limited. Here, however, the clustering at the other end of the scale is rather more marked with fifty-five of the total of eighty-two estates in the table falling at or below the £450 mark. Similarly for the wood-working trades shown in Table 1.5, of the total of sixty-five individuals involved, forty-two left estates valued at £450 or under, fifteen at around £1,000 or upwards, with only five in the area between. The same point could be made for the gun trade, shown in Table 1.6. Again the dual clustering is evident in the trade of gun-maker

Table 1.3 Personal estates in the button trade 1820–40

	£s											Thousands of £s									
	20	50	100	200	300	450	500	600	700	800	900	1	1.5	2	3	4	5	6	7	over 10	over 20
Button-maker		2	3	4		3		6		3		1	3		2	1	1		2	3	2
Glass-button-maker													1								
Metal-button-maker				1	2																
White-metal-button-maker													2	1							
Horn-button-maker														1			1				
Pearl-button-maker	2		1	2	1	1		2		1				1							
Button-stamper	2	1	5	2	2																
Button-turner			2	1	1					1											
Button-burnisher	1		2	1																	
Button-shank-maker				1		1															
Button-solderer				1																	
Button-cardmaker						1															

Total number of estates: 82

Table 1.4 Estimated personal estates in the leather trades 1820–40

	£s											Thousands of £s								
	20	50	100	200	300	450	500	600	700	800	900	1	1.5	2	3	4	5	6	7	8 … 18
Currier			2	2										1	1	1		1	1	
Shoemaker/bootmaker	1		2	4	2	4		1		2		3	1	3						
Cordwainer	2	2	4	4	2	1		1		3		2			2					
Whipmaker		1		1	1	1													1	
Coach-harness-maker		1											1							
Saddler		1	1	2	1	2														1
Saddle-tree-maker			1																	
Tanner	1					1														
Leather-cutter			3	1	1								1							
Leather-seller				2		1												1		

Total number of estates: 82

Table 1.5 Estimated personal estates in wood-working trades* 1820–40

	£s											*Thousands of £s*										
	20	50	100	200	300	450	500	600	700	800	900	1	1.5	2	3	4	5	6	8	10	12	14
Timber merchant	1											1	1	1	1	1			1		1	
Cabinet-maker			3	3	3			3					1									
Chair-maker						1	1															
Box-maker	1	1																				
Woodturner	1	3	1	1	1	1		1										1		1		
Brush-maker		1	1			1						1						1				
Coach-maker	1		1	1	1							1	1		1							
Boat-builder			1	1	1											1						1
Cooper	1		6	1	3																	1

* Excludes building trades
Total number of estates: 65

itself, but all the individuals involved in the subsidiary processes fall at or below the £450 level. As was the case with the leather trades, the upper levels of estates, though high in themselves, do not match the heights of the larger estates of the button-makers of Table 1.3 or of the brassfounders or wireworkers of Table 1.2. Reorganization of the processes of production had of course proceeded much further in terms of the introduction of mechanized factory production in these metal trades than in the more traditionally organized leather and gun trades. This is not to suggest that the latter were in any way 'pre-industrial' in organization, but the tables would suggest that such mechanization extended the possibilities of scale for the entrepreneur quite dramatically.

Similarly the estates of individuals in the building trades shown in Table 1.7 form distinctive groupings at either end of the scale. Most of the estates fall at or below the £450 mark, or at or above the £1,500 mark. But this time the middle ground in this, perhaps the most traditionally organized of all trades, is at its most well defined. The larger estates are certainly present in the table. The large-scale contractor was a growing feature of the building scene at this time, but again none of the estates range as high as those in the most highly mechanized of the metal trades.

In the last analysis, however, do these tables actually suggest anything more than the full spread of opportunity at any one time in a free market economy? Certainly any attempt to provide an alternative explanation must involve an interpretation of the dual clustering of estates. It is, for example, clear that this major differential within manufacturing industry was recognized by contemporaries. It is always difficult, however, to penetrate far beyond that image of small-scale production, projected by the large-scale manufacturer, as characterized by a blend of opportunity, independence, and mobility. The small producer rarely speaks for himself in the available evidence. Thomas Osler, a large-scale glass manufacturer, giving evidence before the Select Committee on Artisans and Machinery in 1824, drew attention to the division in terms of scale within the town's main industries:

> I do not think there are twenty brassfounders in Birmingham who employ so large a capital as twenty thousand pounds each. But there are hundreds of brassfounders who are at work on a

Table 1.6 Estimated personal estates in the gun trade 1820–40

	£s												*Thousands of £s*										
	5	20	50	100	200	300	450	500	600	700	800	900	1	1.5	2	3	4	5	6	7	8	9	10
Gun-maker				1	3	2	3	1	3		3		4	4		4	2						1
Gun-barrel-maker		1			1		2													1			
Gun-furniture-forger				2	3		1																
Gun-barrel-ribber					1	1																	
Gun-barrel-borer		1				1																	
Gun-barrel-fitter				1																			
Gun-locksmith	1	1				1																	
Gunsmith				1																			
Gun-stocker				1	2	1																	
Gun-finisher		1	1	1		1																	

Total number of estates: 59

Table 1.7 Estimated personal estates in the building trades 1820–40

	£s												Thousands of £s												
	5	20	50	100	200	300	450	500	600	700	800	900	1	1.5	2	3	4	5	6	7	8	9	10	11	12
Builder				2	4	3	3		3		5			5	5	2	1	1	1	1					1
Carpenter and joiner	1	2	2	7	9	5	6		1		2		1	1											
Bricklayer		1	1	6	4	3					1					1									
Plumber, glazier, & painter				1	4	5	4	1			2			4		2									
Plasterer							1		1								1								
Stonemason					1	2	2		1		1														
Slater									1						2										
Paviour						3																			
Paper-hanger			1																						
Brick-maker						1	2				1				1			1							

Total number of estates: 133

> capital of perhaps less than £500; for one man makes a drawer knob another a commode handle, another a bellpull, etc., etc. So that though there may be but few who manufacture every species of brass foundry, yet I think I may say that the most voluminous pattern book of the most extensive manufacturer in Birmingham does not contain a single article which a man without £50 may go and manufacture.[20]

Osler's observation of the structure of local industry cannot be divorced from his analysis of the way the system operated. 'In fact,' he claimed, 'if there is a spot in the world in which perfect community of interests betwixt workmen and their employers is to be found, that spot is Birmingham.'[21] Ironically Osler spoke at a time of increasing strike activity, and only five months later a local magistrate complained to the Home Secretary 'that combinations exist in every branch of manufactures'.[22] Nevertheless Osler's interpretation hinged vitally on the entrepreneurial opportunities afforded by small-scale production. Reference to Table 1.2, particularly in relation to the differences in wealth between the categories of 'brassfounder' and 'small-metalware-maker' will serve to confirm Osler's initial observations on the huge differential within the economic structure of the town. He was also, however, making a qualitative judgement on both the viability of the small concerns and the concomitant independence of the small producer. Although the optimism of this kind of contemporary observation has been clearly echoed in the familiar analysis of small-scale industry rendered by recent historians, the interpretation offered here is rather different.

It is argued here that what is reflected in the dual clustering of estates in Tables 1.2–1.7 are the two very different economic universes in which the large and small producers operated. By 1840 the larger manufacturer had appeared as a dominant element in all trades in the town. This was the case whether the industry was a 'traditional' one, such as tailoring, shoemaking, or coopering, or a new and highly mechanized one, such as steel-toymaking or metal-button-making. The presence of the large unit had the effect of reorienting the whole of the production in a way that reduced the small producer's control over the work process (and hence his independence). It also severely restricted the possibility of expansion by the smaller firm, while at the same time, as we have seen, offering itself as an example of the increase in such opportunities.

Both of these effects were the result of the growing dependence of the small firm upon the large. With the large firm the centre of gravity within production, the small producer found himself enmeshed in a relationship of dependency created by price competition and the need to utilize both the credit and market facilities of the larger unit. Firms represented by individuals above the £1,000 personal estate level in Tables 1.2–1.7 are designated 'large' because they were, in varying degrees, free of this dependent relationship, by virtue of their larger capital holding. Above this level individuals are more likely to represent firms that were the dominant element in such a dependency relationship with smaller concerns. Such a relationship operated not only to restrict the growth of the small firm; it also involved the larger firm in exerting control over the way in which small firms were actually run. Increasingly they came into line with the practices of the larger concerns in relation to work discipline and workshop practices. This meant that the workplace conflict between artisan norms and political economy, so familiar to historians in the context of the factory, was also evident in the smaller unit of production. However, in some areas of work, such as gun-making or the building trades, the nature of both the market and the product made it more likely that the small producer was able to retain his artisan–small-master status, and the way of life that this implied, for longer than in trades such as button-making, that were more susceptible to all-embracing forms of economic reorganization.

This analysis has fundamental implications for the understanding of the social relations of production. Between 1815 and 1850 the relationship between large and small units of production altered the nature of small-mastership fundamentally and, hence, also the attitude of the artisan to its status. Where the small master was reduced to a proletarianized outworker the 'safety valve' of upward mobility was no longer effective. On the other hand, where the small producer was remodelled in the image of the larger manufacturer the workplace community of interests between master and man, which had, to some extent, traditionally characterized small-scale production, was no longer possible.

The analysis will be pursued first by examining the competitive pressures that were growing at all levels of production in the decades after 1815. The specific problems this created for the small producer will then be examined along with the differing responses to these problems that were evident in this sector of the economy.

THE RESTRUCTURING OF PRODUCTION

The growth in importance of the large firm in the first half of the nineteenth century should not deceive us into underestimating the importance of capital for the town's industry before this time. The evidence suggests the early decline of the craftsman–retailer, although the persistence of a 'custom-built' section in trades such as jewellery and gun-making can sometimes lead the unwary to see this as a more recent development.[23] By the turn of the century Birmingham was a thriving town of 70,000 inhabitants and had established itself, not only as a centre for industry, but also for trade.[24] The marketing facilities of the town's merchant and factoring houses fed both home and overseas custom. The decentralized workshop network which produced the town's staple goods, primarily cheap and reliable metal goods rather than the highly finished craft product, had long since displayed what David Landes has described elsewhere as 'an orientation to the market instead of the shop'.[25] The workshop system was underpinned and co-ordinated by the circulating capital of the mercantile firms, and sometimes this was enormous. During the American blockade of 1812 Thomas Potts, a manufacturer, explained: 'I know one house that has £70,000 and I know another that has £50,000 and another that has about £45,000 and another that has about £20,000 and another £25,000; they run in that way.'[26]

Such firms continued to play an enabling role within the structure of production throughout the first half of the century. As late as 1876 A.W. Keep began work in his father's merchant warehouse and noted: 'Saturday was the great day when goods came rolling in, many of them still quite warm from the casting shop. These were mostly made by "little men" in the back streets and Black Country.'[27] The enormous personal estates of the merchants and factors who appear in Table 1.2 testify to the continuing viability of merchant enterprise. However, there was a significant absolute decrease in their numbers as the century progressed. Despite an expansion in production generally, in the period, directories indicate that the 175 merchant and factoring firms in operation in 1803 had dropped to 144 by 1833 and to 128 by 1839.[28] Increasingly mercantile firms were moving at least a proportion of their circulating capital into the fixed capital commitment of factory plant. The large firm, which had been so unusual in the area before 1800 (though a number had existed), was becoming, to use John Immer's phrase, 'quite common'.[29]

Immer has rightly taken to task those historians who have underplayed the role of the factory in the economic structure of the town by 1840. The underestimation must partly be laid at the door of Robert Grainger, whose report to the Children's Employment Commission in 1843 has been a major source for the economic history of the town. His statement that 'There are no large and crowded factories such as abound in other districts', in particular, has been used to reinforce the curiously one-dimensional analysis of economic development which has suggested that industrialization simply acted to multiply the number of workshops in operation.[30] Grainger managed to convey the impression that by 1840 the factory was really rather a novel, and as yet largely untried, system of production, by his remark that: 'Of late years a considerable number of new manufactories have been erected upon a much larger and improved plan: some of these buildings contain fine, spacious and lofty workrooms and a few of them may be called splendid constructions.'[31]

These were model factories, like that of James James the screw manufacturer, built during the boom periods of the mid-1820s and mid-1830s. On the other hand, Grainger reported: 'Many of the places of work are inconveniently crowded, shops full of people, built around narrow and confined yards, men, women and children are, to use a homely expression "huddled together".'[32] The implication here is that whereas James's heroic construction was a 'factory' these were simply a number of workshops under a series of small masters. This was, however, not necessarily the case. Both could be, and often were, manifestations of the same phenomenon, both dominated by the large-scale entrepreneur.

Take, for example, the brassworks of James Reynolds Boyce in Alcester Street, visited by Grainger in May 1840.[33] This would have fallen into the latter category of workplace. He found the plant to be old and dilapidated, working conditions crowded, and facilities clearly inadequate. Yet Boyce was himself clearly no small master. He had inherited his business on the death of his father James Boyce in 1831. His father's personal estate at death was estimated at £25,000 with stock and property connected with the business worth £6,000. Besides this he held £2,000 worth of canal shares and annuities, land in Kings Norton, which he farmed himself, and a house at Highgate worth £900. The allocation in his will of £500 a year for his wife is a clear indication of the standard of life enjoyed by the family.[34]

In addition to this qualification, Grainger's report can only really be taken as a glimpse at the extent to which the larger units had developed by the 1840s. Of the sixty-three establishments named in his report, thirteen employed between 150 and 500 workpeople on the premises. A further six establishments were described as being 'extensive', although in these cases no head count was given (for example Robert Winfield's brass foundry, which employed over 100 workpeople in 1835, a workforce that grew to 800 by 1860, fell into this category). Many of the older and larger establishments were actually omitted from the survey. Only two rolling mills appear to have been inspected, yet metal-rolling had been one of the first processes to be mechanized and used an estimated 650 steam horsepower in 1838. Wire mills were also omitted, although an estimated 170 horsepower was used in wire-drawing in the same year.[35] William Fox's Speedwell Mills employed 250 pairs of hands in 1830,[36] whilst T.C. Salt's lamp manufactory employed 120 men by the 1830s.[37] Both factories were in operation at the time of Grainger's survey yet neither appear in the report. Similarly the Eagle Foundry, where George Holyoake and his brothers worked, was omitted and numerous other examples could be given.[38] Grainger, then, provided a useful insight into factory production in the town, rather than a comprehensive review.

An American visiting the town as early as 1811 was impressed with 'the great scale on which manufactories are conducted and the immense power and high perfection of the machines employed'. He was particularly struck by one manufactory where a steam engine of 120 horsepower and 300 workmen produced 300 gun barrels a month.[39] In terms of mechanization, however, it was the decades following the close of the Napoleonic Wars that were really significant. In 1838 a local sub-committee of the Statistical Society reported that: 'From 1780 to 1815, a period of 35 years there were only 42 engines set to work. The total number now at work is 240: of these therefore 198 have been added since 1815 and 120 have been erected since 1830.'[40] By the time of this report there were 3,436 steam horsepower in the town's industries. The fact that this was only one-third of the power being used at this time in the Manchester and Salford area, should not divert us from appreciating the importance of mechanization locally.[41]

This period of increased mechanization coincided with a period of downward spiralling prices for manufactured goods, with most manufacturers, in the decades after 1815, reporting greatly reduced profits. Charles Babbage produced, in 1830, a comprehensive list of hardware products which had fallen in price progressively since 1818. This was updated in 1832 by M.P. Haynes, a manufacturer and a member of the Political Council of the Birmingham Political Union. The table was published in both the establishment and the radical press, and was widely acknowledged as a formal statement of an already accepted fact.[42] Local manufacturers rejected the possibility that over-production at home was the cause of price falls, preferring to interpret them in terms of foreign competition. In 1835, in an editorial on the Prussian Commercial League, the *Birmingham Journal* complained that 'it is now price – lowness of price – that upholds the trade as regards exportation to Germany'.[43] G.F. Muntz, a merchant and manufacturer, reinforced this point to a Select Committee in 1836 by blaming a fall in profits on 'The competition with the continental market; a single alteration of 5 per cent upon any of the Birmingham goods loses the trade'.[44]

This general trend towards price reduction was only slightly offset by the boom periods of 1824–5 and 1834–6, though manufacturers were to look back on 1825 particularly as a year of maximum production when, in the words of T.C. Salt, 'all hands were employed at all hours we could get them to labour'.[45] Above all, it is the extended period of low profits within local industry that is noteworthy. Thomas Attwood, the banker, claimed in 1832 that 'there have been no regular profits made since the war in Birmingham',[46] whilst in 1833 Salt estimated that profit had been absent for at least five years.[47] Even during the boom year of 1836 G.F. Muntz was prepared to claim:

> I believe that in the last two years a great proportion of the tradesmen in our part of the world have not got a single shilling; they have been carrying on business and doing a great return and many of them are in a situation of ruin. They have been doing business for the sake of amusement. . . . I have no doubt that from 1825 to 1835 a great proportion of the tradesmen never got what they spent to live upon; that the reduction, in fact, of the value of their stock, and the value of their different outlay was altogether lost.[48]

These reports of a declining rate of profit must be seen as rather more than the special pleading of currency reformers such as Attwood, Muntz, and Salt. A similar trend is evident, for example, in the cotton textile area of South Lancashire during the same period.[49] Nor is there a real contradiction posed by the correlation of this lengthy period of declining prices with an increase in the total mechanical power used by the town's industry. In periods of boom (such as 1824–5 or 1835–6) manufacturers responded by investment in new plant. In periods of reduced prices, or even of recession, manufacturers attempted to reduce production costs and increase productivity by a variety of innovations and rationalizations. This served to spread capital overheads across a larger volume of output.

Thus, by the 1840s the development of economies of scale, as a result of the cost-reducing incentives of declining prices, alongside investment in new plant in periods of prosperity, resulted in the emergence of a number of large, efficient firms who aimed at low costs per unit of output. A similar pattern has been discerned within the well-documented case of cotton textiles.[50] In the case of the hosiery industry of Nottinghamshire, Charlotte Erickson has gone so far as to suggest that the move from the circulating capital commitment of the domestic system to the fixed capital commitment of the factory, was initially undertaken by those firms whose profit margins were lowest under the older system.[51]

Although there is little concrete evidence to either support or reject such a claim in the case of Birmingham, it is very clear that, in this period of reduced profits, increased mechanization was only one of a number of ways in which production costs were lowered throughout industry. Historians have often seen the opposition offered by workers to the introduction of new machinery as anti-progressive; part of a nostalgic but tenacious retention of pre-industrial norms that was ultimately uninformed by any real understanding of the needs of a modern industrial economy. It should be remembered, however, that for the workforce the 'machinery question' was rarely posed in a very positive fashion in this early period. As an answer to declining prices, caused by increased competition, machinery was seen by the entrepreneur as part of a broad spectrum of innovation designed to lower production costs. For the workforce an increased workload, the dilution of skilled labour, and mechanization were all part of the same package. When Bronterre O'Brien's *Midland Representative* first appeared in the town in April 1831 it defined as a major target for attack by political radicals 'all who have unjustly profited by the frauds and vices of individual competition, aggravated as they must continue to be by the *misapplication of machinery*'.[52] Chartist Henry Watson, who was at one time Chairman of the Unemployed Artisans Committee, complained to a meeting of the BPU in January 1838 that, 'Instead of machinery shortening the term of their toil to give them time and opportunity for moral, mental and intellectual improvement it was made to render them and their labour useless and valueless.'[53] It was not the machine, as such, that was rejected so much as the entire context within which machinery was drawn into play at this time.

Allegations by working people that their individual workloads increased in this period are common. The remarks of both O'Brien and Watson point to the irony of increased workloads that coincided with a period which witnessed an unparalleled application of labour-saving devices in the workplace. The link between low prices for manufactured goods and the necessity for higher levels of output was made by a bankrupt wirework manufacturer in 1829: 'Our manufactories are obliged to make double the quantity of goods for the amount they formerly received and our workmen are obliged to do double the work for the wages they formerly had.'[54] It was the relative rapidity with which the work process was being restructured in this period that is noteworthy, since it was this that rendered 'customary' practice in the workplace such an immediate and relevant yardstick by which the workforce could measure and assess the change. By the 1830s it was a common complaint among artisans that 'the mechanic may labour for 12 or 15 hours a day and earn less than his grandfather did when he laboured only five or six hours a day'.[55]

This restructuring was perhaps most apparent in the increased use of female and child labour. Direct substitution was often implemented as a response to a period of poor trade. Such a period not only increased the need on the part of the entrepreneur to bring about a reorganization in order to arrest a declining rate of profit, it also ensured the tactical weakness of the trade societies who would otherwise have opposed the move. T.C. Salt admitted in 1833 that:

> There are many inferior parts of the work that used to pass through men's hands; we take as much as we can off the men and have it done in parts by the boys or the women and then give it to the men to finish; which when trade was good the men would not submit to . . . formerly when trade was good we did not resort to that screwing system; if we had done so we should not have had a single workman to work for us the next day.[56]

Grainger, collecting evidence for the 1843 report found that many of the manufacturers he interviewed justified the recent extension of child and female labour in terms of the fall in prices. James Pardoe of 'Pardoe and Armstrong', a large gilt-toymaking concern, explained that, 'The custom of substituting boys for journeymen leads to much distress among the adult mechanics. . . . The reduction of prices is so great that masters cannot compete with foreigners unless they adopt this plan.'[57] Such labour dilution itself often served to increase the workload for the remaining male workforce because it involved a reallocation of tasks and a redefinition of functions within the workplace as a whole. In this process the customary or accepted levels of work were easily blurred.

These changes had an impact upon both the large- and the small-scale unit of production. Although it may have been the large firms that were responsible for increasing the tempo of competition, they were not alone in introducing innovation of one kind or another in this period. Yet, strangely, it is sometimes difficult to detect the fundamental nature of the process at work since it left a good deal of the town's overall economic structure apparently unchanged. This point may be explored, in relation to the dilution of labour, by an exercise which compares the occupational statistics available for the Borough of Birmingham in the 1841 and 1851 censuses. There can be little precision in such a venture since the two censuses were constructed rather differently.[58] Nevertheless the general trend that such an exercise indicates ties in closely with the other information, already cited, on the changing age–sex ratio within different trades.

In 1841 the population of the borough stood at 182,922, of which 70,375 were listed in an occupational group of some kind in the census. This means that the working population stood at 38 per cent of the total population. By 1851, from a population of 232,841, the workforce stood at 113,982, or 49 per cent of the population. This may, of course, simply indicate that the 1851 census was a more efficient exercise. On the other hand, the increase appears to have consisted largely of women and children. In 1841, males over the age of 20 made up 63 per cent of the workforce. By 1851 the figure had dropped to 52 per cent.[59]

The increase in women and juvenile workers does not, in itself, 'prove' that substitution was taking place. It does, however, point to a reorganization of work. This is not readily apparent if we concern ourselves only with the overall economic or occupational structure of the town. By the mid-century, for example, it was undoubtedly the metal trades that had undergone most internal reorganization with metal-button-making a leading sector in this respect. A comparison of the figures for the 1841 and 1851 censuses indicates that both sectors of the economy occupied much the same proportion of the workforce between these two dates (Table 1.8). However, an analysis of the shifting age–sex ratio within these groups reveals dramatic changes emphasizing the role increasingly played by female and juvenile workers (Tables 1.9 and 1.10).

The extent of the reorganization implicit in these figures may be appreciated by comparing them with similar figures for a trade that had clearly undergone a good deal less internal reorganization. The gun trade in 1841 occupied around 3 per cent of the total working population, and the figure was the same for 1851. A breakdown of the age–sex ratio within the trade indicates that the drop in adult male workers was much less, between these years, in this trade than in either the metal or the button trade (Table 1.11). The percentage of women and girls employed in the trade did not increase appreciably, the major increase being

Table 1.8 Percentage of total workforce in the metal and button-making trades

	1841	*1851*
	%	%
Metal trades (excludes buttons and guns)	24	23
Button-making	4	4

Table 1.9 Age–sex ratio within the metal trades

	1841	*1851*
	%	%
Men (males over 20)	71	58
Boys (males under 20)	17	24
Women (females over 20)	8	11
Girls (females under 20)	4	7
	100	100

Table 1.10 Age–sex ratio within the button-making trades

	1841	*1851*
	%	%
Men	45	27
Boys	15	16
Women	24	32
Girls	16	25
	100	100

among male workers under the age of 20. Table 1.11 suggests that the gun-workers were rather more successful in preserving the craft basis of their trade than workers in the metal or button trades. The increase of males under 20 also helps to explain why so many of the conflicts between employers and trade societies, in the gun trade, focused on the question of apprenticeship. By the mid-century in this trade there had been less structural reorganization than in some other trades. This (as will be seen later) was largely the result of the nature of the market for guns. It enabled the artisan–small master to preserve his way of life with a greater degree of success than in those trades which had been subject to more extensive reorganization.

Two final points must be made at the conclusion of this section

Table 1.11 Age–sex ratio within the gun trade

	1841	*1851*
	%	%
Men	78	71
Boys	18.4	25
Women	3	3.1
Girls	0.6	0.9
	100	100

on the changing economic context. First, as noted earlier, although the factory lay at the heart of these changes, it was not only the large firm that reorganized work in this period. The next two sections of this chapter attempt to demonstrate that despite the opposition of trade societies and the continued existence of artisan small masters in sections of many trades, the small producer came increasingly to act in ways that reflected the behaviour of his larger counterpart. In this sense the workshop that operated under the price became as much a target for artisan opposition as the factory.

Second, this reorganization of work, which was in itself central to the process of industrialization, was primarily a function of the market rather than a direct product of the machine. As will be seen in the next section, it was the vagaries of the market that served to insulate the gun trade from extensive structural change in the first fifty years of the century and to some extent the same could be said of the building trades, with their seasonal demand.[60] The absence of machinery did not, in itself, prevent a reorganization of work to meet mass demand. This point is most clearly demonstrated in the cases of tailoring, shoemaking, and a host of other technologically 'backward' trades.[61] Some observers have been misled into speaking of the anachronistic survival of 'pre-industrial' enclaves within the world's first industrial society, with the border between 'industrial' and 'pre-industrial' defined by the use of the machine.[62] In the same way the social relations of Birmingham's industries have been seen as inherently harmonious because of this 'pre-industrial' quality. However, superficial similarities between the systems of production in 1800 and in 1850, to be seen for example in the continued reliance on hand technology or the continued typicality of the small workshop, can mask less obvious differences in organization and authority, within the total system of production, that were of rather more importance socially than the similarities themselves.

The reorganization of work to meet the competitive premium on low prices was a feature of all trades in the period but its form varied between trades. In 1833 the artisans of the coopering trade went so far as to advise their employers to combine amongst themselves to maintain uniform prices: 'Viewing the present state of trade through competition we believe that unless some measure be adopted the trade will not be worth following.'[63] Where the possibilities for mechanization were limited the major development lay in a greater emphasis upon the merchant co-ordinator in organizing the process of work and determining the nature of employment. In tailoring and shoemaking, for example, the cheaper end of the trade witnessed a great increase in outworking, since this was seen as a way by which the merchant might decisively breach craft control of the trade. By 1845 the tailors in the town were complaining of:

> unprincipled competition . . . inasmuch as certain Master Tailors have departed from the original mode of employing their workmen on premises under their immediate supervision. . . . The above system of out-door labour has called into existence a certain class of persons who act as middlemen and are vulgarly denominated sweaters who take out large quantities of work in order to secure a large per centage.[64]

As in London (and Paris for that matter), home working in the tailoring trade enabled the merchant co-ordinator to avoid the trade's quality and price controls and its restrictions on the use of female and juvenile labour.

THE PROBLEMS OF THE SMALL PRODUCER

Far from absorbing the smaller units of production, the development of capital intensive industries in Birmingham served to multiply them. This is a familiar development that has been widely observed for other areas and a range of industries.[65] Large brass foundries and wire mills rolled metal that was distributed to small producers to be fashioned into small metalware articles. Even the gun trade, with its more traditional emphasis on the decentralized workshop structure, received an acceleration and expansion by the application of steam to barrel-making in the way that was observed by Simond in 1811. It would be quite wrong, however, to see large-scale industry developing in this period as essentially the servant of the smaller unit. Although this was often the way the large-scale manufacturer sought to present himself, the reverse was actually the case. The centre of gravity within the town's total system of production was shifting towards the larger unit. It was the smaller unit that was now to play the subsidiary role.

Large firms emerged not only to provide the raw material for the small producer but also to complete the finished article. Also entrepreneurs, reluctant to shift all their assets to a fixed capital commitment, often retained a large number of outworkers even where they had established a basis in factory production. Outworkers, in the full variety of forms the term implies, were particularly useful in absorbing demand at peak periods. In 1833, for example, John Turner's button manufactory at Snow Hill employed between 130 and 150 workers on the premises and a further 350 outworkers who, in his own words, were 'either working for us entirely or partially'.[66] Turner, who died in 1840, appears in Table 1.3 as a button-maker with a personal estate of around £16,000. A few months after John Turner's death the works was visited by Grainger, who interviewed Samuel Turner, the dead manufacturer's son. At this stage the firm employed 500 workers and owned market outlets and similar firms in London, Manchester, Leek, and Paris.[67]

The artisan, clearly, could work either inside the factory or outside in his own premises. Yet in the rarefied competitive atmosphere of the three decades following the Napoleonic Wars the difference between the two was often more apparent than real. Either way the smaller concerns worked for the larger, a point that John Turner's grandson made very clear in his contribution to Timmins' volume of essays in 1866: 'As a rule a few larger houses supply the materials to these smaller masters . . . and they take all they produce *thus practically becoming the real employers.*'[68] Similarly William Elliot, whose firm was of a comparable size to Turner's, reported to Grainger in 1840 that he employed, 'when trade is tolerably good, in the manufactory and out of it, about 500 people'.[69] Elliot had inherited the firm from his father who had died in 1831 (he also appears in Table 1.3 as a button-maker, this time with a personal estate of £7,000). The interesting point about the comment by Elliot the younger to Grainger is not so much the size of the firm itself but the fact that he, as an employer, drew little distinction between those he employed inside or outside the factory.

In fact, the subordinate role of the small producer has a long history, as the work of both Franklin Mendels and Hans Medick on the 'proto-industrial' stage of economic development has recently emphasized.[70] Nevertheless the nature of the market and the high reliance upon hand technology (and in some areas the existence of a dual economy of agriculture and domestic industry) had previously given the artisan some degree of independence within this authority structure. The work of Marie Rowlands and of David Hey has given some indications of how this relationship between the small producer and the merchant capitalist might have operated in the metalware trade of the Midlands.[71] Such independence was reflected in 'task-oriented' work rhythms and in the artisan's ready acceptance, in the 1790s, of the libertarian democratic tradition.[72] Nevertheless, the pattern of dependency had itself been long established by the start of the nineteenth century. Over the course of the next fifty years the balance of the relationship moved against the artisan and the small master even though the accelerated pace of industrialization often encouraged the multiplication of the smaller unit.

The relationship between the workshop and the factory during early industrialization has been described by David Landes as 'symbiotic', while for Birmingham itself W.H.B. Court has stressed 'the mutual dependence of both'.[73] Yet even if the relationship was a reciprocal one, as these statements suggest, the pattern of dependency was emphatically biased against the smaller unit. In fact, for any kind of industrial enterprise the twin questions of the viability of the concern and the independence of the producer were determined almost entirely by the nature of the credit and marketing facilities at its command. In this sense merchant capital, or increasingly the larger firms themselves, played an enabling role within the local economy. Richard Tangye, head of a large engineering firm, remarked in his autobiography that: 'One great advantage possessed by manufacturers in Birmingham having but small capital is the practice which has long existed among the factors and merchants of paying cash every Saturday for the supplies of the whole week.'[74] This facility enabled the smaller firm to manage with its cash-flow problems on a week-by-week basis, with the market being provided by the merchant or the larger concern. Nevertheless it is significant that Tangye also attributed his own success, in no small degree, to the extent to which he was able to avoid these channels: 'Instead of relying upon agents who often "sold" us instead of selling our goods we established our own houses at Newcastle upon Tyne, Manchester and Glasgow . . . selling direct to the users . . . instead of through middlemen whose interests were sometimes in contrast with ours.'[75]

Clearly, for a firm to expand fully there was a need to evolve a relatively self-contained marketing structure. Where this was not possible even the larger firms remained tied to the merchant and factor. The relationship between the merchant and his services, and the manufacturer and his product, was a delicately balanced one with credit as its fulcrum. Where the enterprise was large enough for the manufacturer to allow credit to the merchant or factor, rather than vice versa as in the case of the small producer, the relationship was more likely to balance in its favour. James Luckock, a manufacturer of cheap jewellery, found himself in this position in the 1820s. With annual sales of £8,000 and profits of £2,000 per year his was obviously not a concern of comparable size to that of, say, John Turner's button manufactory. Nevertheless the credit equation was resolved in his favour:

> Our mode of doing business was this: we had 20 customers among the Birmingham factors, who, on going on their journies of 2 or 3 months would take about £100 worth of our stock (each) returning to us at the end of each journey what remained and taking from 6 to 15 months credit on the remainder.[76]

Luckock died in 1836 leaving a personal estate of £3,000 which placed him in the lower areas of the 'larger' enterprise section of Table 1.2. It is clear that firms like his, although small in comparison with the larger enterprises of the 'cotton kings', were certainly large enough to escape the pattern of dependency which characterized the small producer proper. In fact, work by V.A.C. Gatrell on Lancashire emphasizes the importance, even in that area, of firms comparable in size to Luckock's. Gatrell has also demonstrated that such concerns lay beyond the reach of the traditional mechanisms of upward economic and social mobility.[77]

The pattern of dependency often began, for the small producer, at the very point of purchasing raw material for manufacture. T.C. Salt, who had a capital of £10,000 tied up in his own lamp-manufacturing concern, explained how, by 1833, the decline in prices and an unstable market had reduced the credit margin that the large firms allowed when supplying raw materials:

> When I first embarked on business in Birmingham [1815], it had been the practice from time immemorial to make all their purchases the first twelvemonth without paying anything, and if you cleared off the purchases of the first twelvemonth in the next twelvemonth it was considered regular payment; now if I purchase metal I pay for it in the same day, cash and that practice is general in the purchase of metals.[78]

This was likely to prejudice the whole nature of the small producer's operation, emphasizing his subordination to either the larger firm or to merchant capital. As Salt observed: 'They go to a merchant, he gives them an order for metal somewhere, taking first of all the profit upon it, and then they bring their goods in at just what prices he pleases.'[79]

In the case of copper, which in the form of brass was central to many of the articles produced in the town, the market had been both opened and dominated by the larger firms since at least the late eighteenth century. By the 1780s the town's industries were using 2,000 tons of copper per year, mostly supplied from Cornwall and smelted in Swansea. In an attempt to cut out the Cornish middleman and establish a reliable supply, the manufacturers of Birmingham, following Matthew Boulton's lead, established a series of companies to both mine and smelt the copper. By 1830 there were five such companies operating in Birmingham each with working capitals of between £20,000 and £100,000 raised on a shareholder basis.[80] At the time of his death in 1827 Anthony Baldwin, for example, who appears in Table 1.3 as a button-maker with a personal estate of £30,000, owned 120 of the 1,000 shares of the Birmingham Mining and Copper Company.[81] Six years earlier five shares in the company had been advertised in *Aris's Gazette* at £100 each.[82] If this price was close to their market value, Baldwin's investment was worth around £12,000.

He also held twenty shares in the Birmingham Brass Company (capital £14,000). Shares in such companies carried a specified allowance of copper or brass for the shareholder. The Birmingham Brass Company, for example, allowed a shareholder 5 hundredweight of brass per share, per quarter. There are no figures available for the Mining and Copper Company, but if its shareholder allowance was similar to this, Baldwin would have had something like 140 tons of copper and brass a year at his disposal.[83] This could be used in his own firm or sold to those smaller firms without such a direct access to a source of supply.

The small firm generally operated on short-term credit, a point which enforced a weekly cycle within its economy. The slim profit margin did not allow the small producer to do what Luckock was able to do, that is, consign a proportion of his stock to a traveller. He had instead, in the words of one small producer, to:

> lookout for ready money customers with whom alone by reason of his want of capital he can at first deal, and whose orders it is absolutely necessary for him to secure. To every story there are two sides. The large manufacturer, or possibly the factor, who gives him these orders knows who he is, how he is circumstanced, and taking the natural trade advantages of his securities, grinds him down to the lowest point consistent with his having any.[84]

The weekly cycle locked the small producer into a viciously inverted political economy whereby he obtained his raw materials in the dearest market and sold his finished goods in the cheapest. What is perhaps remarkable about this passage, however, is the passive acceptance by the small producer himself that the exploitation of his difficulties by the larger manufacturer is part of a 'natural' economic order of things.

Above all, the problems of the small producer were related to the scale of the enterprise which necessarily restricted the range of innovations that could be adopted to broaden the profit margin. T.C. Salt summarized some of these problems:

> in purchasing in small quantities they purchase at a higher price and in manufacturing in small quantities they manufacture with less economy; and they cannot resort to the division of labour, nor to the same convenient machinery.[85]

As the market contracted during a recession it was the small firms who felt the effects first. The larger firms often simply reduced the work that was farmed out to them, hoping to offset fixed capital costs by retaining work for their main plant. W.G. Rimmer has noted that in Leeds at such times the outworking firms 'died like flies in the night'.[86] The weekly economic commitment left little margin for error and the small producer swiftly moved to crisis point. A 'Tradesman of Small Capital' explained the difficulty to the Home Secretary in 1826:

> In my conversations with different gentlemen who have been in the habit of turning tens of thousands in the year, they say that things are so bad they do not care how little they do and that if at the year's end they shall find they have not gained one farthing they shall think themselves fortunate providing they can but escape great loss . . . but then to me and such as me to do nothing is certain ruin because we have nothing to depend upon but trade.[87]

It was really this necessity to keep going on a week-by-week basis, rather than existing in a quarterly or annual credit market, that tied the smaller concerns to the larger. This meant that the viability of these smaller units related directly to their usefulness at any point in time to the larger firm. This was a relationship that enabled the small firm to exist but at the same time kept it small. A shift in the balance of the relationship, created by a fluctuation of the market or technological developments within the factory, could result in the disappearance of the smaller unit providing that particular service or commodity. The fact that production now centred on the large firm made the outworking firms far more precarious than concerns of a comparable size would ever have been within a decentralized workshop system.

The small producer that was most disadvantaged was the garret-master. By 1850 he was present in most trades, and in this year a manufacturer explained the internal economy of the garret-master's operation as it related to pearl-button-making. The description could, however, apply to the making of any small article at this level.

> He could hire the necessary tools for 4 shillings a week and would purchase from the shell dealers as small a quantity as 14

> pounds or 28 pounds of shell for a few shillings or more. Of course in the shell trade as in every other the poor man pays the highest price and a garret master . . . would pay at a rate, almost, if not quite double that which would be paid by the large manufacturer who bought several tons at a time.

At this level the business cycle was emphatically a weekly one, a position which severely prejudiced the sale of the finished article:

> Saturday night brings its wants and liabilities and it becomes imperative for these masters . . . to convert the buttons into money . . . consequently they are obliged to make the round of factors or dealers. . . . If it is early in the day they will not sell them under a fair price but the factor . . . knowing full well that he can get it at a greatly reduced rate as the hour for closing business draws nigh, refuses to purchase at the fair market price. The garret master has no other resource and is pretty certain to return before night and sell his goods for any sum that the factor is pleased to give him.[88]

The garret-master, working alone or with the assistance of his wife or children, faced the problems common to the small producer, but for him they were magnified several times. This is clearly the area where independent production shaded into the largely unskilled sweated trades of Victorian Britain, with their characteristic emphasis upon female and juvenile labour.[89] There has been a tendency to see this whole area as simply a decaying domestic system. In many senses this is, of course, correct. The unit of production was of similar size, co-ordination was by merchant manufacturer, and the family often worked together.

Nevertheless, sweating of this kind was more than a transitional stage in the movement from what Marx referred to as 'manufactures' to modern factory-based industry.[90] Sweating developed as a logical part of the reorganization of some trades to mass produce their respective articles and it always represented one of a series of choices open to the holder of capital, as to the form that production might take. At any point in time he might opt for the fixed capital commitment of the factory with the attendant difficulties and potential rewards. Or he might opt for an extension of production through the outwork system provided that the necessary adjustments to the (mainly human) factors of production could be made. Choice would be directed by the nature of the market and locally available resources in the forms of labour, skill, technology, and capital. The manufacturer could reduce the costs of production himself by recourse to economies of scale within the workplace, or alternatively he could 'persuade' the small producer to accomplish this task for him. In severely undercharging for his labour, and that of his workforce, and in reducing the level of craftsmanship involved in the production of the article, the garret-master was accomplishing all that the machine and the reorganization of the work process aimed for within the factory.

Choice had also, of course, always been an element within the artisan's frame of reference. For generations, with production focused on a decentralized workshop system, the artisan had assumed that he was in a position to choose between working for himself, as a small master, or working for an employer. The operation of small-scale production as a 'safety valve' for social tension depended entirely upon this traditional mobility existing as an accepted reality. It has already been suggested that the growth of the market and the large firm was decisively shifting the pattern of dependency against the small producer in the first half of the period. Added to this was the fact that, in the 1830s and 1840s, increasing numbers of artisans exercised their 'traditional' choice in highly unfavourable circumstances. Unemployment or under-employment forced many artisans into independent production as a means of avoiding parish relief. Speaking of garret-masters in 1833 Salt claimed that 'They certainly have increased from the fact of the manufacturers dismissing their workmen. And the workmen are driven to become little masters.'[91] This meant that for many artisans their experience of being small masters was in fact as garret-masters, the most debased form of small-scale production. Salt suggested that 'in every case the workman would be glad to surrender himself to be employed by the master, for the situation of the little master is deplorable'.[92] Many of the factoring establishments where such small producers made their sales were dubbed 'slaughterhouses', a reference not so much to the retail meat trade as to the 'slaughter of the Innocents'.

Therefore, the accepted pattern was being inverted. Instead of the move to independent production being viewed by the artisan as a process of positive mobility it could, under certain circumstances, be seen as a step down the social scale. Far from easing social tension the multiplication of the smaller units of production at this level only acted to emphasize the changed nature of the economic context in which the artisan existed.

DIFFERING RESPONSES AMONGST SMALL PRODUCERS: SMALL MANUFACTURER AND SMALL MASTER

Small firms thus faced common problems in their role within the town's total system of production. The seriousness of these universal difficulties obviously varied from time to time, and from firm to firm, within the small-producer sector itself. In terms of social relations at the point of production the most crucial factor was the particular frame of reference through which the small producer understood and came to terms with the problems. Here it is vital to differentiate between (a) the *petit-bourgeois* small manufacturer, who drew strength from the image of the entrepreneur as created and modelled by the highly individual values of political economy, and (b) the small master, who related the changing economic context to an artisan-oriented set of collective values. Workplace relations between the small producer and his workforce were almost entirely determined by these two conflicting sets of values.[93]

This section will explore this theme of response within the small-producer sector of the economy. This will be done largely by a case study examination of Charles Walters, a woodscrew manufacturer who left a series of sixteen letters written to his sleeping business partner, T.H. Musgrave of Oxford. Running between January and June 1832 they provide a unique insight into the operation of a small business over a six-month period. Walters is not offered here as a 'typical' small producer, but the letters enable us to understand more fully the problems of the small firm and in particular the relationship that existed between the representatives of small- and large-scale business enterprise. In addition to this, and more importantly, the voice is authentically that of a small manufacturer. The insight given into his attitudes and values can help us to construct a typology of response for this particular economic sector. This is particularly useful in contrasting the attitudes and values of Walters, who clearly did not identify with the world of labour, with those small producers who do appear to have subscribed to artisan values.

The small manufacturer

Charles Walters operated on a working capital of £132 and his weekly profits fluctuated (after paying wages) from 25s to £5. The size of his workforce is never specified in the letters, but his weekly wage bill was around £30. Compared with some of the other screw-makers in the town, his was a very small concern. Grainger, for example, reported in 1841 on four screw manufactories, the largest of which was that of James James. At the time of the report, James employed 300 women and 60 men in a factory which Grainger considered to be a model of its kind: 'This is an admirably conducted establishment, every attention is paid to the comfort of the workpeople, many of whom have been here 15 and 20 years, and upwards.'[94]

The firms of Hawkins and Ledsam, making the same product, employed 190 and 140 hands respectively.[95] The fourth large firm in the trade was owned by T.H. Ryland, who left some details of the firm in his autobiography. The business grew from an initial investment of £2,000 produced entirely through family connections; Ryland was a third-generation industrialist who had also made a judicious marriage. By 1842, he recalls, 'my consumption of wrought iron was 50 tons per week and my returns £4,000 to £5,000 per month'. By 1850 his plant alone was worth £15,000. Nevertheless he still felt justified in reflecting, in his autobiography, 'I began without any capital to speak of'.[96] It is only by examining the scale and problems of a small manufacturer like Walters that such claims can really be put into perspective. Ryland's initial enterprise, though small compared with the size of the same firm over the next decade, was large enough for him to escape the pattern of dependency, relating to marketing, credit, and economies of scale, in which Walters found himself trapped.

Walters' letters clearly reflect the problems posed for the small firm by the emergence of such large-scale units as a response to the market. In one letter he draws attention to:

> The turn given to our affairs by many masters rushing into the Trade with large expectations and fresh capital invited away our forgers by premiums and promises. . . . Mr. Ledsam the present High Bailiff has lately taken out a patent for screws – Mr. James has 300 girls on. In Birmingham a demand for any article meets with a speedy supply – numerous adventurers and

ready capital quickly overstock any that can be made.[97]

There is also the sense, in the correspondence, that this development was something new and different for this particular trade. At one point he complained that:

> Times are not what they were – formerly ignorant men – a sort of upper workman were masters in the Trade – Mr. James came into it, took a lead – killed the price to drive such masters out and now is bringing in men of more general knowledge and of rank in life with himself, and consequently, more able competitors as to quantity and quality.[98]

Clearly Walters could not compete directly with such firms. They attracted the best labour by paying higher wages and produced their goods at the lowest price. James James dominated the market in this way in the 1830s, as Walters put it 'his screws are the best common – but like "Hodges Porter" in India, the name does wonders'.[99] The higher the output the lower the cost of the product and in May he related sadly:

> One or two merchants called upon me because they could not obtain any from Mr. James, but our prices being 30 or 35% higher they found our terms too costly for shipping. . . . Messrs Timothy Smith and Sons purchase £300 every quarter of screws – ours are too costly for their wants.[100]

He seems to have survived this particular problem because he managed to fill a gap in the market which the larger firms had left open. He produced a middle-sized screw which, for technical reasons, the larger firms found difficult to mass produce. Nevertheless he found himself in the grip of the factor who marketed his product. This was a man by the name of Nettlefold, who eventually went into screw production himself in partnership with Joseph Chamberlain. It was vital for a small producer such as Walters to retain total credibility in the eyes of the factor. T.C. Salt explained the economic consequences that accrued if that credibility was dented: 'When the factor goes round and begins to have doubts about this man, in consequence of that doubt he allows a less discount and surcharges him.'[101] Thus it was quite common for a factor to insist on seeing the books of the small firm and to inspect the place of work and even the workforce itself. As

Walters himself put it, 'they deem it wise to look more narrowly into our proceedings and to assist if favourably impressed'.[102] Nettlefold spent some time going over the workshop at the end of which, to Walters' relief, he 'expressed himself in a gratifying way at the regularity of the people and the aspect of things'.[103] Despite this he lived in constant fear that Nettlefold might discover his many unsuccessful attempts to supply other factors in the town. Nettlefold, however, was able to keep a steady economic hold on the concern, facilitating development only in those areas directly of use to him and which did not constitute a threat to his other enterprises. Walters pointed out in March: 'it is not in his interests to assist us further – he gets what he wants and has the preference – he has no mind to supply an opposition to his town trade'.[104]

Above all, it is clear that Nettlefold was able to influence, quite strongly, the way in which the smaller concern developed economically. The 'regularity' of the workforce, of which he so approved in Walters' firm, was a vital element in all of this. The credit and marketing facilities which Nettlefold offered were the vital, enabling elements within production. In order to appear creditworthy the smaller manufacturers had to run their firms in a businesslike way. The form that this took was increasingly defined by the factory discipline of the larger concerns. Grainger, for example, considered James James's screw-manufacturing workforce the best regulated in the town in 1840. For Walters, however, working within a tighter profit margin, the regulation of a workforce, more used to the traditional work patterns of the workshop, was a rather more difficult matter. Only four years after Walters' series of letters, G.F. Muntz, the owner of a steam-powered metal rolling mill, indicated to a Select Committee that he had successfully overcome any desire on the part of his workforce to worship 'Saint Monday':

> What do you call a full week's work?
> Working all the week.
> Do they do it now?
> Some of them do.
> Do they work Mondays and Saturdays?
> My men do always.[105]

Despite the pressure to demonstrate the 'regularity' of his

workforce to his creditors, Walters was signally less successful in this endeavour. His workforce clung tenaciously to its 'task-oriented' work rhythms. These consisted of both weekly and seasonal irregularity.

> Sunday appears to indispose the people and Monday, being a sort of Saint Holiday – among the working classes of the town Thursday generally arrives before all are capable of moving on – one day is a day of exertions, Friday and the quantity set is exceeded – some steady ones approximate daily – I endeavour to move en masse . . . but, as in chemistry there is nobody whose particles are not attracted by the particles of some other body – today they are all unsettled.[106]

His letters (though it must be remembered that they were justificatory letters to a creditor) display no sense of community or identity between Walters and his employees. In one letter he refers to them as 'riff raff' (so much, then, for the closeness of workshop relations).[107] The seasonal calendar of quasi-religious celebrations was only seen by him in economic terms, as complicating his problems of regular output. In February:

> Shrove Tuesday broke in upon the 'even tenor of their sway' and the march of the 7th Hussars complicated our embarrassment. Four of our hands (Females) are induced to enter His Majesty's Service.[108]

Then in April:

> In consequence of Good Friday being a holiday 533 gross were made . . . 647 should have been. . . . This week we commenced working today, Wednesday. Monday and Tuesday being termed 'heaving days'.[109]

Such was the cost in terms of weekly production that he noted by 1 May that 'The holidays, I am sorry to observe, have brought us back into the worst times – and a loss of £4 14s 2d.'[110] With such slim profit margins the process of disciplining the workforce was absolutely crucial to the firm's viability.

The issue of labour discipline was, however, far broader than the question of the regularity of the workforce. Once at the workshop the employees had to be induced to work in ways that were efficient, and so profitable to the employer. Walters' letters are filled with estimated profit margins that assumed the workforce could be induced to work efficiently:

> The Press is at work – the man at 3 shillings per day (daily wages) turns out with ease 5 a minute. . . . Press will cost £11 – wheel and apparatus about £2 10s more – the savings at present 8 shillings per week and with practice will be augmented by putting the man to piece work.[111]

The inefficiency of a workforce unused to running and servicing machinery would jeopardize the viability of the small firm. Walters wasted little sentiment, in March, when a female worker fell into a machine, but he did regret the financial implications. She had, he explained:

> Met with a serious accident by having her gown sleeve loose in cleaning up the machine and needlessly keeping the bank on it wound round the shaft and brought her arm to the saw before she could be extricated – otherwise our profits would have been £8.[112]

In trying to organize the workforce to overcome these kinds of problems Walters attempted to introduce the kinds of rules for personal conduct that are perhaps most familiar to us in the context of the larger factory. He noted with some pride at one point that, 'two mothers of girls working in the factory called to thank me . . . for reclaiming their children from vicious habits to more correct conduct'.[113] He was, however, not always quite so successful and regretfully revealed that in the first week of May 1832 he was compelled to dismiss four of his most skilled workmen, 'on the score of irregularity'.[114]

Maxine Berg has demonstrated the centrality of the ideas of political economy to economic development in the decades after 1820. This process of development, she suggests, was dependent less upon the individual skill of the worker and rather more upon the overall discipline of the total workforce.[115] The continued reliance of small-scale production on skilled work should not mislead us into believing that the same process did not apply to this level of industry. In fact, the imperatives for imposing work discipline were, if anything, expressed more strongly for the small producer than for the 'captains of industry'. It was not just that the slim profit margin of the smaller concerns gave little room for manoeuvre. There was also a conscious attempt by the larger firms to take advantage of the economic dependence of the smaller firms on them, and, through this, to refashion small-scale production in their own image. This was a necessary procedure if the smaller unit was to fulfil, efficiently, its subsidiary or servicing function for the larger unit of production. The pressures upon Walters to induce regularity in his workforce were not purely related to the internal economies of his operation. They also related to a need to appear creditworthy and respectable to the owners of capital upon whom he depended.

Work discipline has generally been understood in relation to the larger firms, hence the phenomenon is commonly referred to as 'factory discipline',[116] and sometimes related directly to the expansion of steam mechanization *per se*.[117] The indications are that the larger, steam-powered firms were successfully disciplining their workforces, from the 1830s onwards, in a variety of ways evolved and perfected by a breed of 'new model employers'.[118]

Although there may be a powerful analogy to be made between the mechanical action of the steam piston and the systemization of human activity which industrialization involved, steam power itself was probably less important in this respect than the actual scale of the enterprise concerned and its concomitant facilities for an overall restructuring of the work process. Mechanization was clearly only one part of this. Thus it was not so much that the scale of the large firm demanded factory discipline, since this was a necessity for the employer at any level of production. Rather it was the case that the scale of the larger firm facilitated the inculcation of labour discipline in ways that were often more problematic for the small producer. Walters, for example, was attempting to operate on a workshop scale and yet to reject workshop norms and values. In the large firm such a rejection undoubtedly induced conflict, as Chapter 2 shows. Here, however, it could often be offset in ways precluded from the small manufacturer by the smallness of his enterprise: perhaps by higher wages for the most skilled in return for regular attendance, or by the provision of alternative facilities in the form of schools, reading rooms, libraries, or recreation facilities.[119] In all of these ways the large-scale manufacturer could present himself as both a philanthropist and a moral reformer through the reorganization of the workforce. If, as Chapter 3 suggests, this was a stance that the workforce did not always find entirely convincing, it represented, in itself, an alternative that was not necessarily open to the small manufacturer.

The small master

The process whereby the small producer was transformed into a *petit-bourgeois* manufacturer may, perhaps, be highlighted by reference to the activities of small producers who resisted the process by appealing to the values of the working community. There is, for example, an obvious difference between Walters, who quite deliberately distanced himself from his workforce, and Robert Basford, described in the local press as a 'master manufacturer' in the bone-button trade. Basford was involved in an incident in October 1837 during a strike in the trade. A crowd of several hundred women, workers from a number of shops on strike, assembled outside the factory of a manufacturer named Weaver, in Bagot Street, calling for his workers to join the strike. The incident turned into a very violent confrontation and women workers who refused to join the strike were badly beaten. The similarity between the action of the crowd on this occasion and the food riot as a traditional form of protest is marked. The press reported:

> They behaved in a very riotous manner and cried out something about three farthings a gross and said 'Turn out the —' meaning the workmen and women 'and we'll tear their livers out if they work at that price'. They brought an effigy made of rags and straw and said it was his wife's picture. . . . They set fire to it and threw it over complainants palings and gates into his yard.

Basford and six women were arrested and tried on charges of assault. In sentencing Basford to three months hard labour at the House of Correction the magistrate admonished him that, 'he ought not to have encouraged them to acts of violence, which, but for his example they might not have attempted'.[120]

Clearly Basford had responded to the economic pressures of the moment, not by further rationalization within the workplace but rather by acting, with his workforce, in a collective manner which reflected the values of the working community. A similar point could perhaps be made about John Watson, a pearl-button-maker interviewed by J.E. White on behalf of the Children's Employment Commission in 1862. The evidence for Birmingham presented in this report mostly consists of large-scale manufacturers extolling the virtues of paternal factory discipline in reforming the wayward habits of their workforce. With Watson's evidence, however, we enter territory bounded by a very different frame of reference. He worked in a loft above a wash-house in conditions that White obviously considered unhealthy. He employed only himself, his son (an adult), and an apprentice. In addition he was Secretary of the Pearl Button Makers' Trade Society and an observer of 'Saint Monday'. His views on working-class morality were rather different from those of most of the other witnesses interviewed by White:

> It is said sometimes that the poverty and ignorance of the pearl button people are owing to their habits of drinking and irregularity. I believe, however, that it is owing to their being so ill paid. A marked improvement in the character of the men has taken place since a rise in wages of a farthing a gross was obtained from the large masters and buyers.[121]

It may be that differences in scale between the respective concerns of Walters and Watson go a long way towards explaining the difference in values. Once past the employment of a handful of workers, the small producer was more likely to be a small manufacturer than a small master. Such a formula, however, could not be applied in a mechanistic fashion. Nor should we, therefore, judge the relationship between the small manufacturer and his workforce in terms that properly relate to the small master.

It was undoubtedly easier for the small master to resist the process of change in some trades than in others. The building trade, despite the rise in importance of the large-scale contractor, retained much that had long been familiar in its internal structure. As suggested earlier, the gun trade was in a similar position. Here contractors were reluctant to shift their circulating capital to a fixed capital commitment. The market, dependent upon international conflict, was hit after 1815 by the longest period of peace for generations. It was this, rather than the absence of large-scale capital in the trade, that was responsible for the slow growth of the factory in this trade. As Richard Prosser, a local civil engineer, informed the Select Committee on the Manufacture of Small Arms in 1854, 'if you gave them 500,000 to make a year there would be no difficulty finding money to erect machinery'.[122] In fact, hand technology was often retained even where an alternative, mechanical means of production was available. This is particularly evident in the slow adaptation of the Blanchard lathe to the production of gun stocks.[123]

The nature of the market served to emphasize the passive, but controlling, role of the merchant–capitalist within the gun trade. This can be seen in a description of gun-making as given by John Adams, a contractor to the Board of Ordnance in 1824. Adams was speaking to a committee of enquiry, headed by the Duke of Wellington and established by the War Office, to investigate allegations of bribery among Ordnance inspectors during the Napoleonic Wars. The account is given in full because it emphasizes the remote centrality of the merchant–capitalist to the process of production:

> The barrels, locks, bayonets and rammers having been received from the Ordnance Office by the contractors for setting up, the barrels are given out to have pins filed off and fitted to a jigger, they are then taken to the view room for inspection and if approved and marked they are given out with the locks and stocks to the rough stockers who, when he had rough stocked the guns took them to the view rooms . . . and if they were marked and passed they were brought to the contractors warehouse who then delivers the rough stock'd guns with the bayonets, rods, brass and iron work to the finishers who first screw the guns together, and in that state take them to the view rooms for inspection and if the work is well performed and the stock good and sound they are marked – the finisher next takes the gun to pieces, sends the barrels to be smoothed and the locks to be hardened and the brass work to be polished. Then the barrels are again to be viewed and if well smoothed, free from cross cracks and the hoops well on they were marked on this state on the tailpin, the stocks were made off, cleansed and oil'd and in this state again taken to the view rooms for final inspection when the viewer has the locks taken off to see if they are properly harden'd and polished and that the side nails are

well received, if the work is all well performed the guns receive the final mark *and are entered into the Office books to the contractors credit.*[124]

By the mid-century even those who controlled such a process were prepared to admit that the industry had fallen behind in terms of rationalization. One witness at the 1854 Select Committee suggested that this process was 'like making the doors of a house in one part of the town, the window frames in another and the floor in another'.[125] An engineer from the Woolwich Arsenal declared to the same Committee that the trade was fifty years behind other industries in the town.[126] This is not, of course, to say that the gun trade in Birmingham had retained a purely craft basis and consisted of retailer–craftsmen. There had been a good deal of restructuring of the work process but what had been retained was the artisanal context for production as a whole.

The gun-maker contractors objected fiercely to the restrictions upon the process of innovation imposed by the mutuality of the workforce and facilitated by the peculiar nature of the market. Above all, this forced them to accept a system of production which tended to preserve an implicit set of values that were being more fiercely eroded in other trades where the avenues for innovation were more obvious. The gun-maker contractors were locked into a continuing relationship with a mode of production, the underlying artisan-based values of which they uniformly rejected. The price, for the contractor, could be a high one. Traditional rhythms of weekly and annual holidays meant that production levels could vary wildly. John Goodman's subcontracting workforce was capable of producing 1,755 guns per week when operating at full capacity. However, depending upon the traditional holiday calendar, production could fluctuate anywhere between this high figure and the lowest weekly total of only ninety-three guns.[127] As Chapter 3 will show, trade societies generally varied in strength from period to period, but they were at their strongest, in the gun trade, at exactly the point at which the contractor had received a large order. The agreement over prices on these occasions could take anywhere up to six weeks to achieve.

These price agreements were also enforced within the trade by collective action. This will be more fully explored in Chapter 3, but the case of James Clare may be taken here as a useful indicator of the general character of this kind of activity. Clare was a small master, working in his own gun-stock-making shop and employing labour on his own behalf. In 1840 he contracted to produce forty gun-stocks at 10 per cent below trade society prices. In consequence of this he found himself hauled before the Gunstockmakers Society and asked to account publicly for his actions. His refusal to recant resulted in his shop being lobbied by 100 members of the Society, who threatened to prevent him from receiving work of any description in the future.[128] Such activity was likely to occur in any trade, as evidenced by the enormous expansion of trade societies in the 1830s and 1840s. Clearly the success of such attempts to maintain control over the labour process varied from trade to trade in relation to the extent and nature of its internal reorganization.

We can, therefore, isolate two very different responses to accelerating industrialization on the part of the small producer: one an individualist and the other a collective response. Through the former the small producer expressed his separation from the working community and by the latter he reaffirmed his role within it. These responses were defined by an approach to the restructuring of the labour process in a period of high competition, and were acted out through a network of relationships with the workforce itself. It was within the context of this differentiation that the increasingly apparent separation of the *petit-bourgeois* manufacturer from the artisan small master was taking place.

2

Politics and small-scale production

The small producer was facing a critical choice: to act with or against his workforce. The choice of action was being presented in very positive ways after about 1820 by both middle-class and working-class agencies. This chapter considers the attempts made to salvage production in an artisanal mode from the engulfing sweep of capital-oriented industrial change, and also discusses the emergence of what might be seen as a specifically *petit-bourgeois* form of radical politics. In both these areas the separation of the working community from its employers in terms of class-specific values and aspirations is clear enough. We should, therefore, see the transformation of the small producer as part of a broader process whereby an older artisan-based culture was under attack. Outside the workplace this process has been explored in the work of (among many others) Hugh Cunningham, Robert Malcolmson, and Peter Bailey.[1] By the 1860s, in Birmingham, Samuel Timmins was able to note approvingly, 'The habits of the people, generally, have changed greatly for the better during the past thirty years. The ''bull-baiting'' and ''cock-fighting'', of sixty years ago, have died out.'[2] Clearly the erosion of the collective culture of the working community outside and inside the workplace were complementary processes and the jealously guarded artisan concept of workplace autonomy was one of the principal fortresses to be stormed.

THE LANGUAGES OF COHESION

Inside the workplace, this process inevitably involved an attack on the small producer as small master, since in this role he embodied the artisan ideal. As Chapter 3 will demonstrate, this was a period in which the working community expressed its values and aspirations in an uncompromising manner. In this respect the small producer who, by his actions, augmented the autonomy of labour over work was paraded as living proof that the restructuring of the labour process was not predetermined by economic inevitability. In the rhetoric of workplace confrontation in these years, the 'honourable' and the 'dishonourable' master appear repeatedly like two characters from a parable. At the successful conclusion of a strike among the wire-drawers in 1845 the Chartist John Mason was called upon to address the men. He took the opportunity to prevail upon 'the working men of all trades to combine to secure proper and just protection for labour generally and to protect those employers who, in the legitimate pursuit of trade, acted honourably, equally to the interests of other employers and to his workmen'.[3] The phrase which Mason used, 'the legitimate pursuit of trade', is vital, since it encapsulated the argument that there was a mode of business practice that was acceptable to the workforce. It was being firmly enunciated in the period under discussion because the action of the majority of employers clearly infringed this unwritten code. By the 1840s, however, large manufacturers frequently referred to what they called the 'legitimate trade', with legitimacy defined by an acceptance through practice of the logic and morality of the market and the primary role of capital.[4]

Striking brass-cock-founders stressed in 1845 the importance of the choice made by the employer in this respect:

> when a bad and unjust practice is introduced into a branch of trade, while the upright and honourable employer refuses to take an oppressive advantage of his workmen, the unjust employer embraces every opportunity to injure his men; and with the advantage of getting his work done at a less rate of wages, is able to injure other employers, by destroying the market price of the trade.[5]

Grievances were almost always articulated by the workforce by reference to an organic community of work within which masters and men shared economic and social interests. When the locksmiths announced the establishment of a society within their trade in 1833 they were careful to point out that 'integrity must be our rule, as much as liberty is our warrant and justice our end, observing honour towards our employers and fidelity to each other'.[6]

As we have already noted, employers themselves made a workplace consensus of interests the legitimation for *their* actions (see pp. 10–13). It is important to note here that we are dealing with appeals to two very different kinds of consensus. The employer's reference to a 'productive class' underpinned his autonomy in the workplace as the authoritative leader of this class. 'I never see my tall chimney with its full and curling volume', wrote one manufacturer in 1831, 'without thinking of the industry it betokens – of the wages it raises for my forty pairs of hands and of the comfort it diffuses amongst the families of my work-people.'[7] The manufacturer's role as the philanthropic provider of employment and material goods justified, theoretically at least, his autonomy over the means of production. This is the vital element left out of most studies of industrial paternalism. For Birmingham, Douglas Reid's recent study misses the way in which paternalism reproduced authority within a very particular context.[8] This was not simply an issue of welfare, with a 'progressive' employer buying hard work and regularity from a grateful workforce. The real issues related to power and its mediation, that is, who had the right to control the determinants of production and even whose workplace it was. The 'reformist' employer, at one with his happy workforce, was a contemporary construction of reality and one which dominates much of the documentation with which historians operate. Its role at the time was to legitimize, and encourage, a specific version of the social relations of production by fixing them to a congruent notion of morality. Reid tells us, 'I have been most reliant on the Liberal press for it was here that I discovered most information.'[9] Here we return to the problem we examined earlier in the context of the Allen–Briggs–Tholfsen model of social relations. A notion of reality was constructed by the middle-class press of the day, and this construction is now reproduced by the historian. Thus when Reid describes James James, the screw manufacturer, as a 'shining example of paternalism' or industrial relations as existing in a state of 'veritable harmony' he is himself using a language that would not have been out of place in the columns of the *Birmingham Journal* in the 1850s.[10] This in itself demonstrates that the construction does not exist outside the language and might lead us to look for alternative versions of contemporary reality that were perhaps less popular with 'the Liberal press'.

Even where employers were able to establish their hegemony over production, the workforce was not the passive recipient of the new order. In her study of factory workers in New Hampshire Tamara Hareven has shown that submissiveness 'was part of a strategy of accommodation that often involved play-acting', and the work of Peter Bailey on role performance would seem to support this point.[11] Anyone who has been booked for speeding and referred to as 'sir' throughout the interview by the policeman involved will appreciate that the language of deference is not one-dimensional. For the workforce, the only acceptable community of interests was one which paid due regard to the rights of labour. In 1833, when the plasterers of Birmingham celebrated the first anniversary of the founding of their trade society, 'The healths of the masters present were drank with the greatest enthusiasm each receiving the hearty honour of three times three.' The *Pioneer*, reporting on the meeting, reflected: 'When masters and men better understand each other we have no doubt that a reciprocity of interests will lead them to seek their mutual benefit.'[12]

In all this talk of consensus and reciprocity from both sides of industry a number of historians of the labour process have divined a 'terrain of compromise' between workers and employers, with the artisan acting as mediator between the employer and the rest of the workforce.[13] Patrick Joyce, for example, argues that historians have, in the past, been too concerned to isolate the conflictual interface between capital and labour, ignoring the more important areas of co-operation through reciprocal interests.[14] The important point, however, is not that employers and workers accepted the notion of reciprocal interests but rather that their notions of reciprocity were themselves in conflict and were expressed in conflictual terms. The plaudits with which the plasterers gloried the 'honourable' masters were, in effect, brickbats directed at the 'dishonourable' masters. Cordwainers on strike in 1834 emphasized the acceptability of masters willing to stand by their agreements: 'thank God we have some few employers in the town who will give their men fair remuneration for labour'.[15] The military-gun-finishers, on strike in 1846, made their point in a similar way: 'We ask for no advance of prices –

we are well convinced the interests of the employers and the workmen are inseparably connected – we wish only to abide by the list price.'[16]

Thus the language of cohesion was also the language of conflict, since it formed a central part of labour's case for the 'legitimate pursuit of trade'. In such cases the enunciation, by the workforce, of a community of interests in the workplace, does not serve to cloud the issue of class relationships, as has often been claimed; rather it helps to clarify it. For employers were being invited, in positive ways, to act as part of the working community. Being part of a community, however, involved accepting its mores and codes which, for obvious reasons, the majority of employers were unwilling to do. Thus the extent to which small mastership actually remained a firm alternative for the artisan became in itself an important measure of the process of change. At the same time, the very existence of a small-master sector in the economy, giving due regard to the claims of labour, was a powerful argument against the freedom of the employer to restructure the work process in response to the apparent dictates of 'economic laws'. The artisan concept of 'legitimate trade' had little to do with a free market economy, a point made by a group of button manufacturers during a strike in 1825. They refused 'to submit to such specific terms and prices as a self-created Union Club shall choose to dictate – a system hostile to free trade [which] if generally adopted must soon annihilate this country as a manufacturing nation'.[17]

For all these reasons the artisan alternative of small mastership came under sharp attack from large-scale employers. In a period of intense competition between large firms, in almost every trade the small master was universally blamed for the lowering of prices. For example, during a dispute in 1835 the operative-screw-locksmiths were informed by their employers 'that a reduction of prices at times has taken place in consequence of competition we have to contend with against small Saturday night men'.[18] It may seem rather odd in a society ostensibly so committed to free enterprise and to the emergence of large firms from small beginnings, that small producers should be so heavily criticized. The point is, of course, that it was the small master rather than the small manufacturer that was being pilloried in these years. The objection was not to the small producer, who ran his business along 'respectable' lines (with 'respectability' defined by the practice of the larger enterprises), but rather to the employer of labour who actively perpetuated the values of the world of labour. J.S. Wright applauded the opportunities for advancement afforded by the predominantly small-scale nature of his trade:

> All that is needed for a workman to start as a master is a peculiarly shaped bench and a leather apron. . . . With these appliances and a steady hand, he may produce scarf-pins, studs, links, lockets, etc. etc. for all of which he will find a ready market on Saturday among the numerous factors.[19]

Yet only a few years earlier Wright had pointed an accusing finger at small producers in his trade during a dispute over declining prices. 'He was of opinion', he explained, 'that much of the evil complained of was caused by small manufacturers, *part of the men*, who sold their work at a reduction because they could not get full price and thus damaged the trade of the capitalist.'[20] Thus he objected to small producers only when they were 'part of the men' and where they refused to accept the rules of the market game. In this case they expressed a heterodox approach to the economy through an attempt to undersell Wright.

Compare any of the heroic explanations of the growth of the factory from the humble workshop, rendered by successful industrialists, with the following description (also by an industrialist) of the making of a small master:

> If a man were of irregular and dissipated habits and did not like to conform to the rules of a shop, or if he had any dispute with his employer he would occasionally become 'saucy' and set up for himself . . . one inducement for them to set up for themselves in this way is the liberty it enables them to take of playing at cards in beer shops and of drinking and smoking away Monday and Tuesday which they cannot have in a regular shop.[21]

This attack, adopting the aspect of a moral crusade, was also levelled at the small master's traditional source of credit from within the working community, the publican. Part of the complex fabric of relationships between the workplace and the public house was the role of the publican as a provider of short-term credit. In return for such a facility the small master might arrange to pay his men their wages in the public house. 'There is a practice calling loudly for legislative interference', announced *Sam Sly's Birmingham Budget* in 1850, 'that of tradesmen paying their men on a Saturday night in public houses. This leads to more drunkenness and vice than anything else whatever.'[22]

The artisan free from the straitjacket of work discipline was a heretic; as a result, by the middle of the century the small master who struggled to be free from the constraints of capital, had become a scapegoat. 'They plunder the honest manufacturer of a remunerating profit', was a fairly typical complaint from a wirework manufacturer in 1830.[23] Nevertheless, as an observer in the brass-foundry trade candidly pointed out, 'it is difficult to say whether [it is] the dishonest competition of men who have capital, or the ruinous trading of men who have none that is the active cause'.[24] This point was picked up from within the working community in the early 1830s. James Morrison, later to edit the *Pioneer*, complained in 1833 that the rules of the game were being laid down in a way that effectively excluded the small master from participation:

> The competition of the wealthy man, then, who by the weight of his capital can bear all before him, can drive out the smaller master by lowering prices; . . . this competition then is fair and honourable. But let it be opposed by the less important manufacturer . . . and his competition becomes 'unlawful, unnecessary and unfeeling'.[25]

When Joseph Parkes reported a discussion with Morrison on trade unions in 1834, he referred to him, helpfully, as a 'master man'.[26] It is, of course, this area of apparent ambiguity in the role of the skilled adult male worker that is the main argument levelled against the conflictual interpretation of social relations at the point of production in this period. The artisan often acted as a sub-contractor or a direct employer of labour, even when the work unit was subsumed within the larger factory. In this respect Robert Sykes's work on the mule-spinners in the 1830s and 1840s suggests that these workers were closer to the 'classic' artisan than the archetypal factory worker.[27] In the view of many recent historians the role of the artisan as sub-contractor fragmented the authority relations of the early industrial workplace, clouded the class issues, and formed the 'terrain of compromise'.[28] This misses the point.

The close proximity between artisans and the small masters in terms of nature, function, and self-image was precisely the cutting edge of working-class consciousness in this period. They represented a labour-oriented mode of production some considerable distance from the reality of the workplace in the period, and this acted as a yardstick with which to measure change. The value system of the artisanal mode of production was very different to the world of the small manufacturer, such that the self-justification of the upwardly mobile *petit bourgeois* was not universally accepted. Later in the century an artisan in the gun trade was to observe that 'to a common observer, he will appear to have mounted as much upon his bad qualities as upon his good ones'.[29] James Morrison, a painter by trade, saw the emergence of capital intensive enterprises as a threat to the traditional choice between wage labour and employer status *within* the working community. This perception took him, and many others, to the notion of a producers' co-operative as a conscious attempt to hive off a section of the market for the exclusive use of the small master operating within an artisanal concept of production.

PRODUCERS' CO-OPERATIVES IN THE 1830s

When Robert Owen appeared in Birmingham in November 1832 to lecture on the nature and purpose of the Labour Exchanges, the scheme was already underway in London.[30] At its heart lay the perception that producers were also, themselves, consumers. The provision of a forum for the exchange of goods would, it was argued, draw the two activities together without utilizing those conventional marketing structures which, as we have seen, operated to damage the interests of traditional producers. Owen clearly felt himself to be in a favourable setting for the establishment of a local branch. In a meeting held in the Public Office in Moor Street, on 14 November, he stressed what he felt to be the potential middle-class support which existed locally for the scheme.

> The men of Birmingham were in a better situation to adopt the plans he had to propose than those of almost any other town or city in the world. It was necessary they should have men at their head who were well known and long-tried leaders of the public cause, and here were the Attwoods, the Scholefields, the Muntzes and the Joneses and many others who had been long

> labouring in the public vineyard ready, he hoped, to come forward.[31]

Owen had been invited to speak by local co-operators, notably the tobacconist William Pare, who had been prominent in early attempts to establish neighbourhood co-operative shops between 1829 and 1832.[32] Owen's optimism over local middle-class patronage was based on his appreciation of the achievements of the Birmingham Political Union (BPU). Birmingham had been the focus of national attention during the Reform Bill campaign when Attwood's BPU appeared to draw together a range of social groups. Owen was particularly attracted by Attwood's claim that the BPU transcended class divisions by drawing employers and employees together within the 'productive class'. On the face of it the town appeared to be a perfect location for a scheme that, while it was aimed at small producers, required an initial benign participation by men of capital. Local co-operators calculated that the £2,000 needed to launch the venture could be raised by the sale of £20 shares to middle-class patrons.[33] The Reform Bill campaign had drawn heavily on working-class goodwill and the Labour Exchange scheme assumed that a reciprocal gesture would be made by the local middle class purchasing shares in an institution which they would not need to use themselves. The scheme's initiators were predominantly small masters and artisans.

The apparent compatibility of co-operative and Attwoodite economic thought also seemed to augur well for the embryonic Exchange. Both stressed that producers were also consumers and sought economic regeneration by drawing the two functions together. For Attwood increased paper money would raise the purchasing power necessary to release production; the co-operators envisaged an economy within which what was produced was to be aligned closely with what was needed. Above all, both Attwood and the co-operators offered an underconsumptionalist critique of the contemporary economic universe. Indeed, when Attwood introduced Owen to the BPU council on 13 November he appeared to be offering substantial support:

> Next to the Reform Bill, which was necessary to all other improvements he (Mr. Attwood) regarded this experiment of Mr. Owen as among those which were of the greatest importance to the country.[34]

Yet only three days later Attwood wrote to Owen withdrawing his active support for the scheme. The letter made his position clear and is quoted here in full.

> In order to prevent the possibility of mistake I beg to say in writing that I will, on no account, consent to attend the meeting at Mr. Beardsworth's, nor will I on any account act as Chairman or President of the intended Association.[35]

The meeting at Beardsworth's, which Attwood refers to, had been set for Monday 26 November and was intended as the launching point for the Exchange. In the week following Attwood's withdrawal Owen gave two more explanatory lectures at the Public Office. Following these, on 25 November, the very eve of the meeting at Beardsworth's, the MP Joshua Scholefield withdrew the support of both himself and his son. His letter to Owen, though more diplomatic than Attwood's, was no less firm in its intent.[36]

The meeting went ahead the next day (26 November) with an audience of 10,000 under the chairmanship of G.F. Muntz.[37] He claimed to have been put under considerable pressure to dissociate himself from the meeting.[38] This had not deterred Muntz, who was a particularly single-minded man. Nevertheless, he did introduce the proceedings in a rather guarded fashion:

> He must say that he had not been able to enter fully into the details of the plan now proposed by Mr. Owen; but so far as he had examined it, he thought there was a great probability of its doing immense good, without the possibility of any evil arising from it.[39]

Although it was agreed at the meeting to establish an Exchange there was a significant delay between this resolution in November 1832 and the actual opening of the institution the following July. In this period it became apparent that there was not the 'respectable' support available. By the middle of December 1832 only £400 of shares had been sold at the £20 price.[40] By the end of January 1833 the committee were urging trade societies to purchase quarter shares at £5.[41] By March the price of shares had been reduced to £1.[42]

This delay reduced a good deal of the movement's momentum, or at least, caused it to be rechannelled into other, often related, ventures. James Morrison had begun publication of the penny, unstamped, weekly newspaper, the *Birmingham Labour Exchange Gazette*, in January 1833. This proved rather premature and by February, after only five issues, it had become clear that, with the delay in establishing the Exchange, there would not be enough news to sustain regular publication. Morrison turned increasingly toward working through the trade societies to achieve Owenite aims.

The failure of the Labour Exchange scheme in Birmingham should be seen within the wider context of an attack on small-scale production within a specifically artisan mode. It was designed to provide a location where the goods produced by the 'legitimate pursuit of trade' could be marketed without the critical mediation of the large-scale producer or the merchant. The *Birmingham Labour Exchange Gazette* noted in January 1833 that 'Scarcely a meeting on the subject . . . passes over unmarked by the outpourings of the vial of wrath of some sufferer under the slaughtering trade.' One of the major figures in the early organization of an Exchange was William Hawkes-Smith, a man who had edited a radical journal, the *Birmingham Inspector*, in 1817. He was quite clear in his own mind that the Exchange would provide a facility for a particular type of producer, writing to Owen in October 1832 that:

> In a manufacturing town like Birmingham the deposits could mostly come from small masters (like the pearl button makers . . . who are pressed by competition to the destruction of profit) – and from outworking operatives who at present, whatever our 'influentials' may say, are many of them almost void of work.[43]

In his analysis Hawkes-Smith pointed to the unitary nature of the 'small masters' and the 'outworking operatives'. The Labour Exchange aimed to reconstitute this organic relationship by eliminating the intrusive element of capitalist marketing which threatened to destroy it. In February 1833 the *Exchange Gazette* reported the recent case of a 'small master who had tried in vain to sell a batch of white metal spoons which had cost him in materials seventeen shillings, and in wages paid six shillings'. The small-scale producer eventually offered the goods to 'a great mercantile house' at the cost price of twenty three shillings, but, as the *Gazette* revealed, with little success:

> The answer was 'we do not want them, but if you choose we

> will give you eighteen shillings per gross'. The unfortunate producer of this mass of useful wealth was obliged by his necessities to accept the offer. Was not this a slaughter house price? Would it have been offered by an Equitable Labour Exchange?[44]

The *Gazette*'s rhetorical questions emphasized the fact that the Exchange would be concerned not simply to provide an extension to the available market but to create an alternative marketing mode. Its very existence would therefore provide a critique of existing structures and might, in a number of ways, threaten them, since the system was designed to lock the small producer into a national as well as local market. William Pare explained at the November meeting that 'the Lancashire people were smothered in their cotton goods, and those of Leicestershire in their hosiery but were in want of infinite variety of articles manufactured in Birmingham and Sheffield'.[45] The necessity for exchanging such goods for what Hawkes-Smith referred to as 'agricultural and colonial produce' was also recognized. Pare was dispatched in July 1833 to the Owenite community of Rahaline in Ireland to establish the basis of this trade.[46]

The Exchange system was designed to deal with an economic problem, but the justification for taking such action was unashamedly political. The founding resolutions of the Birmingham Labour Exchange declared that: 'as it appears government is incompetent to extricate the working classes from the evils arising from overstocked markets it is necessary that the producers of wealth should now make an effort to relieve themselves'.[47] For the labouring community the scheme was part of the next step following a Reform Act that was widely recognized as only the first instalment of piecemeal reform. No sooner had the Act been passed than the working class within the BPU called for universal suffrage and formed the Midland Union of the Working Classes (a Birmingham-based branch of the National Union of the Working Classes).[48] The failure of Attwood and middle-class radicals within the BPU to back this call for universal suffrage emphasized the point of political departure between the middle-class and working-class radical ideals. At the same time, the undignified scramble by the leaders of Attwood's 'productive class' to avoid involvement with the Labour Exchange lent an important ideological dimension to this demarcation point. Their hostility to the scheme demonstrated the incompatibility of the immediate economic aspirations of large-scale capital and small masters within the working community. For not only did the Exchange system threaten to break the hegemonic relationship between large and small enterprises (by circumventing it), but also it justified its function by reference to the centrality of labour, rather than capital, to production through the use of labour notes. The *Birmingham Co-operative Herald* explained in May 1829: 'Capital, then, so far from being the power or source of production, is the product of labour or rather of human co-operation. It did not precede, but followed production.'[49]

Here, then, was a language which universalized the changing nature of production in theoretical and practical terms that challenged capital. Above all, it attempted to throw a life-line to small-scale production in an artisan image. If the intransigence of capital in the face of such a challenge is less than surprising possibly the organizers of the Exchange could be accused of *naïveté* in believing that the middle class would provide the necessary financial backing to launch the scheme. But Attwood and the middle-class radicals of the BPU had traded for years on the supposed compatibility between the interests of masters and men. They were now simply being presented with an opportunity to make good this analysis in practice. There was also a tendency among working-class co-operators to exaggerate Owen's ability to draw in middle-class patronage. In a letter in May 1832 Bronterre O'Brien, who was observing the Reform Bill campaign from Birmingham itself, urged Owen to adopt the BPU's organizational framework. The letter also contained some shrewd observations from O'Brien as to the problems posed by Owen's leadership:

> If these and like duties were performed judiciously and your own peculiar opinions on Religion, Responsibility, etc. – kept in the background, at least for a short time, I believe we could very soon (to use the language of Mr. Attwood) roll up such a massive power – such a giant strength as would be perfectly irresistible.[50]

Similarly Pare had seen Owen's intervention as a crucial element drawing the local middle class into the scheme (although in the event his appearance in the town had the opposite effect). In October Pare wrote to Owen:

> I have had several interviews with Mr. Attwood on this affair and he is very favourably inclined, tho' he thinks it scarcely practicable. He however last Saturday voluntarily proffered to take shares if a Bazaar were established here and I think if you were here *you* would not find it difficult to get *his name* as a sanction to it.[51]

The failure of the Labour Exchange made the distinction between the different forms of small-scale production more apparent than it had ever been before. For 'master men' like Morrison it meant a reaffirmation of the small master's role within the working community by means of active trade unionism. At the start of September 1833 he informed Owen of this development in his thinking:

> I have retired from the Exchange and intend to devote the whole of my time and energies to the Union. . . . You may think it strange that I should leave the Exchange. But my time is up – and it does not give *satisfaction* to be running after the Union. The Union, however, is more likely to accomplish the same great object.[52]

The *Pioneer* began publication in the same month and the first eleven issues of this weekly paper were produced in Birmingham. Morrison adopted a stridently class-conscious stance, announcing in the second issue that 'A grand secret has been unfolded to the world; that labour is the source of all wealth.' This formed part of a broader development of trade-based activity which reasserted the right of workers to organize production. The 'master men' of Birmingham's Central Committee of the United Building Trades (formed in 1833), addressed Walthew, one of the largest contractors in the town, in exactly these terms.

> Aware as we are that it is our labour alone that can carry into effect what you have undertaken . . . and as you had no authority from us to make such an engagement – nor had you any legitimate right to barter our labour at prices fixed by yourself we call upon you to arrange with us a fixed per centage of profit for your own services in conducting the building and in finding the material on which our labour is to be applied.[53]

The same committee reminded the contractors of Manchester that 'labour not capital is the paramount source of legitimate wealth and happiness',[54] and also applauded the '150 masters' who had locally offered support during a strike. The Manchester contractors on this occasion pointed out that the 'masters' were not masters at all, employing in the main only one or two men each.[55] It is important to remember that whilst reinforcing this kind of challenge the *Pioneer* was also exhorting trade organizations to admit as full members those masters who accepted the 'legitimate pursuit of trade'. What was being defined, by both capital and labour, in the struggles of these years, was the role and status of the small producer within very different notions of production.

This confrontation engendered a significant and forthright response from the wealthy middle-class radicals who made up the ruling Political Council within the BPU. They made it clear that the consensus within production to which the *Pioneer* addressed itself was in no way synonymous with that envisaged in their own concept of a 'productive class' united by 'common interests'. As one member of the Council put it in November 1833, 'Every man ought to be allowed to obtain the highest price he could for his labour but it was not right for men to combine to force each other to demand a given price.'[56] At this point there was really only one member of the Council prepared to support the emerging trade societies and that was the soon to be bankrupt draper William Blaxland, who resolved to give his support 'however unpalatable to my brother councillors'.[57] In 1837 G.F. Muntz was to recall his own position a few years earlier: 'Did he not oppose the Trades Union? Did he not tell them that it was neither right nor equitable, nor expedient, to endeavour to obtain those prices by resistance which masters could not afford to give?'[58] The middle-class radicals who had fought so hard for the Reform Bill preferred the bland unity promised by a capital-oriented consensus within production, as enunciated at a public dinner by the borough's merchant MP, Joshua Scholefield: 'He despised the master who would lower wages without sufficient cause; but he believed although there might be some few individuals who would act so, yet generally speaking they were compelled to reduce from necessity.'[59]

Statements like this, appearing as they did in the light of the workers' experience of rapid change in the workplace, simply reiterated the emptiness of 'productive class' rhetoric pedalled so vigorously by men of capital during the Reform Bill campaign. Trade-based organizations (as Chapter 3 of this book will show) kept open this debate on 'the legitimate pursuit of trade' which the ill-fated Labour Exchange scheme had thrown into such fine relief. Through this the evident choice for the small producer between operating in an artisanal or a bourgeois context became clear. Thus the overt hostility of capital to workers' co-operatives and workplace organizations was also an attack on the organic community of interests between masters and men as seen within the 'traditional' artisanal sector.

This attack had an important political dimension and it is this which is most often lost in the talk of class co-operation within the BPU. The conflict between capital and labour over workplace autonomy, within which the small producer was claimed by both sides, was also acted out through antagonistic concepts of the democratic process. The arguments for bourgeois democracy which lay behind the Reform Bill agitation (and the continued demand for household suffrage post-1832) contrasted sharply with calls from within the labouring community for a wider (and very different) form of democracy through universal suffrage. These conflicting conceptions of democratic form will be explored in more detail in later chapters of this book as part of an analysis of the Reform Bill campaign and the early Chartist years. But it is perhaps worthwhile, at this point, to examine the implications of all this for the small producer. For nothing demonstrates the polarization of the options within this level of production more than the emergence of a clear distinction in the 1820s and 1830s between artisan politics and middle-class radicalism within a *petit-bourgeois* context; while the former challenged, the latter actively underpinned the hegemony of capital.

THE CHANGING POLITICS OF THE SMALL PRODUCER: 1790–1850

During the 1830s, wealthy middle-class radicals in the Attwood camp drew heavily upon the imagery of the 1790s to justify their leadership of the movement for parliamentary reform. In this early period the radicalism of a group of wealthy Nonconformists, gathered around Joseph Priestley, had contrasted markedly with the popular Toryism of the crowd expressed in the 'Church and

King' riots of 1791 and the burning of Tom Paine's effigy in the marketplace in 1793.[60] The button manufacturer Benjamin Hadley, secretary of the BPU during the Reform Bill campaign, announced to a meeting of non-electors in 1836:

> I am one of the People (cheers). I was born a reformer and I was reared a reformer. Yes I was born a reformer. I was born on 14 July 1791, at the very moment when Baskerville's house was in flames. . . . At that very moment a troop of horse soldiers came to my father's door demanding money, and what was the cry? Why 'damn your eyes Church and King!' (Cheers and shame).[61]

However powerful the rhetoric, such statements established and drew upon a false continuity within the middle-class commitment to parliamentary reform. After the Priestley riots the wealthy Nonconformists left the movement and it took the radicalism of Thomas Attwood, with a very different political and economic focus, to draw them back in any numbers.[62] Between 1791 and the mid-1820s the reform agitation, fuelled by a Painite conception of libertarianism, was carried on by an amalgam of artisans, small producers, and retail-tradesmen. These social groups provided the backbone of the formal radical organizations of the period, reinforced by street-level popular support at important points. R.B. Rose has argued that in Birmingham the crowd 'changed sides' during the Napoleonic Wars.[63] The replacement of popular Toryism with an equally trenchant popular radicalism can be seen in two days of rioting in November 1816 directed against a Tory newspaper office, and also in the peaceful crowds who met in their thousands at Newhall Hill in 1817 and 1819 to petition for parliamentary reform.[64]

What is most apparent to the historian familiar with the development of Attwood's brand of radicalism in the 1830s is the absence of wealthy support for the parliamentary reform movement in this early phase. It is also clear that the movement assumed an increasingly plebeian complexion as time went on. By the early 1830s the Painite rhetoric of political rights had become not only popular within the working community, but also identifiably *of* that community. In tracing the emergence of a working-class consciousness historians have primarily devoted their attention to developments within that class. What was also important in this process was the residual effect in the development of small producer–lower tradesman radical politics as something quite separate and distinct from the politics of the working community. Bechhofer and Elliott argue that the period saw the replacement of the 'rights of man' by perceptions of the 'rights of property' in the consciousness of an emergent *petite bourgeoisie*.[65] Developing the theme, Geoffrey Crossick has suggested a narrowing down of the political vision as part of this social group's growing self-awareness, manifesting itself primarily in a preoccupation with the local and an absorption with economism.[66] In Birmingham Attwood was able to draw this group into the BPU, where the full force of its energetic radicalism could be constrained within the wider parameters of his brand of radicalism. We may trace the roots of such a development in the preceding decades and see within it some reflections of the new socio-economic configuration within which small-scale production was beginning to exist.

During 1816 and 1817, agitation for parliamentary reform within Birmingham was led by a Hampden Club established under the chairmanship of George Edmonds. The Club was clearly implicated in the riot of November 1816 although Edmonds himself denied its complicity. At the centre of the disturbance was William Askew, subsequently imprisoned for a year for the part he played. A witness at his trial claimed that Askew had addressed the crowd at one point saying: 'I belong to the Hampden Club and the present things won't do.'[67] There was a good deal about this attack on the offices of the Tory *Commercial Herald* to suggest that the boisterous spontaneity of the food riot, which was a feature of the town in the 1800s, had been infused with a broader political perspective directly relevant to the experience of the working people. As the crowd of four or five hundred gathered outside Richard Jabet's office they are reported to have shouted: 'Nine shillings a week, fetch him out, hand him and kill him.' Catching sight of one of the town's constables Elizabeth Martin (who was also prosecuted for her part in the riot) cried: 'Now what do you think of us? Now we will let you know who is to triumph! We'll soon show you!' At this point, according to a witness, she extended 'her arms in a triumphant attitude and by so doing collected a number of persons about her'.[68]

Edmonds himself always saw the Hampden Club's role as being essentially constitutional. He explained in a letter to a tradesman in Bath, 'Hampden Clubs are the only things to prevent a Revolution as they direct the people's efforts into a legal and constitutional path and induce in the people the hope of better times.'[69] Throughout 1817 he chaired a number of mass meetings to petition for reform. The first of these, held at Newhall Hill on 17 January 1817, was attended by an estimated 25,000 people and called upon parliament to reform itself and reduce taxation, the size of the army, and the National Debt.[70] Edmonds felt that the openness of mass meetings, and a reliance upon reviving and utilizing the right of petition, differentiated the post-war agitation from what had gone before. For him 'Jacobin' had simply become a term of pejorative convenience for the opposition. As a Hampden Club handbill put it in December 1816: 'Reformists have long been branded as Jacobins and reform confounded with revolution by those who know the falsehood of the application but have cunning to know the force of a name.'[71]

Perhaps the most celebrated public meeting of these years was that of July 1819, held at Newhall Hill, which elected Sir Charles Wolseley 'Legislatorial Attorney' and charged him with the task of representing Birmingham at the bar of the House of Commons.[72] In John Cartwright's words this was an attempt to effect 'a new mode of application by sending a representative in the form of a living man instead of on parchment paper'.[73] Such a move, as Parssinen has suggested, invoked an anti-parliament tradition present in various forms in the radical movement from the late eighteenth to the mid-nineteenth century.[74] Thus, according to T.J. Wooler, Cartwright, and Edmonds who devised the scheme the 'Legislatorial Attorneys' would represent the sovereign people more fully than the corrupt body at Westminster because of the purity of the process behind their election. Of course, none of the organizers imagined that these individuals (there were to have been other meetings at Leeds and Manchester) would be allowed to present their case at Westminster. Nevertheless in turning them away the government would be demonstrating that the right of petition, the only real mechanism for redress built into the system, was effectively dead. Edmonds told the crowds gathered at Newhall Hill on 12 July: 'The effect to be produced is not upon the House but upon the country and public opinion.'[75] The point was not lost on Lord Liverpool's government, who responded with a Royal Proclamation, declaring the meetings illegal, and the arrest of the organizers.

Edmonds' commitment to constitutionalism brought him, in this way, to a lengthy trial for seditious conspiracy and nine months in Warwick gaol. He was also clearly in conflict with other elements within the radical movement at this time. He disapproved of the schoolmaster Charles Whitworth's attempts to support the Oliver uprising after the Hampden Clubs were declared illegal in 1817. The magistrate Isaac Spooner reported on 27 May that 4,000 men were ready to rise in the area.[76] Edmonds also stood apart from a Union Society established in the wake of 'Peterloo'. Whitworth was elected Chairman of this organization, which was rumoured to be arming itself in October 1819.[77] In the same month an anonymous broadside appeared on the walls of the town with the message: 'Let us fight nobly and if we fall the motto on our tomb shall be "Our country's cause and liberty".'[78] In January 1820 Whitworth was imprisoned for having published a Union Society handbill which included the following verse:

> Britons arise and yet be free,
> Defend your rights and liberty,
> Boroughmongers long have shared the spoil
> The working class shares all the toil,
> Now or never strike the blow,
> Exert yourselves and crush the foe!!![79]

It was, however, the embryonic radical movement that was crushed rather than 'the foe'. The Birmingham Loyal Association for the Suppression and Refutation of Blasphemy and Sedition was formed in the town in 1819, its Tory originators using the London-based Association for the Refutation of Infidel Publications as its model.[80] By 1821 they had initiated successful prosecutions against a number of local radicals. The Loyal Association drew its membership from the local Pitt Club and represented a powerful axis between town and county society. In William Hamper, Theodore Price, William Bedford, N.G. Clarke, and the Revd J.H. Spry the Association boasted the support of men who combined wealth with the exercise of authority as magistrates. It also spoke through the medium of *Aris's Gazette*, edited by local banker Paul Moon James. 'It is from editors like you', Edmonds claimed in 1819, 'the press is perverted to most partial and unprincipled ends.'[81] The Association worked in close liaison with the Home Office in issuing anti-radical literature and prosecuting seditious publications locally. By January 1820 Theodore Price, Chairman of the Association, was able to assure Lord Sidmouth, 'We pledged ourselves to prosecute sedition and we have kept our word.'[82]

Thus the radical movement was attacked effectively from the pulpit, the Press, and the magistrates' bench in a local campaign complemented by the repressive policies of Liverpool's government. This clearly created problems of strategy for local reform organizations who trod the familiar path between constitutionalism and revolution. The programme of the Birmingham Hampden Club in 1816 reflected that of Cartwright's parent organization and also Burdett's Union Society. The Club called for 'Representation at least co-extensive with direct taxation', and a system of annual parliaments.[83] Edmonds, in his 1817 series of public meetings, almost always referred to a 'general suffrage' and it is likely that his terms of reference were kept deliberately ambiguous in order to draw in the wealthier support he had long hoped for. The Unitarian William Hawkes-Smith shared this view. Nevertheless, he closed his radical journal, the *Birmingham Inspector*, in August 1817 because of what he called:

> the complete apathy of the middle and higher classes among us. Their indifference to the welfare of the country in every instance except where their own petty profits are concerned; their fixed determination not themselves to originate any action which should assert the broad principles of moral and constitutional rights, nor support those who might commence such proceedings.[84]

A similar point was made by James Luckock in 1822, when he lamented that 'the higher we go for respectability and virtue, the more likely are our expectations to end in disappointment and mortification'.[85] The veracity of his statement, however, could be aptly demonstrated by his own rather peripheral involvement in the movement. Luckock, as the manager of a manufactured jewellery business, had been active in radical politics as a member of Priestley's congregation in the early 1790s. He was also a founder member of the Birmingham Society for Constitutional Information (BSCI) formed in 1792 in the wake of the 'Church and King' riots, and later succeeded by a local branch of the

London Corresponding Society.[86] By the post-war period, he was running his own business with some success. His memoir, written in 1825, reveals, however, a rather ambivalent attitude towards the predominantly plebeian Hampden Club:

> I had been casually acquainted with Edmonds for some time previously to the establishment of the Club, and for the sake of knowing what was going forward among them I was introduced by him to some of their meetings though I never became a member.[87]

Luckock put his faith in the degree of middle-class support the movement would gain once its constitutional nature was established. In this he suffered an early disappointment when he was unable to drum up support among fellow Unitarians for a public meeting of January 1817 which attracted a crowd of over 20,000.[88] The illegal status of the Hampden Club did little to encourage 'respectable' support and Luckock himself was clearly uncomfortable rubbing shoulders with the likes of Askew and Whitworth which it did attract:

> I saw the necessity for more caution than they as a body might be supposed to possess; and aware of the obloquy and malignant opposition they had to encounter I thought it my duty so far to identify myself with them as to know the exact state of their opinions and intentions. If I could not control I found that I could moderate their zeal so as to guard them from violence.[89]

The less than enthusiastic support for radicalism in the post-war period, by men who had previously been its firm advocates, can be witnessed again in the actions of the Hill family. Thomas Wright Hill, a one-time follower of Priestley and, like Luckock, a founder member of the BSCI, was, by 1817, running a flourishing school for gentlemen in Edgbaston with his three sons.[90] One of these sons, Roland Hill, noted the progress of the local Hampden Club in his journal:

> It consists chiefly of the working class although some of its members have a right to rank higher. I am on account of our profession obliged to keep clear of anything political, as most of our friends in promoting the success of the school, are on the opposite side in politics, so that however I may wish success to

> the reformists I am equally inactive on both sides except that I do not scruple to sign any petition, the object of which is to produce a reform. My brother Edwin who is a saw-maker and, of course, unfettered, is a member of the Hampden Club.[91]

The vital factor here is Roland's dependent economic relationship with the town's wealthier elements. This precluded his participation whereas his brother, as a small master, was independent enough to join.

There appear to be three important elements in the waning enthusiasm for radicalism by Luckock and Hill, both 'survivors' from 1791; the success of their business ventures, the growing articulacy of the artisan leadership within the movement, and the lack of support from wealthy sections of local society (or outright opposition in the case of the Loyal Association). Perhaps the most significant of these was the second, for it was effecting a polarization within even the more active supporters of reform. By 1820, in the face of intransigence from local wealth, the ambiguity of earlier radical demands had disappeared and universal suffrage had become the central pillar of a movement that was successfully broadening its base. When T.J. Wooler entered the town in 1822, having served fifteen months in Warwick gaol for his part in the 'Legislatorial Attorney' meeting, he was greeted by a crowd he estimated to be 40,000 strong. The horses were taken from his carriage and he was drawn through the streets in triumph. Later, at a dinner in his honour nearly 1,000 radicals heard him defend the principle of universal suffrage: 'When the opponents of Universal Suffrage could show him a man upon whom the state laid no burdens he would admit they had discovered a man who was not entitled to vote.'[92] He defined his position primarily against that of Thomas Attwood, whose economic writings were gaining some support in the town, and who had declined an invitation to attend the dinner. Attwood's letter of refusal, which was read aloud by Wooler to the assembled company, hinged primarily on the rejection of a property-free franchise. Wooler made his contempt clear.

> In thus recommending a great and vital change in the existing state of Parliament Mr. Attwood would be fearful of calling in the aid of universal suffrage without the qualification of property, which in his judgement would necessarily lead to the

right of *sitting in Parliament without the qualification of property.*[93]

At the same meeting George Ragg, an ex-weaver recently released from Warwick after serving nine months for selling the *Republican* and the *Black Book* at his newspaper shop,[94] delivered a moving speech. After his incarceration Ragg had to support himself with crutches in order to speak: 'Feeble as he was, he hoped he would live to see his persecutors brought to the punishment they so richly deserved at the hands of the people.'[95] The notion of 'the people' that Ragg invoked was clearly far broader in concept than just the working community. In these years, despite the crisis of the post-war economy, the radical movement rarely drew upon an economic critique to back the demand for political rights. Yet the potentially broad social appeal of the Painite rhetoric of rights was being narrowed, in practice, by middle-class passivity or outright opposition to political reform on these terms.

THE EMERGENCE OF *PETIT-BOURGEOIS* POLITICS: 1820–50

As political rights became equated in the working community with the demand for universal suffrage, so this measure, in turn, became the 'test' of the radical. Those radicals who themselves feared an articulate emergent working-class leadership, and aimed at a property-based franchise were increasingly marginalized within the movement. This led them into a very different form of radical politics. In Birmingham this can perhaps best be illustrated by the case of Joseph Russell, radical bookseller of Moor Street. During the repression of the post-war years Russell was twice imprisoned for selling radical literature. In March 1818 he was arrested for selling Hone's *Parodies* and as his trial dragged on into 1819 he became a *cause célèbre* both locally and nationally. His eventual conviction and imprisonment for six months was condemned by Edmonds as 'the diabolical persecution of an innocent man'.[96] This was a conclusion that must have been difficult to take issue with since Hone had himself previously been acquitted for actually writing the *Parodies*. Sidmouth, whose harvest of successful prosecutions against the radical press had been woefully small in London, took heart from this and wrote, in August 1819 to Bedford, a Birmingham magistrate: 'The result of Russell's trial will, I trust, operate as an encouragement to magistrates in every part of the Kingdom to show their confidence in the intelligence and integrity of British juries on all similar occasions.'[97] Russell, in fact, was the first of a number of local radicals to be imprisoned. Nevertheless, on his release, he continued his radical activities and, thanks to the efforts of the Loyal Association, was returned to gaol in November 1820, for three months, convicted of selling the third issue of the *Republican*.[98]

Russell's radical credentials were impeccable, but even he found it difficult to exist within the reform movement in the early 1820s because he rejected the principle of universal suffrage. He was forced to defend himself publicly at a dinner held in January 1823 to celebrate the release of Coventry radical W.G. Lewis, the last of the organizers of the 'Legislatorial Attorney' meeting to emerge from imprisonment. Russell's statement, however, only served to emphasize the distance between his own position and the direction which the movement as a whole was taking:

> I have long desired to come fairly before you, and clear myself from that misrepresentation with which I have been assailed; it has been asserted I have turned my coat with regard to politics, this I distinctly deny, and challenge proof to the contrary. I have always said that universal suffrage would, in the present state of society, be productive of evils equal to those it would cure. I have ever been the supporter of the right and expediency of household suffrage on the most extended scale.[99]

As Russell pointed out, he had remained consistent in his viewpoint, but the change of direction towards a radical commitment to universal suffrage had left him high and dry. Edmonds, on the other hand, was later to pinpoint a qualitative change in his own perspective as a result of his experience in this period. Although never slow to conjure up the imagery of the fugitive Hampden Club days when, in his own words, 'a few working men determined on boldly exhibiting their farthing candle',[100] he had, by 1830, taken a significant step away from the world of the 'freeborn Englishman'. In its place, he offered something that was rather more utilitarian in its nature. At a public meeting called by the newly formed BPU he defended piecemeal reform in these terms:

> He warned the meeting against being led away by those theorists who would accept nothing unless they got all – who, if they could not obtain what they wanted at once, were unwilling to receive it by slow degree and who were too fond of claiming things merely because they considered them as rights, without first taking into consideration the first and most vital rule by which they ought to be regulated – the happiness of the people. It mattered not whether the elective franchise was universal, or extended merely to householders, if both equally tended to confer happiness on the people. . . . Another capital error in the view and measures of ultra-Reformers, *and he confessed he himself had been once subject to the delusion* was, that they were too much enchanted with a beautiful theory and forgot altogether the varied thoughts, prejudices and motives of mankind.[101]

It is clear that during the 1820s, by becoming a point of polarization within the radical tradition, universal suffrage assumed a practical and symbolic significance which it had never held previously. Of course, men like Russell and Edmonds still saw themselves as representing 'the people', but they had narrowed the operable definition of the term to specify the small ratepayer and householder rather than the wider community which the term had the potential to embrace. At the same time, the notion, now being clearly articulated, that political participation could only be validated by ownership of property in some degree, drew the ratepayer lobby towards Attwood's brand of populism. Thus, the importance of 'ratepayer politics' in defining *class* positions was not simply that many of its platforms excluded the working community in a residual way, but rather that its constituent elements took their very substance by being defined *against* the working community. Non-ownership of property invalidated the case for working-class admission to the political system. It also made the working community a potentially voracious tax-eater in its absorption of rates in the form of poor relief.

Much of this can be seen in Russell's *Birmingham Independent*, which he published between August 1827 and June 1828. Through this he expounded a pugnacious *petit-bourgeois* radicalism which championed the needs and aspirations of what he referred to as 'resident active tradesmen'.[102] His case for admitting 'lesser ratepayers' to the parliamentary franchise stressed the economic position of the small producer:

> for let it never be forgotten that the individual of limited means has a more immediate interest in the enactment of prudent and just laws than the man of larger possessions. On the former national difficulties press with an accumulated weight and often times in almost an instantaneous manner, whilst local injustice frequently prevails over such an individual from want of means to combat its power. From both the one and the other the wealthy in most cases are secure; nay it frequently happens that the rich capitalist adds to his possessions whilst the man dependent upon the produce of his industry for the comforts of his existence is doomed to suffer grievous privations.[103]

This position was extended by attacks on the perceived maladministration of local affairs through the Street Commissioners, the Court Leet, and the Guardians of the Poor, all of which were seen to be squandering ratepayers' money. Russell lamented that 'unfortunately the possession of wealth or the obsequious obedience to its possessors is the principle consideration in the appointment to local authority'.[104] This, of course, was not an attack by the unpropertied upon the propertied but rather a variation of the productive class–unproductive class dichotomy which Attwood was so fond of making. The working community was never seen as a repository of potential electors whose admission to local and national politics would rectify the abuses which so concerned the *Independent*. Rather, as tax-eaters they were a further threat to the 'active tradesmen'. In September 1827 Russell appealed to the 'mechanics of Birmingham' to assist in keeping rates low:

> You have an opportunity individually to limit one portion, and that the most considerable of parochial demands, viz. the Poor's Rates, by abstaining from becoming chargeable to the same, except in cases of real necessity; this would in many instances not only assist in producing a change for the better in your domestic circles by increasing your temperance and economy and by adding respectability to your character, but render you of more consideration in the eyes of your employer, and consequently produce a more adequate reward for your respective labours.[105]

A similar format was present in Joseph Allday's *Monthly Argus and Public Censor*, published between 1829 and 1834. Allday, a bankrupt wirework and fender manufacturer, consistently attacked the control by the wealthy of the organs of local government. He evinced a particular dislike for the successful manufacturer who moved to Edgbaston or Handsworth 'while his less fortunate neighbours Bill Garlic and John Hardware are left to bear the burden of the rates'.[106] A Tory in politics, Allday was careful to define his brand of radicalism as a rejection of the Painite tradition:

> We are reformers – not such reformers as Hunt and Cobbett, nor such levellers as Taylor and Carlile. We are willing to follow in the ranks of such men . . . such ultra Tory reformers as the Marquis of Blandford and Mr. Attwood.[107]

Like Russell he saw the working community as a threat in a number of ways. The economic pressures upon the small manufacturer were caused, in Allday's view, by a combination of the 'factor's awful authority' and the willingness of artisans to establish themselves as small masters. He saw the establishment of producers' co-operatives as an unmitigated evil that promised to be 'subversive, not only of Christian faith, but of social union'.[108] It was, above all, the facility which the co-operatives afforded of small-scale production within an artisan image that he feared most:

> The first step taken by the co-operators has been to exterminate small shopkeepers. In Birmingham there are no less than three 'stores' for the sale of groceries and provisions. They have even opened a 'Bazaar' for the sale of fancy goods. When their funds accumulate they will root out the more extensive dealers until at last – like Pharoah's lean kine – these fellows will eat up all the vending worth taking hold of.[109]

Allday estimated in 1830 that one-seventh of the population were recipients of poor relief and that these included 'some who keep dogs and pigeons, some who keep fowls and rabbits and some who get drunk two or three nights a week'.[110] His answer was to publish and circulate an alphabetical list of the recipients of poor relief. 'The only objection', he pointed out, 'is that the publication of such a paper would wound the feelings of many worthy people who receive parish relief – but are the feelings of the paupers to stand in competition with the pockets of the rate-payers?'[111]

Attwood's BPU drew heavily upon the support of the *petit-bourgeois* groups which Russell and Allday addressed in their respective publications. From the outset the Union pledged itself 'To prevent and redress as far as practicable, all local public wrongs and oppressions and all local encroachments upon the rights, interests and privileges of the community'.[112] Thus the demand for a moderate extension of the parliamentary franchise was complemented throughout the 1830s by an attack on the oligarchical control of the Street Commissioners, Guardians, Court Leet, and Vestry by a small group of wealthy local families. This culminated in the successful campaign for a Charter of Incorporation in 1838. The aggressive economism of *petit-bourgeois* radicalism was often at odds with the way the leaders of the working community perceived and expressed their interests. When the Poor Law Commissioners took evidence in Birmingham, William Boultbee, a member of the BPU Political Council, was at hand to urge them 'that no relief should be given in money, from having observed the inducement which it creates in itself to the poor to seek relief from the parish and the temptation which it presents to them, when obtained, for misapplication'.[113] Thomas Baker, an operative, on the other hand gave voice to a deeply ingrained working-class principle only three years later when addressing a public meeting: 'It was his opinion that every man who was able and willing to work but who could not procure it had an undoubted right to relief from the land or the property of the country.'[114]

In 1837 local radicals in the Reform Association (a precursor of the BPU in its second phase) successfully fought the Guardians' election. Of a reform list of 108 candidates 85 were elected including 60 men who had never been Guardians previously (amongst them eleven retailers).[115] This was followed by an ostentatious celebration of economism as the parish plate was sold at public auction to indicate the end of lavish Guardians' dinners at the expense of ratepayers. For the working community, however, this change in local administration resulted in a reduction in relief available. During the intense distress of the winter of 1837, for example, the parish authorities attempted to force the Irish community beyond the pale of poor relief. Thomas Finigan, an urban missionary in some of the worst affected parts of the town, recorded in his journal for February 1838 that 'the unfortunate natives of Ireland who had the temerity to present themselves and crave even a mouthful of bread at the workhouse door were spurned away with contempt and inhuman scorn'.[116] Under the new Guardians the Overseers applied the Settlement Laws to the letter, such that Michael Hare, a spokesman for the 'Irish mechanics', pointed out in the same month that they would have been better off under the rigours of the New Poor Law, 'for it made it imperative on the parish officers to relieve all cases of urgent distress whether or not the parties were parishioners'.[117] Criticism of the local administration of poor relief was extensive within the working community, providing as it did a foretaste of the radical middle class as local officials. This would later be extended with the incorporation of the town, in 1838, and the election of a radical corporation, culminating in the irony of ex-BPU middle-class radicals trying the Bull Ring rioters in 1839.[118] At a public meeting in February 1838 the 'radical' Guardians were closely questioned by an audience made up of working people. One speaker from the floor put the point directly: 'He asked Mr. Salt, who was one of the Guardians of the Poor, and he asked the Overseers how it was that the people were thus permitted to die for want of food.'[119] Yet when R.K. Douglas, editor of the radical *Birmingham Journal* (and himself one of the new Guardians), came to review this period of local administration he had nothing but praise for his fellow officials:

> They had carefully watched the conduct of the Overseers, in their capacity as Guardians and the result was that they had acted on all occasions with liberality and great humanity; and if they appeared rigid in some instances, it was only from a conviction that they must derive the means of their liberality from a class of the community who were very ill able to afford them.[120]

Within Chartism the working community was able to retain and develop the breadth of political vision present in the older radical tradition. They refused to support Attwood's revamped Political Union in 1837 because it aimed primarily at local reform and the granting of a Charter of Incorporation. Their support was only earned when Attwood reluctantly accepted the principle of universal suffrage. The granting of corporate status to the borough meant that the wider perspective of the working community was irretrievably divided from the concerns of active local middle-class groups. Under the provisions of the 1835 Municipal Corporations Act a property-related franchise reflected the tacit agreement that the working class should be excluded as active political participants. Whilst this development will be more fully analysed in Chapter 5 as a crucial point of departure between the radical ideals, it should be noted here that the new town council provided a firm focus for the major thrust of *petit-bourgeois* politics. By 1841 about one-third of the council can be said to have fallen into the small manufacturer–retailer category. This group maintained an organizational base in reform associations in Duddeston-cum-Nechells and Deritend and Bordesley. Although they, in reality, represented a small ratepayer interest, they exerted political leverage on the wealthier local elite by purporting to also represent the unenfranchised in a very direct way. They were, for example, drawn into Sturge's initiative for complete suffrage, but stood by the Complete Suffrage Union (CSU) when it split with the Chartists. In October 1839, when the Duddeston-cum-Nechells Reform Society failed in an attempt to obtain the election of two small manufacturer members in a Ward contest, it made no secret of the way it perceived its historic mission:

> That the members of this Society, seeing to what coercion and tyranny the working classes of this Ward would be subjected if they were under the undissipated influence of the factions who have now, by fraud, intimidation and corruption, gained a temporary advantage over them, do hereby solemnly pledge themselves to continue their bond of union and to prosecute the great principles for which they are united with increased zeal, energy and determination.[121]

Local Chartist groups were largely unimpressed by what they saw as a straightforward exercise in economism (often at working-class expense), clothed in grandiose rhetoric to increase its effectiveness in the intra-class struggle which municipal politics had become. In 1843 the Deritend and Bordesley Reform Association's annual dinner opened with the twin toasts: 'The six points of parliamentary reform' and 'Free trade throughout the world'. Guest speaker Councillor Benjamin Giles of the Duddeston-cum-

Nechells Society proclaimed their local success: 'in place of profligate expenditure they had adopted a system of economy – that they had, in Duddeston, saved the hamlets £2,000 in highway rates'. It was, he assured the diners, 'the perseverance of working men that had done this'.[122] His use of the term 'working men' suggests a very specific interpretation within this context. In purporting to represent a wide section of society, *petit-bourgeois* radicalism was busily annexing elements of a language that would legitimate that claim within, what was in reality, the narrowly restricted world of municipal politics. The argument of Birmingham's wealthier middle-class radicals, such as Attwood, Muntz, and Scholefield, had always been that since the interests of capital and labour were identical, productive capitalists could effectively represent the 'people'. The *petit-bourgeois* claim to be the 'people' was based upon the same assumption and related directly to a capital-oriented perception of consensus at the point of production. The work of E.P. Hennock has stressed the importance of the 'resident active tradesmen', as Russell called them, on the town council in the 1850s. During this period they operated as a self-avowed 'Economy party' led by Joseph Allday.[123] The emergence by the mid-century, of a specifically *petit-bourgeois* mode of political expression, defining itself against the collectivity of the working community, must be seen as a reflection of the changing role of the small producer within the broad spectrum of production. Economically and socially tied to large-scale capital, working-class notions of what constituted the 'legitimate pursuit of trade' were rejected along with the boisterous mutuality of working-class culture. Politically this group's vision had narrowed to a form of ratepayer populism, some considerable distance from the world of the 'free-born Englishman', and which both accepted and underpinned the values of liberal individualism.

CONCLUSIONS ON SMALL PRODUCERS

Industrialization did not eliminate small producers but it did recast them into a different form. Elsewhere Leonore Davidoff and Catherine Hall have charted the emergence of a specifically *petit-bourgeois* lifestyle in this period, centred on the house and emphasizing the woman's role as home-maker.[124] In an area of predominantly small-scale production such as Birmingham we can see other facets of this important social development through an examination of the ways in which the fundamental relationships at the point of production were evaluated by those involved. Clearly both capital and labour prized the small producer, not only as an important element in the pragmatic organization of the industrial system, but also as being symbolic of very different approaches to production itself. At the start of our period the economic and social nexus between the artisan and small master was strong: by the mid-nineteenth century that between capital and the small producer was stronger, and here was a fundamental change. The small master operating in an artisanal mode had not disappeared but he had been marginalized. In his place stood the small manufacturer as a representative of the ethos of individualism and keystone of the Victorian gospel of achievement. Moreover, the outer boundaries of the *petit-bourgeois* universe were marked firmly by the collectivity of the working community. At its most articulate and active, artisan workplace autonomy and the concept of participatory democracy at the heart of the working-class political vision undermined the small producer's new roles as organizer of production and aspirant within a bourgeois social hierarchy. In order to understand this we must ascribe a social value to language in context. Notions of workplace consensus, the ethos of competition, control of production, and democratization were not universal in their nature; rather they had, by the 1830s, become avowedly class-specific in their use and application.

3

'The worst of democracies': the internal life of the workplace

INTRODUCTION: ARTISANS AND OTHERS REVISITED

Over the last twenty-five years a good deal of the academic debate about the social impact of industrialization has focused on the issue of conflict in the workplace and its precise role in the creation of class consciousness. In particular, the relationship between trade unions and political radicalism has been a major area of debate. Edward Thompson's socialist–humanist analysis has presented a working class whose multiform organizations, both inside and outside the workplace, fed a unitary class consciousness by 1832.[1] Extending this view Prothero, working on London, and Sykes, concentrating on south-east Lancashire, have charted in some detail the precise points of organizational contact between trades unions and an emergent Chartist movement.[2] Their work represents a forthright challenge to the 'compartmentalist' analysis of Rowe, Musson, and Thomis, and also some of the earlier Chartist historians, who saw trade unionism and Chartism as (in Sykes's words) 'two very separate, almost hermetic movements'.[3] But this notion of a working-class expression of trenchant opposition to the growth of capitalism has been questioned more recently by two modes of analysis of rather more profound significance than the compartmentalist school can ever aspire to.

First, there are what might be termed the 'new consensualists', mentioned at the beginning of the last chapter. As a corrective to conflictual models of the resolution of workplace issues, a number of historians have drawn attention to the co-operative interface of consensus between skilled workers and employers through the various stages of capitalist development. Far from the emergence of 'modern' industry requiring wholesale deskilling as a destructive exercise perpetrated via new technology, it is argued, the role of skill within industrial production was renegotiated at different stages and relocated within the labour process on the basis of compromise and agreement.[4] Within this 'terrain of compromise' the skilled worker's role as an intermediary moving between the employers and the wider workforce is necessarily stressed, with the implication that this imbued the demarcation of the 'frontier of control' with a degree of imprecision which impeded clear notions of antipathy between workers and employers. Zeitlin and Sabel have recently argued that community co-operation was a characteristic of areas whose structures of production featured small workshops with a high emphasis on skill. Reid maintains that in Birmingham between 1800 and 1875 a moral consensus grew between a 'conscious minority' of skilled workers and their employers, separating them from the mass of the working class.[5] Joyce's analysis, whilst it does not reject the conflictual element in workplace relations, does stress that there was also an area of reciprocal interests between skilled workers and employers that was at least as important, yet which has been largely ignored by historians.[6]

The second major, relevant, critique is the product of a continuing debate within the English Marxist tradition. Some years ago Perry Anderson and Tom Nairn eloquently laid the basis for an explanation of Chartist failure in terms of an absence of revolutionary theory.[7] Anderson's more recent work has confirmed his doubt about the existence of a working class in this period in terms of both 'its objective composition as a social force and its subjective outlook as a political force'.[8] Gareth Stedman-Jones's essay in *The Chartist Experience* locates much of this kind of analysis within the language used by Chartists and pre-Chartist radicals. Here, he argues, the rhetoric of the 'industrious classes' provided fruitful grounds for co-operation between employers and employees, against a common (and traditional) enemy in the aristocrats and placemen of 'Old Corruption'. Part of Chartism's failure to engage capitalism as a process is related to its inability to embrace the working community as a totality in either language or (consequently) ideology. Thus artisan notions of labour as property may have blunted, rather than sharpened, the conflict with the employer class, leading Chartists to seek alliances with middle-class groups against the 'idle classes'. Implicitly, therefore, in defending the property of skill the artisan had rather more in common with other property-holders than with the property-less common labourers. A significant factor in the argument (as it is in the work of Rowe, Musson, and Thomis, though their thrust is qualitatively different) is the apparent lack of extensive support for Chartism from the trade societies.[9]

There is a certain resonance between these two critical approaches, and it is no surprise therefore that, for example, Joyce should find Stedman-Jones's essay 'both stimulating and persuasive'.[10] Labour history, as it has emerged over the last few decades, has demonstrated a marked unwillingness to explore the issue of division within the working class. Both these approaches, in their different ways, address this silence. Much of the debate hinges on the role of the skilled worker, and, whilst his participation in both workplace conflicts and radical movements is not itself in doubt, it is the significance which attaches to these areas of activity, their relationship to each other, and the ways in which they were acted out through the experience of change that causes controversy. Prothero, for example, in his excellent book on John Gast, points out that 'It now seems generally recognised that artisans were the backbone of the first workers' movement everywhere.'[11] Two areas which have not been explored, however, and which are thrown into fine relief by the approaches cited above, concern the relationship between the artisan and the rest of the community and that between the rest of the working community and the political movement. To extend Prothero's metaphor we might ask what the precise relationship was between the 'backbone' and the rest of the body?[12]

The genealogy of these difficulties is clear enough. They began with a methodological problem: that the artisan is simply the most visible member of the working community and therefore most histories of that community are histories of the artisan. This is surely the implication inherent within Thompson's *The Making of the English Working Class* (1963). But arguably a methodological problem has become synonymous with an analytical weakness: that class consciousness has come to mean artisan consciousness, with the term 'artisan' broadened to include the self-image of the degraded outworker. 'It is true for England as elsewhere in Europe', concludes Prothero (quoting Sewell), 'that "much of what historians mean when they speak of the rise of the working class is artisans becoming politically active''.'[13] If this is so then class consciousness has been narrowed down, in practice, to the view of the adult skilled male worker.[14] This unsatisfactory situation has not been helped by the tendency of those historians who *have* explored the broader nature of popular culture to divorce their analysis from a consideration of the political context.[15] What has been lost are the class-specific notions of social order embedded in labour's attempt to control the labour process in this period, and the relationship between these configurations and a perception of the political ordering of society. At the same time, both of these elements need to be located within the culture of the working community in a way that, for example, the historians of leisure have often been reluctant to do. On the one hand we have had, to use Linebaugh's phrase, 'Labour history without the labour process', and on the other, to take Eley and Neild's point, a social history that 'ignores politics'.[16] The reconstruction of values at the point of production, however, will enable us to contextualize the political ethos of the community in ways that are not possible otherwise. Thus we will aim, in this chapter, to relate the strategies adopted by labour to control work at the point of production, to the radical political configurations of the day.

This will be approached in four ways. First, and most straightforwardly, by relating the chronology of workplace confrontation to the development of political agitation. This will then be extended by a second section, which explores the construction of social order at the heart of workplace organization and the way particularist definitions of democracy resonated through those forms. We will then consider the attempt by labour to establish community solidarities by defining the workplace as the exclusive territory of the workforce. It will be argued throughout that the values of labour at the point of production revolved around the notion of the worker as an independent producer with a concomitant right to organize work through systems of sub-contract reflecting a hierarchical order. Thus the final section will deal with the attempt by employers to modify work structures to create a system of production that was capital-oriented rather than labour-centred. These four areas of discussion should enable us to identify the values that tied the working community together, despite internal divisions, and which enabled Chartism to articulate the wider community solidarities.

THE CHRONOLOGY OF CONFLICT

In Birmingham, in the three decades following 1820, working people seized the opportunity provided by periods of good trade to improve their conditions of work and, above all, to consolidate and extend their control of the job. Employers demanded reductions and hastened the move to a more fully integrated mode of production wherever the circumstances weakened labour's hold. In a remarkably frank interview in 1833 the lamp manufacturer T.C. Salt explained the relationship between crisis and innovation:

> there are many inferior parts of the work that used to pass through men's hands; we take as much as we can off the men and have it done in parts by the boys or the women and then give it to the men to finish; which when trade was good the men would not submit to . . . formerly when trade was good we did not resort to that screwing system; if we had done so we should not have had a single workman to work for us next day.[17]

Such restructuring in the face of a declining rate of profit was referred to as the implementation of 'readier methods of working', a term which (like our own euphemism 'rationalization') clearly embraced a sense of unavoidable economic pragmatism which historians always seem to have found hard to resist. To the workforce, however, changes of this nature did not seem inevitable and the assumptions which lay behind them were openly contested. Ninety-two strikes, across a wide variety of trades, have been traced for the period 1830–50 in Birmingham, and this is clearly only the tip of the iceberg. These strikes show a marked increase in years of good trade, 1824–6, 1833–5, and (particularly) 1845–7. In common with the rest of industrial Britain, Birmingham experienced depression in 1816–18, 1819–23, 1826–33, 1837–42, and 1847–8. In 1837, at the start of another crisis, an operative, Thomas Baker, summarized his experience of the previous two decades for the benefit of a town's meeting:

> For twenty years past they had been subject, at various times to fluctuations in trade which had brought the labouring classes to great abjectness and misery. . . . In the year 1816 they were in an alarming state of distress from want of trade and in consequence of that depression the working men had to undergo a great reduction in the price of labour. They however bore up

against it. . . . It was true that in the year of 1818 a gleam of hope came forth and in many instances a partial rise in prices took place but they were not restored to that eminence from which they were cast down in 1816. Well, after they were emerging from their difficulties they were thrown back into still greater distress. In 1826 and several successive years they had again to experience the greatest possible evils from want of labour or anything like a fair remuneration for it. And it was only for the last two years that they had had anything like what was called prosperity; that is work sufficient for the people, but certainly not such wages as enabled them to put by anything for a rainy day (hear, hear).[18]

It is clear that in the middle years of the 1820s, 1830s, and 1840s the trades organized to hold ground or to claw back that which had been lost. The intervening periods of relative industrial inactivity coincide with periods of acceleration in the development of political movements in the town.[19] But it would be to wrench trade society and radical political activity from the specific context in which they emerged in these years, to suggest that the former was derivative purely of a craft consciousness and the latter of an embryonic class consciousness.[20] When Thomas Shortt, Chartist and Birmingham-based secretary of the Operative Stone Masons, was criticized in 1841 by the masons of Canterbury for disseminating his political views via union literature, he replied:

I have, however, yet to learn what difference it makes to the working-man whether his employer reduces his wages sixpence per day or the self constituted 'authorities of the land' impose a political tax on his food etc., etc., to that amount or that there is more virtue in resisting the one than in resisting the other seeing that the effects of both are the same.[21]

Politics had long been part of the culture of the workplace, a visitor to the town at the turn of the century remarking that:

The manufactories, my friend, have their politicians and republicans as well as the barbers shops and ale houses, yea and their revolutionists, Robespierres, and atheists, are as numerous and fierce, and it is as common to hear the downfall of states, the high and low church party, the indivisibility of the great nation, the imperfection of thrones and dominions, and the perfectability of human nature, the bill of rights or the bill of wrongs, discussed and determined in casting a button, or pointing a pin as at the Devil Tavern or Robin Hood Society.[22]

In terms of the oscillation in prominence between political and industrial activity it is useful for the earlier part of the period to consider the evidence of Table 3.1, showing the numbers of friendly societies registering their rules in the years 1794–1826.

Table 3.1 Friendly societies in Birmingham registering rules 1794–1826[23]

1794	19	1811	5
1795	22	1812	8
1796	2	1813	2
1797	5	1814	5
1798	1	1815	4
1799	2	1816	4
1800	1	1817	3
1801	2	1818	2
1802	2	1819	2
1803	1	1820	–
1804	–	1821	1
1805	–	1822	2
1806	3	1823	–
1807	4	1824	102
1808	1	1825	22
1809	3	1826	8
1810	2		

In small-scale industries, what were effectively trade societies often took friendly society forms. It is difficult to believe, for example, that the Friendly Society of Cabinetmakers, which registered its rules in 1810, a period of intense conflict between masters and men in the trade, was anything other than a trade union.[24] The button-burnishers formed the Loyal Albion Lodge in 1810 after a dispute over prices.[25] As a member later recalled, 'We had a sick and burial club, our only legal hold in those days, but our principal object was to keep up wages.'[26] The table indicates a high level of registration in the mid-1790s, a period in which, after the setback of the 'Church and King' riots in 1791, political radicalism began to establish a foothold.[27] After the passing of the Two Acts in 1795 registration dropped dramatically. The registration of rules offered security, at law, of funds but carried the disadvantage of making a society visible and subject to the invigilation of the authorities. As a result, societies were inclined not to register.[28] After the passing of the Combination

Acts registration remained low, although a few societies chose to register in the 1811–12 period. These were years characterized by food riots, combinations (at least twenty-seven trades demanded price increases in 1810), and political radicalism such that one authority has suggested that it was a period in which 'the Birmingham working class leapt from the pre-political into the political age'.[29] The pattern of registration suggests that in the repression of the post-war years the societies remained hidden whilst political radicalism moved towards a mass base. With the repeal of the Combination Acts in 1824 a very large number of societies surfaced and registered (102 as compared with none the previous year). This was also a period of intense trade society activity. In August 1824 a local magistrate, the Revd J.H. Spry, reported to the Home Office:

> I am sorry to say that combinations exist in every branch of manufactures. . . . I have reason to believe that the old disturbers of the public peace are endeavouring to take advantage of the state of things and give the discontents of the area a political bias.[30]

There were similar 'explosions' of activity in the middle years of the 1830s and the 1840s. Trades involved in this kind of activity covered a wide range, from traditional crafts characteristic of most expanding urban centres (shoemakers, tailors, etc.), to the more obviously 'industrial' occupations (wire-drawers, cock-founders, etc.). They were often 'new' trades, such as button-burnishers, or old ones put to new methods of production, perhaps involving steam power (glass-workers, steel-toymakers, etc.). The agitation around the Reform Bill in Birmingham involved the commitment of many trade societies as such. John Collins, later to figure so prominently in the town's Chartist movement, served his political apprenticeship 'with that branch of the agitation which belonged to the trade societies'.[31] Charles Walters, visiting the Eagle Foundry (where trade organizations were strong) in May 1832, found himself the object of political intimidation: 'a man threatened me in a half joke to drop on me if I did not hoist the Union blue'.[32] In the first burst of euphoria after the passing of the Bill the 'United Trades', formed in 1830 in connection with Doherty's 'National Association', held a procession through the town led by James Morrison (later to edit the *Pioneer*) as the leader of the

Operative Builders. Those trades participating included the carpenters and joiners, brush-makers, gun-makers, pin-makers, sawyers, masons, farriers, jewellers, gilt-toymakers, piercers and stampers, plumbers, painters and glaziers, bricklayers, silk-hatters, plasterers, and tailors.[33]

By October 1832 the United Trades Union was sharing in the general disillusionment with the Bill and was instrumental in calling a meeting to establish a Midland branch of the National Union of the Working Classes.[34] The years 1833–5 saw a great burst of trade activity, with strikes and prosecutions in a wide variety of trades. With sixteen societies adopting the new label 'United' there is much evidence of the formation of new societies and the consolidation of old ones.[35]

United Trades support for the Derby lockouts and the Dorchester Labourers[36] was, perhaps, most marked in the familiar case of the building trades.[37] In December 1833 the ceremony of laying the foundation stone of the Builders' Guildhall was attended by a range of organized trades parading with flags, banners, and bands.[38] Much of the Owenite influence in evidence at this time was promoted by the architect Joseph Hansom.[39] Nevertheless, despite his aspirations to being what he termed, in a letter to Owen, 'the Moses of the Deliverance of the Labourites',[40] he found the builders, and the other trades involved with their activities, to be fiercely independent. His speech at the laying of the Guildhall foundation stone is indicative of a divergence of views:

> He would conclude by exhorting them to abide by their workshops, insisting on, and obtaining, the fair privileges of trade, of which they were the best judges, and turning themselves away from political and other controversial matters about which they knew but little and it would be unprofitable to learn more.[41]

This forthright statement could perhaps be used to substantiate the claim, commonly made, that trade organizations were little concerned with political affairs. Hansom's views, however, clearly conflicted with those of the Operative Carpenters, whose banner on this occasion read, 'Unhappy heroic Poland! The injuries of thy martyred sons shall recoil with tenfold vengeance on the heads of thy unmerciful oppressors.'[42]

In fact, the growing involvement of trade-based organizations in political activity is perhaps the clearest indication of a changing emphasis within their viewpoint and function. Obviously this should not be overstated. The society was primarily the organization of the particular trade and, as such, was concerned to protect the direct interests of its members. Such sectionalism, however, did not preclude the wider vision of class awareness, especially in the wake of a Reform Act which betrayed the political aspirations of the workforce. The experience of industrialization may have varied from trade to trade, as did the organizational ability to act collectively, nevertheless there were many aspects of this experience that were common to all trades; the renewed vigour of the political response in the 1830s was an important element in this universality.

There is a dichotomy here between the specific interests of individual trades and their more general political commitment that is in no way contradictory. Take, for example, trade unionism in its most visionary form in the period, the Grand National Consolidated Trades Union (GNCTU). This insisted in its rules that 'Unionists should lose no opportunity of mutually encouraging and assisting each other in bringing about A DIFFERENT ORDER OF THINGS, in which the really useful and intelligent part of society only shall have the direction of its affairs.'[43] This was seen as perfectly compatible with rule 28, that 'No subject which does not immediately concern the interests of the Trade shall be discussed at any meetings of Committees or Lodges.'[44] The definition of what might 'immediately concern the interests of the Trade' was being broadened. Thus Joseph Parkes noted in his report to Abercromby in 1834 a certain ambiguity between the objectives and the leadership of the trades societies:

> You are of course well aware that most of these and former societies or combinations of the working classes are formed and gathered by the 'active spirits' – men of energetic and instructed minds – that in their objects they are always ostensibly, and generally really, unconnected with politics, tho' usually led by the most violent and least instructed of the Radical classes.[45]

Certainly the expansion of work-based organizations in the mid-1830s was one of a number of factors which made co-operation along the lines of the Reform Bill campaign unrealistic when the

Birmingham Political Union (BPU) was revamped in 1837. The issue of workplace conflict was a particular point of tension between the middle-class and working-class membership of the Union during the build-up to the Chartist period, and this in itself gives a valuable insight into the Chartist consciousness. The Charter, and its implicit social programme, represented the demands of an independent and articulate working-class leadership to whom the changing workshop experience of the preceding decade had been vital in the establishment of class perspectives. As Chapters 4 and 5 of this book will show, tension within the BPU focused firmly on the issue of universal suffrage and its acceptance in form and principle. By this stage the experience of the workplace was severely testing the bland unity projected by Attwood's 'productive class' rhetoric.

The period 1843–7 represents another escalation of trade society activity. How many of the societies survived the economic setbacks of the late 1830s is difficult to tell. But overall this was a period of reorganization even for those trades able to exert a constant presence. For example, the pearl-button-makers, active in the early 1830s as the 'United Pearl Button Makers', brought 500 men out on strike in 1839; the society was reorganized extensively in 1843 and struck on a similar scale in 1849.[46] The brass-cock-founders society, formed in the late 1820s, was active in the 1830s. They pledged financial support to the Chartist Convention in 1839, struck for fifteen weeks in 1840, and then reorganized internally for a successful strike against discount in 1845.[47] Trades societies with national links similarly reorganized in the mid-1840s, particularly the cabinet-makers, shoemakers, and tailors.[48] The last two trades certainly reorganized with a Chartist orientation. Nationally the shoemakers were organized, after 1844, into the Cordwainers (alternatively 'Boot and Shoemakers') National Mutual Assistance Association, with a London-based executive under the Chartist Hunnibell.[49] In Birmingham the boot- and shoemakers were led by John Mason, the Chartist lecturer who made such an impression on Thomas Cooper in 1840.[50] Mason and the Birmingham branch called in 1845, for 'a more efficient means of national unity', and were particularly critical of the central executive's failure to support a strike in Bradford that year. As Mason himself put it: 'Better, infinitely better, that Bradford had been supported till the last fraction had been contributed – as evidence of our iron resolve to resist any and every reduction on the price of competition.'[51]

Similarly, the tailors reorganized nationally. In 1844 the United Tailors' Protection Society was formed in London with a Chartist orientation and the *Northern Star* as its official organ.[52] The Secretary of the Society, T.W. Parker, on a speaking tour in 1845, addressed three tailors' meetings in Birmingham, at one of which 1,000 people were present and two sections of the union formed. The following year the tailors struck against structural changes in the industry.[53] New societies appeared in trades that previously had been relatively unorganized. The fire-iron-makers formed a society in 1845 and the following year brought 140 members out on strike against the price erosions of the previous decade.[54] The Edge Tool Makers' Friendly Society was formed in 1843 and soon boasted 200 members. In 1845 it conducted a successful ten-week strike. Significantly, the previous year it had passed a resolution of thanks to the editors of the *Northern Star* 'for their readiness at all times to assist the oppressed against the oppressor'.[55]

This 'pendulum' motion between political action and trade-based organization is generally seen, by historians, as simply a periodic reversion to craft sectionalism following the failure of political movements. This interpretation both assumes and maintains the exclusivity of the two forms. In fact, the 'pendulum effect' was the result of the closeness of the two modes of action and it was this that made them interchangeable according to economic circumstance. Organization within the workplace developed within a mental framework defined by the political experiences of the preceding years. The closeness of mainstream Chartism to such trade-based activity, in the London of the 1840s, has been explored by Prothero.[56] In Birmingham this proximity found expression in the formation of the Central Committee of Trades in 1845. At a meeting of the wire-drawers striking against discount in March 1845, John Mason was asked to speak by the chairman, 'as he had rendered great services to his fellow workmen in the various trades of Birmingham'.[57] The Central Committee was established in August of the same year to co-ordinate strike activity in the area. It met on the first of every month and aimed to organize financial support for strikes that it considered justified and to intercede with employers where this was required.

The first dispute supported by the Committee was that of the Operative Pinmakers, striking in September 1845. The Committee provided funds and issued a statement condemning the employer involved.[58] It later supported the building workers during a general strike of the trade in April and May 1846. On this occasion the Committee condemned 'the illegal and tyrannical conduct pursued by a section of the building masters towards their workmen', and lobbied parliament for a revision of the labour laws.[59] In September 1846 Mason was a guest at a dinner given by the flint-glass-makers to celebrate the release of three of their members from gaol. In calling upon Mason to respond to the toast, John Culley, secretary of the glass-makers, referred to him as 'a gentleman to whose exertions and abilities they the working men . . . of the glass trade of Birmingham were bound to regard as the instrument of attaining the triumph of one of the most important strikes which had occurred in the trade'.[60] The Committee was still active in 1848, again in support of a glass-workers' strike. At this point it consisted of a pearl-button-maker, a pin-maker, a carpenter, a plane-maker, and Mason, who was still chairman.[61] The work of the Committee exemplifies the link, in terms of collective action, between those trades such as pin-making, wire-drawing, and glass-making, that were mechanized and factoryized and those, such as shoemaking or the building trades, that were still organized along apparently traditional lines.

Such a review of the 1820–50 period in Birmingham may serve to make the 'terrain of compromise' look like a battle-scarred wasteland, but this is really only a starting-point for a fuller analysis. These phenomena must be related to the broader nature of the work experience if we are fully to answer our central questions regarding the class status of skill and the relationship between industrial and political action. So far the case has been argued through a circular form of logic: in order to demonstrate the conflictual nature of the social relations of production we produce only evidence of conflict to confirm our initial assumptions. It is vital, therefore, that this evidence of the chronology of conflict be located within the day-by-day experience of the workplace.

THE WORKPLACE AND NOTIONS OF SOCIAL ORDER

The growth of industrial capitalist ascendancy in the economic and social sphere was accompanied by an extensive and active public debate on the nature of social order and its political context. Clearly this was not an abstract debate: the Reform Act of 1832 and its concomitant, the Municipal Corporations Act, were fairly hefty statements in favour of representation as a bourgeois democracy with participation qualified by property. For their part, however, working people were themselves involved in acting out particular notions of social order in their daily lives through their relationship with other members of the working community. It is important to our full understanding of Chartism that we recognize the existence of such a dialogue in practice. In the defeat of that movement we may perceive not only the physical 'capturing' of a political system but also a redefinition of politics. Thus capital came to dominate not only the system of representation but also the definition of what representation should be. The objection to Chartism was not simply that it promised to swell the total number of voters but rather that it promoted an unacceptable concept of democracy. Significantly, the fears aroused by the Chartist notion of democracy by participation may be explored by examining the critique of workplace organizations offered by outsiders to the working community.

Commenting on the Glasgow spinners' organizations of the 1830s, Sir Archibald Alison declared them to be 'an example of democratic ambition on a large scale'; and, in a powerful association of ideas, argued that 'a committee for assassination was appointed by universal suffrage'.[62] Tufnell was equally succinct: 'Were we asked to give a definition of a trades union, we should say that it was a society whose constitution is the worst of democracies – where power is based on outrage, – whose practice is tyranny – and whose end is self destruction.'[63] In much the same vein the *Birmingham Advertiser* commented on the shoemakers' practice of stationing a man outside shops working below the price to note the names of men reporting to work: 'Here is an enemy secretly and silently at work undermining the dearest right of the whole community and bending our best interests to suit the convenience of a set of democratical tyrants.'[64]

These then were the key anti-union images of the period: their existence represented 'democratic ambition', their organizations were 'the worst of democracies', and their organizers, 'democratical tyrants'. What comes across strongly here is not simply that the demands of workplace organizations were considered to be unreasonable because they flew in the face of market logic, but rather that the demands had no legitimacy because they stemmed from organizations *based upon illegitimate notions of representation.* Sir David Sandford, who had been an active supporter of the Reform Bill, put forward a widely held view of the unions in 1834: 'This I cannot avoid designating as the tyranny of the multitude: and that man is ill versed who does not hold the tyranny of the many to be equally hateful with the tyranny of the few.'[65] Writers addressing the issue of trade unions in *Blackwood's Magazine* referred, in 1834, to 'a tyranny of numbers'[66] and, in 1838, to the 'unrestrained and irresistible tyranny of the majority'.[67] During a trial of striking glass-workers in 1848, Birmingham magistrate and manufacturer Charles Geach argued the reverse case, based on the same concept of illegitimacy. 'It was not even, in many cases, the tyranny of the many over the few', he explained to a courtroom packed with union members, 'it was, from their peculiar organisation, the tyranny of the few over the many'.[68]

To the middle-class observer these workplace organizations were living proofs of the impracticality of a more extensive representation than that achieved in 1832. The apparent ambiguity over whether they embraced the 'tyranny of the few' or the 'tyranny of the many' was actually a dispute of degree, rather than kind, which, in itself, echoed Burke's classic attack on representation by right: 'In this political traffick the leaders will be obliged to bow to the ignorance of their followers and the followers become subservient to the worst designs of their leaders.'[69]

Turning to the participants in workplace organizations we may chart the dimensions of a rather different notion of the representation of interests. A certain amount of documentation exists in the rules of early unions which draws heavily on a morality stressing the obligations conferred upon the individual by their membership of the work-group, rather than the freedom of the individual to pursue their own perception of their best interest. Fines were often exacted for non-attendance and executive posts were rotated.[70] Alternatively these posts might be filled by nomination followed by ballot or open vote. In Birmingham the silver-platers and the smiths fined members who refused to stand after being so nominated two shillings and sixpence, whilst among the carpenters the fine was one shilling.

There is a clear distinction to be made here between the concept of a representative democracy and that of a participatory democratic form. It is a distinction that has been clouded by an insistence that the latter was simply an earlier and less-sophisticated version of the former. Thus Gosden refers to the participatory structures of friendly societies as 'a form of primitive democracy', a term that is also favoured by Matsumura with reference to the organizations of the flint-glass-workers.[71] Alternatively H.A. Turner, in his study of the cotton unions, has suggested that such procedures reflected a conscious attempt on the part of the workforce to prevent the emergence of an élite of leaders who might be distanced from both the realities of the workplace and the feelings of the membership.[72] This is obviously a compelling analysis for any historian writing from the context of a highly formalized twentieth-century trade union movement facing exactly this problem. However, it seems more likely that, in the context of the three decades following 1820, these regulations were an attempt to legitimate the view of the organization as being a collective expression rather than the view of specific individuals. This was clearly perplexing to observers such as Tufnell, who, as we have seen, found it genuinely difficult to determine whether the committees controlled the members or *vice versa*.[73]

Within the societies the process of debate was carefully protected by the rules, again to legitimize the notion of a collective view. Drunkenness on lodge nights was invariably a fineable offence. The stonemasons fined men one penny if they did not address the president as 'Worthy President' and fellow masons as 'Brother'.[74] In the Birmingham carpenters' society, rule 12 stipulated 'That no member be allowed to speak twice on one subject, except the proposer and seconder of the motion, who will be allowed to reply'.[75] A graduated fine of sixpence for the first offence and a shilling for the second reinforced this particular regulation. Often trade society rules incorporated elaborate grievance procedures, which could be implemented if any members felt they required internal arbitration of a dispute with other members.[76]

Where the rules of formal trade societies have survived from other areas they suggest that the participatory forms of organization that characterized the Birmingham trades were far from unique. Yet there is rather more to the history of workplace organizations in these years than the emergence of formally constituted trade societies. Most trade-based action was the work, not of formal trade societies but rather of groups of workers acting together to deal with a specific problem in their shop or in their trade. To call these groups 'societies' is often to imbue them with a structural formalism which they did not possess. Thomas Winters, corresponding secretary of the National Association of the United Trades, made precisely this point to a Select Committee in referring to an outbreak of strikes in 1853: 'there were strikes in every town, whether the workmen were in society or out of society. I think there were more strikes among those out of society than among those in society.'[77]

There were a number of facets to the relationship between 'formal' and what might be called 'informal trade unionism', which may be of relevance here. Although there were particular periods when workplace activity as a whole increased, it is as well to remember that in an economy as diversified as Birmingham's we are not dealing with an automatic mechanism. The variables involved were the relationship between groups of workers, market needs, and the organizational ability to apply customary practices. This relationship could vary dramatically for different groups of workers within the same trade or for different trades within the same manufactory. An example might illustrate the point. It comes from a letter to G.J. Holyoake from his mother in 1845:

> you want to know how trade is at the foundry the moulders are very well of but the smiths are not so well the moulders have decline working by the piece the work now for weekly wages the have turned out twice within this three months for advance of wages and have got it but there is no chance for the smiths but we must do as well as we can.[78]

Holyoake himself recalled that in the foundry in the 1830s, 'Piece workers and day workers were so continually subjected to reduced prices and wages that they never felt certain on Monday morning what they would receive on Saturday evening.'[79] In such a situation of prevailing uncertainty the opportunities for taking successful industrial action varied from group to group and from period to period. But the willingness to utilize a shift in market needs to resist change or regain ground was a common factor across the industrial spectrum. This essentially opportunist element projects much of the activity into the category of 'ephemeral action'.[80] Trades organized and reorganized according to circumstances and the study of many of the trades involved will not reward, in any direct sense, that search for organizational continuity that has marked trade union historiography for so long. Even where formal structures were established they often seem to have carried an acceptance of their own *de facto* brevity. The United Brethren of Wire Workers and Weavers imposed a fine of ten shillings and sixpence on any member heard 'publicly or privately' to propose the dissolution of the society. On the other hand, it was often the case that where highly formalized frameworks had been established work-groups preferred to use informal methods for settling local disputes. In 1868 T.J. Wilkinson, the Birmingham-based secretary of the Flint Glass Makers' Society, explained to a Royal Commission that 'nineteen cases out of twenty are settled by the men and the employers amongst themselves and we do not know anything about it'.[81] Reports of a shoemakers' strike in 1844 suggest the adoption of a temporary formalism to meet the needs of the moment. The *Birmingham Journal* reported a case in which two men were charged with conspiracy to raise wages:

> It appeared that four or five weeks ago forty or fifty shoemakers took an empty house in Pinfold Street where they commenced meeting every other day to regulate what they termed their trade affairs. They elected a President and moved resolutions to the effect that there should be a turn out and strike for higher wages.[82]

This case echoes the findings of Nassau Senior during his investigation into unions in 1832. One Lancashire manufacturer complained that 'One of the last strikes was among the piecers, boys from nine to twelve years old. They elected their delegates and President, held their meetings under a gas lamp, stopped the work of their parents by refusing their services and succeeded in their object.'[83] In both these cases groups organized to take advantage of a specific moment and sought to legitimize their demands by a transitory formalism which embraced a clear, democratic form.

Historians have often been puzzled by non-continuous forms of labour organization, generally seen to be 'ephemeral action'. More usefully, John Rule has recently drawn attention to what he calls the 'habits of association' within the workforce, which resulted in a 'spectrum of responses with *recurrent* forms linking the ephemeral with the continuous'.[84] Richard Price, in his study of the building trades, argues that even by the middle decade of the nineteenth century it was rather more important for workers to be 'in union' than that they be 'in the union'.[85] David Wilson has coined the term 'ad hoc unionism' to describe the extensive activities of Portsmouth dock-workers who lacked formal unions until the late nineteenth century.[86] Clearly, alongside the history of formal trade unionism, which historians have always been anxious to explore, we require a history of 'informal' unionism.

Yet such an analysis must be pushed one step further. Of course, we may see the formal trade union as part of a wider phenomenon whereby work-groups evolved less-formalized trade associations. At the same time, however, this kind of activity, the 'ad hoc' strike, wage demand, or riot, was arguably only the most explosive and visible manifestation of a broader set of largely implicit rules by which the work-group related one to another at the point of production. There was much of this in Wilkinson's evidence in 1868. Asked if it was union rules that regulated the capacity of production, he answered:

> I may simply say that the old custom of the trade, independently of the union, before the union came into existence, in a great measure brings about the two moves or journey system, and it regulated a certain amount of produce per turn, that is according to a given time.[87]

With regard to promotion within the work-group in the glass trade:

> I can say that I commenced work when very young in the trade myself and I know I was kept back, not from any rule of the society, but from the understood custom of the trade, and that is thirty years ago.[88]

Only a year earlier William Broadhead had explained, to another Commission, that 'rattening' was not sanctioned by any of the rules of the Sheffield saw-grinders, rather it had 'simply been an understanding'.[89] Similar 'understandings' existed in relation to most aspects of work in most trades and though we may see them most clearly at times of conflict they were part of the internal organization of work at *all* times. Take, for example, Birmingham's extensive heavy steel toy trade which produced a variety of workmen's tools. In 1810 employers were lobbied by workers in the trade for 'an advance on the price of our work'. There is no evidence to suggest that a trade society existed but a memorial to the employers, which appeared in the local press, was signed by ten workmen 'on behalf of our brother journeymen'.[90] Possibly the lack of formal organization could be explained by the existence of the Combination Laws, yet the memorial itself contravened this legislation since it constituted an action 'in restraint of trade'. In 1825 employers in the trade introduced a system of deducting discount from the prices paid. This was widely resented and gave rise to a protracted strike in 1833.[91] Immediately following this successful action a union was formed. This in itself is a notable sequence of events: the strike creating the union rather than *vice versa*. After two years, however, the union was discontinued. Despite this the prices, reluctantly acceded to by employers in 1833, were still being paid by the middle of the century. In addition labour also clearly had some control over the pace of work since it was customary at this time for the men to play cricket on a Monday afternoon if the weather was fine.[92] Needless to say the weather was not usually a variable factor of production where the labour process was controlled by capital. Yet if labour's ability to control work is to be judged on its ability to create formal organizations then clearly this trade has an unimpressive record, since it possessed a trade union for only two years of the first half of the century. In this case, however, we can see a process operating whereby ground gained by an 'ad hoc' strike was held through the informal structures of 'understandings', which made up the face-to-face relationship of the workforce at the point of production. It is, however, not unlikely that the historian of conventional trade unionism would select the two-year period of formal organization as the most significant development in the trade's labour organization in this period. To the workers involved it must have seemed otherwise. It is only by exploring this network of informal 'understandings' on work organization that we can begin to piece together a labour-oriented perception of social order which involved all workers, not simply the artisans. One of the major difficulties in doing so, however, lies in the impenetrability of the workplace during this period.

THE TERRITORIAL IMPERATIVES OF WORK

There is a certain openness about the later nineteenth-century workplace that is apparently absent in the earlier period.[93] From 1850 a plethora of documentation was created by both the growing interventionist role of the state and the gradual ascription of an accredited role to formal trade unions representing a minority of workers. Nevertheless the relative opacity of earlier workplace culture cannot be explained simply by reference to those difficulties of documentation that confront, say, the historian of eighteenth-century plebeian life. There are certain aspects of the early nineteenth-century working-class experience that are fairly well documented and therefore eminently retrievable. This is particularly true of the 1830s and the 1840s; the many social histories of radical politics that have emerged since Edward Thompson's pioneering work in 1963 furnish examples of those aspects of its affairs that the working class of the time chose to conduct in full view of the public gaze. The predominantly constitutional nature of Chartism, for example, demanded that a large proportion of the movement's business be overtly visible. The same cannot be said of many aspects of workplace culture in the same period. Here the relationship between what was made public and what was held secret was of crucial importance for what has been called by Richard Price the 'autonomous regulation' of work by the workforce.[94] This is not to suggest a contradiction or a disjunction between the Chartist political consciousness and the way the working community sought to control its immediate working environment. The line between the covert and the overt was drawn, in both cases, according to strategic considerations. Historians have, for obvious reasons, been constrained to concentrate on that which was made public. But in the three decades following 1820 the opacity of the workplace was consciously fostered, through secrecy, ritual, and folk violence, reinforced through the wider culture of the working community. If the historian has to struggle to understand the internal life of the workshops and factories in this period it is arguably because the workforce intended *all* outsiders to find themselves in precisely that position and thus be reminded of their alien status. As long as the workplace retained its enigmatic quality it could be controlled by those whose position within its highly integrated culture made them privy to its internal complexities.

Certainly the early industrial workshop or factory was no place for the sensitive or proselytizing outsider, and it was with great trepidation that strangers ventured over the threshold. This did not always reflect a concern for the privacy of the working community. The domestic urban missionaries, for example, who in Birmingham would happily enter the working-class home, uninvited and unannounced, to deliver their moral strictures, only rarely appear to have penetrated the workplace. This was not because they considered it unimportant in terms of its influence upon the moral condition of the individual. Rather the reverse was the case: the workplace was seen as the repository of every value that was calculated to undermine the missionaries' efforts. Edward Derrington drew attention in 1839 to the independence that the experience of work afforded otherwise pliable Sunday School scholars: 'the youths have at a very early age', he complained, 'been their own or nearly their own masters'.[95] Such independence threatened to undo the work of the rational recreationalists, for, as Derrington added, 'they are the fighters – the pigeon flyers – dog fighters and gamblers'.[96] Another missionary, Peter Sibree, recorded with some concern the case of a widow in his district who had supervised the running of a manufactory since the recent death of her husband. The woman explained to him 'that her children had been brought under the teaching of the Gospel among the Wesleyans, but now they were unhappily infidel having imbibed the notions from some of the workmen'.[97] This interesting case of employees inculcating their employers with their values may be a reversal of the flow of that particular traffic that we have come to expect, but it does serve to emphasize the powerful, and obvious, concentration of those values within the workplace.

Despite this the missionaries directed their attentions toward the working-class home, only rarely setting foot in the workplace. William Jackson, a missionary in Birmingham from 1842 until 1847, congratulated himself upon having entered and preached in a fire-iron workshop in 1846: 'I this day engaged in an effort from which some four years ago at the start of my missionary labours I should probably have shrunk.'[98] Jackson's obvious reticence to enter the workplace had not been assuaged by an experience only five months earlier. 'While urging the importance of divine things' in a nailer's shop, he was stopped and challenged to open debate by an 'infidel' workman.[99] On those few occasions when he preached to the navigators digging a canal through his district Jackson thought it wise to take along Edward Derrington for support. Jackson subsequently professed himself to be impressed by 'the willingness with which these apparently repulsive characters listened to our serious remarks'.[100] Derrington's abiding memory of one such visit, however, was of 'an hour's close argument' with an 'infidel' navigator who 'eulogised Robert Owen as a most benevolent man'.[101]

To these harbingers of the evangelical ethic the workplace and its reflected image, the public house, represented the strongest points of an unknown culture. Here were twin streams feeding the same collective values and beliefs, enabling the working community to add a frustratingly complex dimension to the missionaries' essentially straightforward message of sin and repentance. A button-shank-maker in Staniforth Street, for example, felt that his absence from church required no explanation 'while the clergy in the town were all Tories'.[102] Commenting on a similar case in his district Derrington lamented 'there is much of this kind of skepticism among the lower orders of mankind, the men are instructed in it at the public house and then they bring it home to their wives and spend the Sabbath in conference on these subjects aided by some of the low publications of the present day'.[103] A dying workman in Digbeth ignored Sibree's exhortations to repent at his last, only asking the anxious priest 'Do you think the present ministers will go out?' There was more than a little of the smug in Sibree's journal comment, 'He died soon after, a sad warning to all working men who, like him, spend their Sabbaths in the alehouse.'[104]

This kind of observation was far more than a simple equation between drink and morality. When the workplace was reinforced by an active relationship with the public house, working-class culture appeared at its most impenetrable. Eschewing both, the missionaries aimed their best endeavours toward the home and haunted the working-class wife while her husband was at work.

Derrington, in 1843, was dismayed, however, to find that regular missionary visits to one woman in his district did little to influence her husband's pattern of behaviour: 'he goes out and spends his evenings at the public house', she explained; 'I talk with him when he tells me that he has heard as good as I have at the Lodge.'[105] The same priest despaired when he discovered the existence of a network of 'Female lodges where mothers and single females go to drink ale till twelve or one o'clock'.[106]

The symbiosis of the workplace and the public house represented, to the outsider, a culture that embraced not only drunkenness, violence, and sensuality, but also radical politics, Owenite infidelity, and, at times, an almost puritanical concept of moral justice. Once within either institution intruders were confronted by an alternative set of values and beliefs that would intimidate them both physically and intellectually. Such an emphasis on the separate nature of workplace culture was essential to the maintenance of working-class control of the labour process. The abiding belief at the heart of workplace organization in the period was that the employer's appropriate role was to initiate the process of production and to market the finished product. What came between (the nature and pace of production) was properly the responsibility of labour. Within even the smallest Birmingham workshop workers expected to be left to organize themselves by operating in work-groups, called 'gangs', 'crews', 'sets', 'shops', or 'chairs', according to the trade, each with its own inherent hierarchy. The agreed head of each group negotiated for work with the employer and ensured its equitable distribution within the group.

Of course, the introduction of 'readier methods of working' presumed autonomy over work on the part of the employer, since they involved a higher degree of intervention and supervision than was possible with the 'customary' modes of operation. Thus the major issue in the early industrial workplace was that of authority. This is a point that is sometimes lost in studying the minutiae of individual strike causation. Even as an apprentice rule-maker in Birmingham during the 1840s, Dyke Wilkinson felt fully justified in deciding upon his own working rhythms. While he worked he kept a volume of literature open on his bench. He explained in his autobiography, 'Burns, Byron, Oliver Goldsmith and Pope were my saints: Shakespeare was my God.'[107] To avoid detection from his employer he constructed a false tool-rack within which the volume could be secreted in case '"Mr. John" paid one of his flying visits'. Wilkinson recalls: 'I never scrupled about using it . . . because I was at this time a sort of piece worker – that is my day's work was set me, and it had to be done before I could leave the place. So while I filed and chiselled and drilled I had ever the beloved little volume before me, and was committing its choicest bits to memory.' 'Mr. John's' authority was hardly stamped efficiently upon the workshop as a whole. In order to facilitate fuller surveillance of work in progress he, at one point, took to approaching the shop wearing carpet slippers to soften his footsteps. 'This so exasperated the lads', Wilkinson remembered, 'they took to shying at him rotten potatoes, stale bread, and, I am ashamed to say, on occasions things of a worse description.'[108] As a last resort 'Mr. John' drilled a 'secret' hole in the wall of the shop to facilitate surveillance, a contrivance which Wilkinson countered with a long piece of pointed wire applied from the other side of the hole. This was rather more than the conflict of paternal authority with the spirit of youth, for Wilkinson (who was not apparently a member of any trade society, although the rule-makers struck in 1845) argued firmly from the premises of the working community. 'You are no master of mine', he informed his employer at one point, 'but only a man who buys my labour for a good deal less than its worth.' The case brings to mind Marx's analysis that where production was based ultimately upon handicraft skill and manual strength 'capital is constantly compelled to wrestle with the insubordination of the workers'.[109]

The rules by which labour governed itself, and thus controlled work, were only rarely given the status of written agreements. Yet the 'understandings' were tangible enough entities for all that. In 1838 a button-burnisher, Joseph Corbett, found himself expelled from the Loyal Albions for defying their 'long established laws and practices'. He had contested the regulation of apprenticeship exercised by the lodge. They banned the taking of apprentices for a year but Corbett had accepted a boy to accommodate his employer. This focused sharply on a critical issue regarding the exercise of authority in the workplace and Corbett clearly appreciated this, explaining: 'I would not be a party in telling a master that he should not put a boy into his own workshop.' For their part the trade lodge refused to retain a member who had declared, by his actions, 'that we had no right to judge for ourselves'. The fact that Corbett could point out in mitigation that 'we have no written regulations . . . there being none to refer to',[110] did nothing to reduce the heinous nature of his offence in the eyes of his workmates. Anybody that was part of the face-to-face relationship of the work-group could be expected to know the correct way to act. Similarly the Birmingham lodge of the Britannia-metal-workers, established in the late 1830s, operated a rigorous closed-shop policy, yet as one member admitted:

> There is no rule of the union which forbids a master to employ other workmen than members of the union, but in an establishment where unionists are employed they do not and will not associate with others except members of their own body which is pretty much the same as forbidding them to work in that establishment.[111]

The brass-cock-founders in Birmingham exerted an organizational pressure, albeit of a highly 'spasmodic' nature, from the late 1820s onwards. An observer in 1851 found 'so much jealousy between masters and men that it is extremely difficult to procure information from either of them on any point connected with the trade'. Even he, however, was able to establish that 'by a rule of the union no journeyman can have more than one boy to work under him'.[112] Despite this very clear understanding within the work-group the brass-cock-founders had no written rules until 1885.[113] This did not prevent them from referring to 'legitimate practice' as a yardstick by which to measure the imposition of change in the workplace during their frequent disputes with their masters.

Thus, even where labour formalized its organizational structure it made little attempt to systematize the organization of work into a formal framework visible to employers and workers alike. Rather the reverse was the case as the 1820s, and 1830s particularly, saw attempts made to mystify custom. Those societies which did emerge clearly placed a premium on secrecy. The United Order of Smiths, formed in 1839, fined heavily 'any member divulging any of the transactions of the Order to any persons not a member'.[114] In their reorganization of 1833 the Birmingham carpenters found it necessary, for the first time, to introduce the paraphernalia of tylers and passwords to ensure the secrecy of lodge night. Their rules were adamant on this point: 'That should either of the tylers admit any member without the password, or otherwise give any member the password without obtaining the consent of the President they shall be fined threepence each.'[115]

Such provisions were often reinforced by oaths taken at elaborate initiation ceremonies. In November 1833 William Boultbee, a member of the Political Council of the Birmingham Political Union, warned the local trades against following the advice 'of men who were leading them to take oaths which were unlawful and to enter into secret combinations . . . for however secret they might imagine their plans were kept the government would have spies among them and . . . they would be betrayed'.[116] The detailed accounts that we have of these ceremonies would suggest that Boultbee was substantially correct in his judgement. The initiation rites of the Leeds wool-combers, the London tailors, the West Country weavers, the Kidderminster carpet-weavers, the Tolpuddle labourers, and the Operative Stone Masons are sufficiently similar in style to suggest a universal format with only minor local variations.[117] The blindfold initiate calling for admittance to the lodge room, the chanted liturgy of psalms and Old Testament extracts, and the oath of secrecy administered by a surpliced official are recurring elements in all these ceremonies.[118] Such activities appear to have been fairly widespread in the 1830s. John Doherty's claim, to the 1838 Select Committee on Combinations of Workmen, that secret oaths had not been taken by the spinners since the repeal of the Combinations Acts was, in all probability, a piece of post-Dorchester back-pedalling.[119] In Birmingham, James Morrison's denials of the extensive use of such forms, in March 1834, can also be accounted for in much the same way.[120] In September 1833 he had written to Owen urging him to include provision for initiation rituals in the rules of the GNCTU: 'I know you consider these ceremonies as so many relics of barbarism. But the spirit of the times requires some concessions to popular prejudice and by conceding a little we may gain much.'[121]

It is possible to see these kinds of ritual as 'traditional' in that they linked the working community with an apparently tangible past. Nevertheless, it is likely that such forms were, during the 1820s and 1830s, far more elaborately developed than at any point in the past. Richard Carlile considered these kinds of ceremony to be 'a wrong start' for the unions of the early 1830s, and he advised: 'Let them be wise and do without secrets: and then they will be approaching a more respectable situation.'[122] It seems likely that such initiations represented an extension of the theatre inherent in the culture of the workplace rather than the continuation of specific forms. There are echoes here of the collective activity of workplace trials, 'foot ales', 'marriage ales', apprenticeship rituals, and the exacting of the 'shifting shilling' from workers moving jobs within the workplace. Thompson has noted the closeness of extravagant theatre alongside the friendly society function of these early organizations; this particular combination of features is demonstrated amply in a letter being carried by the President of the Leamington Lodge of Irish Labourers Conjunction Union when he was arrested in Birmingham in 1834:

> Mr. Boulton we are sorry that it was Not in our power to answer your parcel dated Feby the 25th concerning the signs and passwords we could not send we had not got them we had a little dispute with the Grand Lodge. Mr. Boulton you are requested to attend the Delegate Meeting. Personally all Presidents in the Kingdom must attend by Monday morning By 9 o'clock or he be fined ten shillings you must be in full uniform you must bring your white surplice and cap with you there is to be presidents in attendance All belonging to our Society all to join our conjunctive bond to pledge themselves to secure the Society you are to take a balance an account of the tramps you have relieved and a certificate from the Siety and you must make this declaration on oath that the above contents are true.[123]

There is, of course, no need to search too far for the origins of a tradition of secrecy within organizations that were explicitly illegal from 1800 to 1824 and of rather dubious legal status thereafter. Nevertheless the emphasis upon secrecy through association cannot be entirely accounted for by pointing to the quasi-legal status of trade societies throughout the period. The tradition of organization within the workplace was never an entirely anonymous one. Even during the period when the Combination Acts were at their most effective wage demands were (as we saw earlier in the case of the steel-toymakers) often accompanied by the signatures of workplace representatives. Where it suited them to do so workplace organizers were perfectly prepared to make public their activities in restraint of trade.

The theatre of trade secrecy, in fact, faced two ways, both into the working community and out from it. Morrison stressed this bifurcation in March 1834 while answering Carlile's case against lodge initiations. 'Their ceremony', he claimed, 'is a public etiquette to keep each lodge in order.'[124] Much of the *Pioneer* was directed at the 'initiated bees', but Morrison was adamant that the ceremonies to which he referred involved an 'affirmation' of loyalty rather than a secret oath. In this respect we should be careful not to confuse secret oaths with oaths of secrecy (although the judgement upon the Dorchester labourers indicated that the law made no such distinction). If the London tailors had wished their rituals to be completely covert they would presumably not have carried out initiations in batches of 200 men, and would also have found somewhere a little less public than the Rotunda for the ceremony. Likewise in 1834 the Birmingham lodge of the Operative Stone Masons actually published their Initiating Parts, in printed form, complete with oath of secrecy.[125]

The same public use of 'secret' (or at least mysterious) ceremonial can be seen in the funeral processions that were increasingly a feature of trade activities in the early 1830s. In February and March 1834 the *Pioneer* reported elaborate processions of this sort in Derby, Nottingham, and Hinckley. In June, James Preston of Birmingham was followed to his grave by the officers and full membership of his own woodsawyers' society and representatives of the other branches of the building trades. Each man carried a small bunch of thyme. After lowering the coffin and singing the doxology, 'the trades came two by two to the grave, dividing at the foot, one on each side, shook hands and dropped the thyme on the coffin, and returned in procession to the deceased's house'.[126]

The initiation and funeral ceremonies should be seen as part of the same matrix of 'mysterious' brotherliness. Together they expressed visually the separate and distinct nature of the values that characterized the working community. In this way they were a formal declaration of what was recognized informally in every aspect of working-class culture. The clear message of the trade funeral, irrespective of the way the actual detail of the mummery varied from area to area, or between village and town, was that the individual who respected collective values was, in turn, deserving of collective respect.

What also comes across from an examination of these ceremonial forms is their hierarchical and male-centred nature. Women were clearly involved but marginalized in ways that Dorothy Thompson has suggested also applied to the Chartist movement.[127] Writing of the Nottingham hosiery industry, Sonya Rose has argued that the particular construction of masculinity which became a feature of the workplace in this period was an adaptation and extension of traditional forms within the context of developing capitalism. This point is perhaps supported by the carpenters' motto of 1834, 'May carpenters be men, and nought but men carpenters'.[128] Here the point is less that the carpenters were threatened by female labour but rather that 'correct' behaviour in the workplace had become equated with the expression of masculinity. The development of gender differentiation, in this way, is also an important reminder that whatever its commitment to libertarian politics, the community of work was not a community of equals.

The ceremonial, with its obscure forms, also served notice upon the wider public that the visible manifestations of workplace organization were simply the tip of a much larger iceberg, most of which was hidden from view. Thus the implicit secrecy of the initiation ceremony and the 'mysteries' of the trade funeral were ably complemented by the occasional rather more straightforward display of strength. In taking to the streets of Birmingham in August 1832, for example, the United Trades were achieving more than the celebration of the Reform Bill's passing, which was the ostensible purpose of the procession. They were also demonstrating the existence of sixteen unions able to parade their members under their respective flags and banners behind a workingmen's committee headed by Morrison.[129] In a similar kind of public statement the building trades, late in 1833, began work on their own guildhall. This was to be a magnificent classical edifice, designed as the physical embodiment of the objectives behind workplace organization. In the words of the United Trades Committee, it would 'give permanency and efficiency to the efforts of the working-builders to obtain and secure sufficient wages and full employment for every member of their body'.[130] The planned provision, within the guildhall, of schools for both children and adults, represents an attempt to construct facilities that served the specific and distinct needs of the working community. The ceremony of laying the foundation stone was a celebration of these aspirations. Accompanied by two bands of music the lodges of the eight branches of the building trades marched through the main streets of the town alongside the coopers, silk-hatters, pearl-button-makers, heavy-steel-toymakers, tailors, comb-makers, shoemakers, and locksmiths. The *Pioneer* noted that it was 'a procession of an entirely new and important character'.[131]

The attempt to mystify the workplace in the late 1820s and early 1830s (a move checked by the Tolpuddle judgements), was only an extension of the notion of custom as a series of tacit, and often highly flexible, agreements between groups of workers in particular contexts. Such modes united workers rather than divided them, although custom was often reinforced by apparently sectional forms of cultural organization. Drinking patterns within the working community were traditionally defined in occupational terms. An observer in 1805 noted that, 'for instance, the first rank namely the japanners rarely associate in their hours of relaxation with the workers of copper, brass, iron, etc. the latter frequent common pot-houses, the former get into the third and fourth inns and club rooms'.[132] Certainly trade clubs, and less-formal associations of workers, focused on specific houses, and although any extension of such territorial imperatives could be interpreted as representing a deeply sectional consciousness within the working community as a whole, in fact this was a critical device enabling the work-group to internalize and enforce consensus values. By the 1830s there was a widespread and growing acceptance that the problems facing individual trades were actually universal. Nevertheless the form taken by infringement necessarily varied in particular detail from trade to trade, and control of work therefore required a firm grasp upon the immediate environment of the workplace itself. While the workplace and the public house were firmly integrated the distinctiveness of the line between work and leisure was by no means apparent. The unwritten lore of the shop could therefore be reflected and reinforced outside the workplace.

When Thomas Parrish, a carpenter, arrived from Coventry in November 1833 to take up work he found himself making the unsought acquaintance of a number of society men. The contractor that Parrish had agreed to work for was in dispute with the men. The society had passed a resolution agreeing that 'Old Barnett shall be put upon the shelf and shall not have a man to work for him.'[133] Parrish was now 'persuaded' to leave his new-found employment and for this purpose was taken to the 'Falstaff' in Holland Street, where the carpenters met. Here he was invited into an upstairs room to undergo a ceremony of initiation including the swearing of an oath. When he refused he was attacked by Josiah Knight, the landlord of the 'Falstaff', armed with a red-hot poker. By now Parrish was convinced that the professions of 'brotherly love and friendship' offered by his hosts were likely to prove to be hollow and he bolted, pursued from the district by a group of twenty men. Such cases of intimidation were a prominent feature of most trade disputes at this time and could be multiplied countless times for each industrial centre. But two points are perhaps worth noting. First, as in so many of these cases it was within the public house itself that the violence took place. Second, the role of the landlord in this particular case is significant, since he was clearly deeply involved with the carpenters' trade organization. An ex-carpenter himself, Knight was described by Barnett at his subsequent trial, as 'the organ of this society'. In his own defence Knight explained defiantly that 'the object of the society was to keep men just and honest together and it would take something to frighten him from doing that which he considered for the general good of mankind'.[134]

Knight's typicality as a landlord is, of course, impossible to estimate. Certainly the prevalence of exclusive dealing directed at publicans, particularly at election time, would seem to suggest that many landlords were themselves at odds with the values of the wider community.[135] Nevertheless, within a certain strata of public house, it is likely that the integration of work and leisure was almost total and that the nexus between the two provided a barrier to those self-destructive elements with which the working community was imbued by a free market economy in a state of high competition.

For the manufacturer seeking to reorganize work through a new labour discipline the problem of 'drink' was rather more than simply the problem of drunkenness and its attendant irregularity within the workplace. The employer was far more likely to extend his workplace authority where the cultural controls built into the working community were undermined or rejected from within. Thus the worker who was inclined to accept the subordinate role of labour within the workplace had also to reject certain aspects of the wider culture of his own community. Joseph Corbett suggested in 1838 that his dispute with his fellow button-burnishers stemmed directly from his own acceptance of temperance: 'I had declined visiting the lodge so long objecting to its being held at a public house, having adopted the temperance principle.'[136] The Loyal Albion's reply was perhaps predictable: 'His first leaving the Lodge was not from temperance principles as he states.' Instead, according to the Albion, this was a fundamental dispute over workplace authority: 'There has not existed a good understanding for the last three or four years in consequence of his overbearing conduct towards his shopmates.'[137]

Employers for their part assiduously cultivated the notion of a tripartite correlation between drink, immorality, and customary modes of work organization. In 1820 the master bootmakers discountenanced their journeyman's claims to low wages with the assertion that 'a bootman with full work who earns but seventeen shillings a week must play at least two days in the week unless he be a very dilatory workman'.[138] The employers of the Operative Screw Locksmiths, rejecting the claims of their striking workforce in 1835, declared that 'the true state of the case is this – they want to get as much money in three days as will support their families and supply them to get drunk and attend men fights, dog fights, etc., the other three days of the week'.[139] The economic heterodoxy of artisanal rhythms of production came increasingly to be equated with social deviance in its broadest sense. As one manufacturer put it in 1851, 'there are many trades in which the workmen are intemperate. These are principally the trades in which work is given out and no regular factory discipline is observed.'[140] In the same year another manufacturer argued that 'The union . . . had a direct tendency to bring the men a good deal together, and, as they met in public houses, it led to drinking and dissipated habits.'[141]

The corollary to all of this was a marked belief, among middle-class observers, that the period saw the emergence of an upper echelon of the working class who rejected drink as part of a wider emulative process. Wish-fulfilment on the part of employers and calculated role-playing by skilled workers have often been taken to constitute a substantial reality, and such images have been energetically incorporated into 'labour aristocracy' theory by historians.[142] However, as Bailey has demonstrated, the rough–

respectable typology was itself the product of a bourgeois culture within which 'thinking and drinking' were considered to be mutually exclusive activities.[143] While observers happily charted the decline of an older, boisterous popular culture alongside the adoption of thrift and temperance among the 'respectable' working class, the changes that were taking place often looked rather more complex to the members of the working community. A 92-year-old worker from the light steel toy trade argued in 1851 that 'There is less fighting now than in my day . . . but I think there is more drinking nowadays.'[144] William Bramwell has argued that in Birmingham the public house remained the centre of this community and that the emergence of an elite strata of 'temperance artisans' was 'largely illusory'.[145]

In fact, notions of 'respectability' remained class-specific throughout the period and definitions of respectable behaviour should not be divorced from the broader context of workplace–community relations. Morality as a set of collective values, protected and expressed by the community as a group, lay at the heart of the democratic forms of the workplace. In the main, middle-class observers comprehended neither the values nor the forms they related to, though they acknowledged a causal link between the two. When the gun-finishers struck work against a reduction of prices in 1846 they found it necessary to revoke publicly their employers' picture of them as an 'idle and dissolute body'.[146] At a meeting to answer similar allegations in 1852 James Pomeroy, an operative gun-maker, made a vigorous defence of the trustworthiness and respectability of the members of his trade:

> He looked upon the masters as nothing more than clerks to the Board [of Ordnance], for they merely took out orders and then entrusted the production entirely to the men – never seeing the guns till they were finished. If they were dissipated and not to be trusted how dare they do this?[147]

Many contemporary observers (and, one suspects, not a few modern historians) would have seen such a forthright assertion of respectability as strange, coming as it did from the lips of a man imprisoned for eighteen months, in 1839, for throwing stones at policemen during the Bull Ring riots. Pomeroy had been carrying a dagger at the time and threatened one policeman with the words, 'you bloody bugger I'll settle you'. A prison visitor found him able to read and write well and he spent some of his period of enforced idleness in improving his ability with arithmetic.[148] Pomeroy, like so many others, did not fit neatly into the 'rough–respectable' model of class behaviour which has been an implicit element in much recent research on workplace organization. Here a twin absorption with a stereotyped 'respectable' artisan and with the emergence of modes of arbitration post-1850, has led historians to select only the most peaceful of approaches to disputes as constituting 'normal trade society methods'.[149] In this way the distinction between the craft worker and the rest of the working community has been artificially emphasized and extended. On the one hand, the skilled worker is presented as normative, peacefully relying on negotiation through formally constituted organizations tolerated by employers. On the other hand, the less skilled are seen as having been deviant elements, utilizing 'primitive' forms of wage bargaining by riot. This analysis is often pursued even when it was clearly craft workers who were rioting and justifying violent action in ways relevant to the whole community.

In 1836 Angus M'Greggor of the Birmingham stonemasons expounded the logic of a collective morality that would have to be enforced collectively: 'the member who claims the support of the society in preference to working for under wages is *legally entitled* to it because he resists an infringement on established custom'. Transgressors were, in M'Greggor's view, subject to the same code of ethics, since 'the experience of all ages testifies the universality of punishing the aggressions of individuals against the general rights of society, hence it is our *undeniable right* to prevent masons from persisting in conduct which ruins the mason's trade'.[150] The pursuit of this strategy, argued in terms of overt legality, often took the community outside the law. Here the informality of workplace organization was most marked. One manufacturer reported of the tacit agreements of the filesmiths: 'that if any member of the trade has been guilty of bearing the indignity of allowing his master to employ a boy to do work which (although a boy is perfectly competent to do it) is considered man's work, he is in a manner outlawed, no man will work in the same shop with him afterwards'.[151] The tin-plate-workers were similarly active, another manufacturer reporting:

> If a workman proves unruly and not willing to be bound by the union it is very easy to make the place too hot for him; he finds his tools missing, his coat stolen, his hat smashed, remarks of a personal nature chalked on his bench.[152]

These were simply extensions of the normal workplace mechanisms controlling work in its social context. In the case of strikes these mechanisms became located within the wider community, and there were many examples of this in Birmingham.

In July 1825 three Birmingham carpenters were arraigned at Warwick charged with riotous assembly and assault. Three months earlier carpenters striking for a raise in the price made the rounds of the workshops, as a group, drawing the men out and confiscating the tools of any men refusing to join the strike. One carpenter, Sampson Webb, refusing to join was pelted with mud and thrown into a canal. James Rogers, appearing for the defence, was careful to point out that although a carpenter, and part of what he claimed was a fifty-strong delegation of the trade that confronted Webb, he was not a member of any association. The *Chronicle* dropped its usual euphemistic niceties of description in reporting his evidence, clearly seeing Webb as a victim of the 'tyranny of the many'.

> In a few minutes Webb came out when Jones said to him 'Ah Sam, I did not think you had been a man of this kind; I thought you would have stood up for the good of the trade'. Webb turned round, said he was independent of them and they might kiss his — ; as he said this he pulled up his coat and applied his hand to the part in a very insulting way. The hissing and groaning began now.[153]

Similarly, in 1831, a blank-tray-maker was assaulted and thrown into the canal by a crowd of 100 for contravening 'some regulations which they had entered into respecting their trade'. When the case was heard at sessions he was unable to produce a single witness.[154] In 1835 the attention of the crowd was turned on a glass manufacturer in a dispute concerning the introduction of new machinery. At the trial of some glass-workers involved in the affair, prosecuting council claimed:

> that only a few days ago Mr. Gould's premises were set on fire and there was not the least doubt that the fire was the work of

> an incendiary. He sincerely hoped that the magistrates . . . would protect Mr. Gould from the tyranny of mob-law, the worst of all despotisms.[155]

The cases of the horn-button rioters of 1837, and of the lobbying of James Clare's workshop in 1840 have already been discussed.[156] In 1844 two shoemakers were prosecuted for an assault committed under a conspiracy to raise wages. Again prosecuting council's remarks suggest fairly extensive crowd activity: 'the police would be able to speak to [about] the generally disturbed state of the neighbourhood during the last few weeks in consequence of the gross misconduct of the accused and their associates'.[157] Similarly, in 1848, during a strike which a glass manufacturer imported French labour to break, it was John Steven, a tailor, who was prosecuted as a result of a riot at the factory gates. All this suggests the drawing in of the wider community at these key points.[158]

Over the last twenty years a good deal of work on 'the crowd' has stressed its function as the ultimate arbiter on a range of issues. Although essentially 'informal' in its nature, such an approach to trade issues was fully supported within the 'formal' end of the organizational spectrum, where the option of collective violence was often taken. In 1834 Parkes raised the point with James Morrison:

> I asked the 'Head piece' why if the unions discouraged all (violent) acts they defended persons who broke the law. He said that it was necessary to hold the Unions together to befriend members however imprudent or wrong-doing.[159]

Behind such support lay a universal legitimation through a morality which assumed labour's centrality in the chain of production. The cordwainers, striking in the same year, condemned employers attempting

> to sink into the lowest depths of wretchedness that portion of the community upon whose industry the great machine of society moves and upon that industry alone depends the cultivation of those morals which render us acceptable in the eyes of God and man. Then he is a sinner against God and a violator of every moral law, who advocated the degradation of the mechanic and drives into a state of brutalisation his fellow being.[160]

The same blend of the labour theory of value justified through biblical rhetoric is to be found in the letter from a tin-plate-worker to the *Birmingham Journal* in 1841:

> Men are at liberty to form associations for the prosecution of felons; and I do not know of a worse species of felony than that of robbing a man of the fruits of his honest labour. I really cannot see the moral difference between the workman robbing his master and the master robbing his workman. The same law which says 'Thou shalt not steal' says also 'Thou shalt not covet anything that is thy neighbour's. . . . The men that oppress the hireling in wages rob God as well as man.[161]

This letter, in its restraint, would qualify for admission to even the most Whiggish interpretation of working-class history. The same cannot be said of that received by a scale-beam manufacturer in 1843. But though the letters may reflect a disparity of literacy, and certainly of intent, the appeal in both is essentially to the same corpus of values:

> Sir – of all the bloody roges that ever I herd tell of you are the bigest. You rob your men you rebell against God and you are no better than a murderer, for a murderer is subject to the laws and only injers one but you injer all in the trade. You robe both master and man and you will ruin yourself. I believe you are going to turn your men out next Saturday but we will murder you. We have a plan to work upon that can blow your bloody branes out and it shall be done there is twenty of us united together and we shall cach you on the bonce. I thought I would lett you know because you will know what it is for.
>
> One of the Witfield men.[162]

The tenor of both letters (and particularly the line 'You robe both master and man' in the second), is a reminder that the obligations of the workplace were considered to be reciprocal. The biblical references remind the reader of the sacrosanct nature of the way work was organized. Behind both letters were a set of assumptions about the way work should be controlled which employers had to contest if they were to introduce 'readier methods of working'.

THE ASSAULT ON CUSTOMARY WORK STRUCTURES

The organization of work, as far as the labouring community was concerned, involved a series of mutually beneficial agreements between employers and employees. In this respect it resembled the projections of political economy. However, just as the economist's notion of agreements forged by free agents in an atmosphere of equality was some distance from reality, so labour contrived to present its case in ways that would reinforce its own authority. In labour's projection the formulation of the substantive context within which the reciprocal relationships of production operated was determined by custom. In turn, the exact content of custom would be determined by labour. Thus the precise context in which the autonomous regulation of work was set varied enormously. The Birmingham coopers, for example, found support for their case in the works of Euclid, Locke, and Shakespeare. This impressive collection of literary authorities apparently condemned the kinds of incursion into the cooper's trade which employers were perpetrating in 1834.[163] Drawing two such incursions from the lengthy list provided, and juxtaposing them, serves to remind us of the complexity of customary formulations. On the one hand, the coopers lamented the erosion of payments in kind: 'you have taken the privilege of our chips without an equivalent either in beer or beer money'. The workers' loss of 'chips' (offcuts of wood created in the process of production, used as firewood) and similar fringe benefits in other trades was clearly central to the perception of change.[164] The prolonged strike of 1829 among the linen-weavers of Barnsley was provoked by the loss of 'fents' (the equivalent of chips in this branch of textiles).[165] On the other hand, however, the coopers also castigated their employers for the *introduction* of payments in kind:

> you think, as a matter of course that we must get in timber hoops etc., and perhaps for three or four hours labour, you deign to bestow among four or five half a gallon of beer – a gracious boon! Why not pay according to time and labour.[166]

Thus fringe benefits, unless monitored carefully, were themselves open to abuse. Within the workplace an accepted perquisite which overstepped a customary demarcation line could easily assume the aspect of truck payment. Clearly, it was the workforce that was to decide where the line was drawn.

Throughout this period labour insisted that its centrality in the chain of production allowed it a determining relationship with the product itself. The 'custom of the trade' was invoked, not as a misguided attempt to recreate a mythical 'golden age' but as a consensus agreement on acceptable practice, validated by informal 'understandings' between workers, against which the process of change could be measured and judged. Take, for example, the case of two Birmingham glassblowers who appeared in court in 1846 charged under the Master and Servant legislation for absenting themselves from their work. The glassblowers throughout the town were on strike over an attempt by a local glass manufacturer, William Gammon, to raise the production levels by simply increasing the number of articles to be made in a 'move', or work-period. The men felt this exceeded 'the usage and custom of the trade'. The demand for increased production was arbitrary, unaccompanied by increased remuneration, but it was also perfectly legal, the men having bound themselves by agreement to 'do eleven moves a day as reckoned in the house of Mr. Gammon'. Once custom was ignored in this reckoning, production levels could be set as high as the manufacturer required. Defending counsel made customary practice the cornerstone of his case asking: 'What is a move? . . . he held that the only rule they could adopt as a guide to the settlement of that question was the usual custom of the trade – not the mere will of any individual firm.' But the magistrate, Charles Shaw, a local merchant and manufacturer, dismissed this argument. When the two men refused the option of a return to work, he imprisoned them for a month with hard labour.[167] A similar case before the same magistrate in 1848 reached the same conclusion. On this occasion Shaw made it clear where his sympathies lay, by explaining that he 'bore Mr. Harris [the plaintiff manufacturer] out in every word as to the impossibility of anyone maintaining his trade in the face of other persons underselling him'.[168]

Custom was consistently confronted with the logic of the market, a rationale commanded by the employer and provided with an enabling context by the recurrent crises in production that characterized the three decades that followed 1820.[169] With the onset of crisis the imperatives to restructure work at all levels of the economy were more obvious than ever. Large firms had a fixed-capital investment to protect. As we have seen, for smaller firms competition was intensified at precisely the moment when credit availability was reduced and the dependence upon the marketing facilities of the larger firms was most marked. Crisis, however, also provided the opportunity to restructure work at all levels by loosening labour's hold on the work process in the way suggested by T.C. Salt in an earlier chapter.[170] With the advent of severe crisis in 1847, following as it did four years of relatively good trade and accompanying labour organization, G.F. Muntz announced that:

> The working men have been able to get higher wages, but the master men of Birmingham, who have to live on the produce of their businesses, and to compete with the other manufacturers of the world have been sorely prejudiced by the effect of high wages. [171]

It would be too much, of course, to argue that capital actually welcomed the onset of depression. Even it preferred the vibrant tussles of periods of good trade to the uncertainty of economic crisis. For T.H. Ryland the pressure of this period was so great that he gave up production altogether in 1849:

> So, it went on till I could bear the anxiety no longer and in October I suddenly stopped . . . I had suffered so much anxiety for many months that the day I stopped was to me a day of deliverance and, considering what I had gone through, I might say, of happiness. I had not lived on my creditors; on the average of the fourteen years I had not drawn from the earnings of the business £200 per year, not so much as some of my workpeople had. Every penny went to maintain the works; I don't know how much, but in buildings, engines, machinery, tools, etc., at the very least £14,000.[172]

Undoubtedly, capital at all levels was constrained to see the troughs of trade as the very sternest test which individualism could provide for them. But by the 1840s they were also viewed as part of a natural order of things from which industry might emerge leaner and fitter. 'There is a cycle of national prosperity and adversity', announced the *Birmingham Journal* in March 1847, 'almost as certain of recurrence as the alterations of productive and unproductive harvests.'[173]

It was argued in the first part of this book that the distinction between the artisan–master and the *petit-bourgeois* manufacturer in large part hinged upon a rejection or acceptance of this orthodox middle-class view of the 'natural order'. As we have seen, the internal dynamic of such an economic ordering was competition, an ethos consistently questioned by the rhetoric of the working community. By the 1850s most trades had registered a marked decline in prices over the previous ten years. The gun-makers complained in 1852 that their prices had been reduced by 40–50 per cent in this period: 'This state of things', they claimed, 'had not been brought about by the strange revolutionary power of steam or machinery, but it was owing to the effects of severe competition among the masters.'[174] In accepting the legitimacy of forms of competition which underpinned the position of large-scale capital at the expense of the smaller concern the small manufacturer accepted his position within a hierarchy of economic relationships. Artisan rhetoric questioned the validity of the hierarchy itself. *Petit-bourgeois* producers were constrained to take such a view partly because it gave expression to the economic reality of this relationship between unequal partners in the broader system of production, but also because it was this conception of a 'natural order of things' which legitimized their autonomy over work in their own concerns. Their insistence upon dominion over labour (essential if their concerns were to flourish in a situation of intensified competition) only acted to reinforce their own subordination to large-scale capital. This was the underlying assumption of what capital referred to as the 'legitimate' trade, that is to say, the section of any industry which accepted the legitimacy of market forces in defining its obligations.

The attack on custom, which such an approach to production implied, therefore proceeded on a broad front. The major concentration, however, was upon the relationship between the skilled artisan and the rest of the workforce. The artisan, of course, was central to labour's case for its control of work, since he epitomized the notion of the worker as independent producer. However far this notion was from the reality of the employment structure we will invariably find the concept embodied in the organization of work in this period, since it was this which validated the determining relationship between the worker and the product. The property of skill was possessed by a minority of workers but it was a unique form of property in that it could only manifest itself fully through expression in the collective forms of a labour-oriented work structure.[175] The terminology used varied from trade to trade but the 'gang' system of work organization, in both workshop and factory, placed the artisan at the head of a hierarchy reproduced many times within the same workplace. The 'gang' (or 'set', 'chair', 'crew', or 'shop' according to the trade) produced an article and then 'sold' it to the employer. Thus in one sense almost every skilled artisan was a small master, employing as he did underhands or apprentices and taking responsibility for the 'sale' of the goods to the employer, and the payment of wages. In the metal-button trade, for example, work was organized around four processes: cutting and soldering, both carried out by women paid a weekly rate; stamping, carried out by men on a higher weekly rate; and burnishing, the most skilful operation, carried out by men working by the piece.[176] Button-shanking was a separate trade with its own hierarchy. Within the button-making gangs only the burnishers were formally organized and they carried responsibility for the organization of the work-groups. As an observer noted of the horn-button trade, 'The manufacturer . . . has merely a nominal control over a large proportion of the persons who work in his establishment. He neither engages them, pays them nor dismisses them. They are the servants of his servants.'[177]

The skilled worker's role in this kind of work organization has recently been interpreted as that of the mediator, and in this respect he is seen as a crucial landmark in the topography of the 'terrain of compromise'. Lazonick, for example, argues that the 'gang' system survived in cotton-spinning because it provided a useful way for employers to manage large workforces.[178] As far as labour was concerned, however, the utility of a traditional form of sub-contract lay in the fact that through it the employer was kept away from the product during the process of production. In this sense it should be seen as an expression of the territorial imperatives explored earlier in this chapter. This is partly demonstrated by the fact that wherever possible employers sought either to abolish or to distort the gang system in ways that fragmented the collective unity of the workforce. This was certainly the case with Joseph Gillott's new, large-scale steel-pen manufactory. The *Morning Chronicle* investigator was struck, when he visited the establishment in 1850, by the absence of sub-contracting, noting that 'There is no sub-employing. Every person is directly hired and paid by the manufacturer', and that consequently 'all the workpeople are directly responsible to the employer'. As a result there was much about the conduct of the workforce that the investigator admired, particularly in the discipline of the unskilled female labour:

> Unlike too many of the women employed in the manufactories of Birmingham, they are extremely neat in person and attire. . . . There is no talking in the room. The only sounds to be heard are the working hand press and the clinking of the small pieces of metal as they fall from the block into the receptacle prepared for them.[179]

This all contrasted markedly with other establishments where the small gang system held sway and the employer's presence was less in evidence. In Gillott's works the role of the 'ganger' was replaced by a supervisor, in this case an engineer:

> Each division of the workshop is superintended by a tool-maker, whose business it is to keep the punches and presses in good working condition, to superintend the work generally and to keep order among the workpeople.[180]

Nevertheless, the abolition of sub-contracting and the gangs, and their replacement with direct employment and a system of paid supervisors, was an unusual achievement. Working people clung tenaciously to the traditional system but in the process it underwent profound changes. The attempts that have recently been made to focus on continuities in work structures have led historians to underestimate the significance of these changes.[181] Certainly in Birmingham the situation was different to that described in cotton-spinning by Lazonick. The working-class perception of the 'gang' or 'set' was of a small group of perhaps half a dozen people at the most. In the glass trade, with its clearly defined informal understandings, the work-group was four: workman, servitor, footmaker, and taker-in, constituting a 'chair'.[182] The smallness of the group tied the skilled to the unskilled in a direct way. In some cases the work-group had clearly built into it a promotional scale. Glass and mule-spinning are perhaps the best examples, but the concern to maintain apprenticeship regulation throughout the trades suggests that there was an accepted mode of upward mobility within the work-group generally. Alternatively, the smallness of the group might facilitate family operations, as one button-maker recalled:

> In the year 1799 . . . being then in my seventh year I began work in the hard white metal button trade, along with my father and mother, who both worked for one large manufacturer in the town. I continued to assist them daily for ten or eleven hours a day until I was twelve years of age. They received wages for me, but how much my labour earned I cannot say.[183]

As far as the employer was concerned, however, the larger the gang the better. The contrast between the two views of ostensibly the same system can perhaps be seen in the brass-lamp trade. In 1851 an operative in the trade explained the system and its reward structure as follows:

> An average day-workman gets about £1 1s a week. The wages of the piece-workman differ according to his ability, and to the number of men or boys working under him. A workman has ordinarily from three to six persons working under him, called his 'crew'. By the aid of his crew he may earn from 35s to £2 a week.[184]

The same workman also observed that 'There are some manufactories in the town where the crew or gang system is not admitted.' A manufacturer in the trade, interviewed at the same time, however, spoke in favour of the system:

> The 'gang' system . . . is the only one which can be satisfactorily adopted in a large establishment, because of the infinite variety of work required to make a lamp. There may, for instance, be a score of men occupied upon different parts of one lamp burner, and these being placed under one person the work is greatly facilitated. . . . The heads of the gangs make from £2 to £3 per week. One man in our employ has invested his savings so well that he is the owner of eleven small houses.[185]

Thus by 1851 in this single trade there were three systems of work organization in existence: the traditional (and worker-favoured) small gang, the employer-favoured large gang, or the direct supervision of work in the absence of gangs.

The large gang, of course, was the natural consequence of the dilution of skill which labour opposed so rigorously throughout the period. One small manufacturer, bankrupted in the 1840s, took to producing lamps in Vienna which competed successfully with local lamps on the home market. The ex-patriot's explanation of his new-found success was simple: 'I have but one man to pay: I give him twelve shillings a week; he is a sort of superior servant, but to the others I pay from seven shillings to nine shillings a week and that is the way I undersell you.'[186] Here the crucial factor was as much the proportion of skilled to unskilled as the lowness of wages across the board. A lowering of wages increased the willingness of skilled workers to extend their responsibilities. A caster in the brass trade explained the operation of this mechanism in 1851.

> About fifteen years ago, a caster, having three boys under him, could earn about 30s a week, but at present he could only earn about £1 a week. Manufacturers, in consideration of the low rate of wages, generally allowed the men to manage two or three 'shops', a shop consisting of about three boys.[187]

In the brass-nail trade at the same time, the *Chronicle* investigator found that it had become common 'for the sake of economizing wages to substitute the labour of women for that of men in the manufactories'.[188] The case was cited of one establishment whose workforce of sixty-five people included only six men. Similarly, in the silver-plating trade, which by the mid-century had adopted Elkington's new electro-plating process, a manufacturer explained that 'The proportion of women has increased because now a man can keep a greater number of women fully employed.'[189]

This process was not simply a dilution of skill, it also changed the nature of the relationship between skilled and unskilled labour. The manufacturer, as others have pointed out, remained in need of skill to operate effectively. However, restructuring emphasized the supervisory capacity of the skilled men and changed the orientation of that supervision.

To the working community, there was nothing fixed or inevitable about these changes. Whatever might be said about the logic of the market, work was reorganized in this way because manufacturers took particular decisions on how they wished to operate and utilized the moment to restructure the labour process to their own advantage. Where such moves could be resisted they were. The variation in practice within the lamp trade has already been noted. Similarly, in the brass-thimble trade in 1851, an observer summarized the position thus:

> The proportion of men varies *according to the manner in which the manufactory is conducted*. In some cases the men are said to number one-third of the whole, and in others it is stated that men are only employed as tool-makers, and to superintend in the workshops in the same manner as in the principle steel pen and Florentine button manufactories.[190]

If recession both emphasized the necessity and provided the opportunity for employers to reorganize work there were clearly a number of alternative strategies, in the face of crisis, which were more acceptable within a labour-oriented approach to production. The Britannia-metal-workers, in the depression of 1848, opted to work half-time in order to share the available work throughout the workforce. 'By such trials as these', argued one worker, 'we are bound together by sympathy and goodwill.'[191] In addition it was often possible to turn to 'independent' production. One manufacturer of saddlers' ironmongery complained that 'Whenever there is a scarcity of work the men immediately begin to manufacture for themselves',[192] while in the gilt-toy trade in 1846 a manufacturer noted workers setting up business for themselves rather than agreeing to 'some new regulations that were about to be introduced'.[193]

Although this notion of the worker as independent producer lay at the heart of labour's case to control work the implications of such an analysis were changing in the three decades following 1820. Through the introduction of the discount system, for example, manufacturers attempted to make the ganger accept the full responsibilities of independent production within the economic context of the time. Just as the competing manufacturer would allow a discount upon his book prices to his customers, so he came to expect a discount to be allowed upon the price of articles 'sold' to him, in the workplace, by the artisan. Whereas in the marketplace what was actually a method of undercutting prices could be passed off as a reduction for cash payment, swiftness of payment, or some such justification, in the workplace it was seen for what it was, an attempt to reduce wages which affected not only the artisan but also the workpeople of his 'set'. In a number of trades it became standard practice for employers to apply the discount system whenever economic circumstances placed the ball in their court. This was at the centre of many disputes. The cabinet-case-makers struck against discounts of five to seven shillings in the pound in 1824.[194] The bootmakers, during a strike in 1830, named eight firms about to introduce a 25 per cent discount.[195] A denial from the employers in this case did not dispute that a discount existed, but merely asserted that it stood at 10 per cent. The operative filesmiths lobbied for abolition of the system in 1824 and again in 1845.[196] The rule-makers struck against it in 1846 describing it as 'detrimental to our interests as workmen and unjust as a practice'.[197] When the brass-cock-founders struck against the system in 1828, their employers informed the public that the men could earn thirty to fifty shillings a week. This calculation, however, did not take account of the 15–20 per cent discount deducted and emphasizes the usefulness of the system, to employers, as a means of undercutting wages whilst adhering ostensibly to agreed prices. On this occasion the brass-cock-founders pointed out in reply to the employers' statement: 'The Journeymen do not ask an advance on the lists of prices but merely that no discount be deducted from such a list – as they cannot, single handed, earn more than from 18s to 22s per week.'[198] An agreement was reached and price lists adhered to until the bad trade of the late 1830s when discountage was reintroduced. By 1845, when the Union reorganized to oppose it successfully, discount on wages stood at 25 per cent paid in addition to 5 per cent deduction for shop rent.[199] The heavy-steel-toymakers found a wage increase obtained earlier drawn back by the introduction of discountage in the late 1820s. In 1833 they reorganized as the 'United Steel Toy Makers' and successfully struck against it.[200] For the wire-drawers, who objected to discount as 'a practice neither just in itself, nor a custom in other branches of trade',[201] the system had been first introduced in 1822. It spread throughout the trade, as was explained by a wire-drawer during a strike against the system in 1845:

> It was soon introduced in other factories and in a few years it was raised to ten per cent of deduction. But that was not all; their wages had been reduced within fifteen years thirty per cent so that their just remuneration was being cut down by a double process.[202]

The tin-plate-workers found a discount of 10–15 per cent imposed on them during the recession of 1841.[203]

It is perhaps significant that it was at the end of the wire-drawers' successful strike against discount in 1845 that John Mason, the Chartist, called upon 'the working men of all trades to combine to secure proper and just protection for labour generally, and to protect those employers who, in the legitimate pursuit of trade, acted honourably, equally to the interests of other employers and to his workmen'.[204] Here were two areas which clearly fell outside the 'legitimate pursuit of trade'. The increased size of gangs gave the artisan the role of the highly paid supervisor of large numbers of workers, the discount system imbued him with the responsibilities of the entrepreneur, whilst conferring none of the attendant benefits. Both were distortions of his traditional relationship with the unskilled sector of the workforce.

Writing of the Lancashire cotton industry in the third quarter of the nineteenth century, Patrick Joyce has referred to a '*de facto* acknowledgement [by the employers], at first grudging and then more open minded, that the unions were essential for the successful running of the industry'.[205] The emergence of modes of arbitration and conciliation in this period has been a commonly recognized aspect of trade union history. In its Birmingham context this development has been explored by the research work of Alan Hooper.[206] We may, however, question the extent to which this very gradual acceptance of formal unions represented an unqualified triumph for labour.[207] Their newly accredited role was part of a wider and more effective form of labour discipline than it had been possible for employers to impose earlier in the century.

For the 'new model employers', as they have come to be known, the advantage of drawing the unions into the open was that the trade union was always rather more narrowly representative than 'the trade'.[208] The informality of the latter distinction always had the potential to draw in the wider workforce in ways that we have seen. However, following the defeat of the Chartist political initiative and the apparent failure of autonomous regulation to substantially alter the nature of structural economic change, the tacit acceptance of trade unions by employers at least held the possibility of 'official' recognition in a workplace relationship between manufacturer and employer which was increasingly being defined in specifically legal terms.[209] Also, it should be emphasized that even where the overall pattern was of subordination this did not in itself obviate the possibility of continuing resistance on the part of a labour force learning the rules of the game. It did, however, restrict the context within which the game itself was to be played. This point was demonstrated by some research carried out in Birmingham by Robert Martineau in 1859 on behalf of his aunt, Harriet Martineau, who was preparing an attack on trade unions for the *Edinburgh Review*. At one point he interviewed a tin-plate manufacturer called Blewitt and uncovered the kind of contest over control so characteristic of the workplace in the first half of the century. The firm had a long history of industrial conflict, and it is quite clear that the employer had the utmost difficulty in making direct workplace contact with his employees' organization:

> I asked him if he would get me a copy of the laws of the union; he said he would try but thought they would not be much use if he did, as they would be sure to show nothing but the most innocent objects, such as the relief of men out of work, the giving them money to get from a town where work was slack to another where it was good and so forth. But he said he would try; though he must do it through his foreman, for just now he is rather afraid of a coming strike.[210]

On the other hand, Martineau also interviewed Dr George Lloyd of Lloyd and Summerfield, an extensive glass-making concern. Here rather a different situation existed. The trade had been shaken the previous year by a decisive confrontation in which the Flint Glassmakers' Society found themselves locked out and defeated by a powerful employers' association. Rather than abolishing the union, however, the employers took the opportunity to refashion it:

> In answer to my question as to why when the masters appeared to have it in their power . . . they did not break up the union altogether, he said they could have done so if all the masters had acted together but that as some would not, it made it difficult, besides, if the men abide by the laws of the union the masters have drawn up the latter will have nothing to complain of.[211]

Of course, the future for formal trade unions was not always as bleak as Summerfield's comment might suggest. Price has warned against accepting mechanistic conceptions of 'real' subordination and argues persuasively that the English working class continued to erect informal structures at work to contest capitalist domination of the labour process.[212] In addition, Peter Bailey's work has shown that the 'respectability' of the mid-Victorian working class cannot be directly equated with bourgeois norms (in the way that, for example, Lacqueur's work on early Sunday schools suggests).[213] The manufacturer sought to restructure work, and argued that, by a remarkable coincidence of fortune, this was synonymous with a moral regeneration. Thus the exemplary factory of Joseph Gillott was admired by the *Morning Chronicle* investigator, not simply because its operations were organized to produce efficiently and profitably, but also because of a certain moral ambiance. Gillott insisted that his employees 'should be recommended for good moral conduct, for steadiness and for cleanliness by a Sunday-school teacher, a clergyman or other respectable person before he will admit them to his employ'.[214] This was the morality of economic rationalism, as Reid's essay on the eradication of Saint Monday demonstrates.[215] Yet the underlying assumptions behind this perception of social order were widely criticized from within the working community. As an old workman in the light-steel-toy trade put it in 1851, 'there is nothing but rubbish made now – stuff that I would not pick out of the dirt, and should be ashamed to work at'.[216] Similarly, one old workman in the brass trade, interviewed in the same year, argued that 'the manufacturers of the present day made their profits out of savings that would have been despised by the masters in his younger days'.[217]

The Webbs (and many others since) were surely right to identify a qualitative difference between the trade unions of the third quarter of the nineteenth century, and what had gone before. What they overlooked, however, was the significance of these earlier forms. Here the emphasis on control of the job through tacit understandings and an oscillation, in organizational terms, between formalism and spontaneous informality, created the particular context against which capital attempted to assert its will. The gradual (if grudging) acceptance of trade unions, and the pressure for moral renewal through changes in popular culture, were both part of an attempt to breach the informality of the workplace by making explicit, in a changed form acceptable to capital, what had previously been largely implicit in the social organization of the working community. The conversion of the labour-centred Saint Monday into a formally agreed Saturday half-holiday in the 1860s is only the most obvious example. Robert Whitfield, for example, used the tactical advantage of the economic crisis of 1847 to introduce a compulsory sick-benefit club for his workers: 'Every man above 21 years of age . . . is compelled to contribute . . . 2s 6d as entrance money, which sum is considered as paid instead of the usual foot ales or drinking money.'[218] This represents rather more than a stage in the evolution of workmen's insurance entitlement. Whitfield had transposed the 'foot-ale', part of the network of workplace 'understandings', into something at once more formal and more clearly acceptable to him.

CONCLUSION

How has all this answered the questions with which we began this chapter? We have argued that labour's attempt to control production in this period cannot be reduced to a crude head-count of formal organizations. That it ever could be is a misconception which, in entering the mainstream of social historiography, has distorted the workplace experience by isolating the artisan from the rest of the working community. The time has come to stop thinking of workplace organization as the occasional characteristic of certain aristocratic groups of craft workers. It is more constructive to think in terms of a network of tacit agreements on workplace procedures, deeply imbedded at all levels of the working community, operating with degrees of effectiveness which varied, to enhance labour's control of work; and that occasionally these procedures were formalized. Unfortunately historians have taken these comparatively rare occasions of formalism and called them the 'history of early nineteenth century trade unionism'. They then ask subsidiary questions, for example, 'How does the "history of trade unions" relate to the "history of Chartism"?' We should, of course, be raising the broader issue of the relationship between worker organization at the point of production generally (both formal and informal: the explosive confrontation and the day-to-day organization of work) and the notion of the political world evident in a movement such as Chartism. We cannot, therefore, judge this relationship, as many have done, in terms of the degree of support for Chartism from trade societies.[219] This is to impose a retrospective formalism on labour organizations that would not have been recognized at the time. When the working people of Birmingham contributed to the Chartist National Rent in 1839 they did not, in the main, do so through identifiable trade societies. Rather they contributed politically, as they acted industrially, through the work-group. Thus the list includes (to name but a very few typical entries): 'Workmen of Mr. Griffiths, £2'; 'Messrs Perton and Sabins workmen, Caroline St, 15s'; 'Ladies clog makers, Park St, 10s'; 'A penny subscription, Mr. Ratcliffes workmen, 5s 10d'; 'Mr. Edwards and shopmates, 10s'; 'Journeymen and assistants of Messrs Gilberts platers, £1 13s 11d'; 'George Pitt, plasterer and shopmates, 17s'; 'Workmen of Mr. Thomas Smith, Holloway Head, 10s 2d'.[220]

It is perhaps a fault of some of the more recent work carried out on the labour process that it ignores the social values which accrued to production and which actually created the particular context within which economic change took place. Once we read these values back into the story we can dispense with the notion that the workforce sought to accommodate capitalism in this period. In this chapter we have examined the ways in which the structures and organizations of the workplace expressed a coherent view, not only of work, but also of the social order. This was the social meaning of work that was projected into Chartism's democratic form. The community of work was clearly a fiercely hierarchical (and patriarchal) society, whose internal make-up was accepted as being anything but monolithic.[221] Just as importantly, the unwritten lore of the workshop was based on a concept of morality which stressed the obligations of the individual to the group rather than the freedom of the individual to act without restraint. The critics of labour's workplace organization were swift to observe that this was a construction of personal liberties that was at odds with the dominant liberal orthodoxy. There is a clear resonance between the workplace as the 'worst of democracies' and a political vision with an emphasis on participation and accountability brought about by universal suffrage and annual parliaments. This can only be fully appreciated by exploring the inherent differences between the middle-class and working-class political visions in this period. It is a task to which the remainder of this book is devoted.

4

'Riding the tiger': middle-class and working-class radicalism in the Reform Bill campaign

In Birmingham the political agitations of the 1830s drew together the energies of middle- and working-class radicals and directed them at apparently similar goals. This unity of action, institutionalized within the Birmingham Political Union (BPU), is widely acknowledged to have been the expression of a set of socially cohesive relations of production. Such an analysis has been central to the way in which historians have judged the emergence of Liberalism. The continuity of class alliances from the Reform Bill campaign, through Chartism, to Chamberlain's town council has provided a microcosm of the emergence of consensus politics within a British framework. It is important to emphasize here that this a model of politics which hinges directly on the relationship between the classes at the point of production: 'The Liberalism of Joseph Chamberlain gained sustenance from this soil', argues Briggs.[1] Where disunity is evident within this continuum it is invariably explained in Parsonian terms. The local middle class were important in the genesis of Chartism but were frightened off by what Briggs calls the 'oratorical fireworks' of O'Connor and Stephens.[2] More spectacularly Tholfsen laments the advent of what he calls the 'Chartist crisis' of 1838–9: 'Birmingham', he tells us, 'was soon to have its first and last experience with the politics of class struggle.'[3] Carlos Flick, the most recent historian of the BPU, confirms this view of a Chartist crisis created by exogenous factors, reminding his readers twelve times in the space of forty pages that Feargus O'Connor was Irish.[4]

Geomorphic metaphors are recurrent in the reproduction of this model. Briggs argued in 1952 that 'down to 1914 the business world of the city still resembled the Warwickshire landscape, a rolling country with no projecting peaks'.[5] Through his local study he had managed to map the 'terrain of compromise' nearly thirty years before Elbaum, Lazonick, Wilkinson, and Zeitlin stumbled across it.[6] In fact, this model simply reproduces the dominant discourse of the period in question, that of successful businessmen presenting their activities as a reflection of the common will and the general good. In the last two chapters of this book such a notion of consensus will be questioned through a narrative analysis of the BPU in both phases of its operation, 1830–4 and 1837–9. Two major areas of tension will be identified and explored: the intra-class competition between middle-class radicals and the traditional Tory–aristocratic connection, and the conflict between working-class and middle-class visions of democratic politics which lived out an uneasy co-existence within the BPU.

Recently David Cannadine has pointed out that the importance of the Tory, county-connected group within the town has been ignored through a myopic concern to write the history of the town in Whig-liberal terms.[7] The BPU drew its strength from large-scale capitalists such as Attwood, Muntz, Scholefield, and Salt, operating closely with small-scale producers expressing the ratepayer politics identified earlier in this book. Opposition from Tory groups within the town made it imperative that the BPU create as wide a popular base as possible, thereby establishing its claim to represent the 'People'. Within the BPU middle-class and working-class members were clearly divided by the issue of universal suffrage. It is easy to underestimate the significance of this conflict particularly if Chartist ideology is seen as a kind of 'rag-bag' of ideas inherited from an earlier age and of little direct relevance to the social and economic position of the men and women who were Chartists.[8] In fact, the issue of universal suffrage was at the heart of a distinction between a bourgeois democracy, with political action legitimized by property, and a participatory democracy of the sort working people practised within the workplace. Attwood, as leader of the BPU, was 'riding the tiger' through the 1830s, dependent on the support of the working class, yet fearful of its notion of politics. The Bull Ring riots of July 1839 were not the aberration that they invariably appear to be in orthodox accounts. Rather they were the expression of precisely these areas of tension.

In arguing that a very distinctive political programme was crystallizing within the working community we have recognized the need to explore two hitherto much neglected areas: the perception of work (particularly the way labour saw its organization) and the understanding of political form. It has been suggested that these two areas were interconnected in fundamental ways and that the nature of the one resounded within the other. In an innovative essay Eileen Yeo has recently raised this crucial issue of the relationship between radicalism and working-class culture. 'It is interesting to speculate', she suggests, 'upon how Parliamentary democracy might have been different had it been won by the Chartists and erected upon a foundation of vigorous local activity.'[9] Such speculation is both worthwhile and difficult, since we have generally assumed in the past that working people saw their political world through the eyes of other social groups or individuals, middle-class reformers, eighteenth-century radicals, the dominant Chartist leaders, and so on. As with the problem identified earlier, of mistaking artisan history for working-class history, a methodological difficulty has resulted in an analytical weakness. The rest of this chapter will amply demonstrate, for example, that though working people participated in the Reform Bill campaign, their views were rarely reported. The final chapter will show that though this was less the case during the Chartist period the point holds good, generally, for both periods of activity. There is, therefore, an important level of political activity that can be pieced together only from scraps, hints, implications, and deductions. This means that we must be particularly sensitive to those points at which the dominant discourse was interrupted and challenged. Hence the significance attached, in what follows, to the issue of universal suffrage.

Throughout these two campaigns the radical middle class worked hard to retain control of a broad movement. As part of the strategy for doing so they kept open a deliberately ambiguous dialogue on universal suffrage and at the same time attempted to create a false link between themselves and an earlier (and more radical) reforming tradition. The ultimate failure of this strategy can be seen in the fact that the BPU broke up in 1834 and 1839, amid extreme acrimony, over class-specific issues. In 1833–4 working people attempted to use the proffered goodwill of large-scale capitalists to push for both universal suffrage (through the

Midland Union of the Working Classes) and at the same time to save artisanal production through the producers' co-operative. These two initiatives, undertaken simultaneously, reflect the closeness of work and politics in the minds of working-class activists. The opposition which they encountered from middle-class radicals is significant in the same way. Small manufacturers, however, adhered closely to the political lines established by the BPU. Attwood's persistent commitment to household suffrage linked the franchise to a property qualification that was within their reach. Economically they sought to align their businesses with the world of large-scale capital. In household suffrage they would have a political identity within that world and one which also expressed the dominion over labour which they sought and needed in the workplace.

THE MIDDLE CLASS AND RADICAL POLITICAL REFORM

Even as Birmingham's post-war radicals were being prosecuted and imprisoned in the early 1820s the need for some kind of adjustment to the system of parliamentary representation was gaining wide acceptance among the local middle class. By 1827 this consolidated around Tennyson's scheme to transfer the East Retford seat to the town.[10] A meeting of ratepayers in June 1828 elected a committee under the chairmanship of Joseph Parkes, a local attorney, to lobby in favour of the move. The committee consisted of a broad sweep of 'respectable' support, including Attwood, Scholefield, and thirty of the thirty-nine members of the Chamber of Commerce.[11] This represented a tentative movement toward limited reform through a process of lobbying that was carefully confined to the local elite. The support of *Aris's Gazette* for the measure, given the paper's unstinting opposition to the post-war radical movement, may serve as some measure of the distance between the middle-class and the working-class reform programmes at this point. After the election of the committee the *Gazette* reassured its readership:

> We are aware some among our townsmen hesitate to lead the public feeling upon the subject, on the ground of the inconvenience generally attendant upon elections in which the franchise

is exercised by a large body of the middle and lower ranks of society. In conferring such a privilege on a populous town like our own may we not however, safely rely on the wisdom and experience of the legislature so to restrict the right of voting and to impose such regulations as shall greatly obviate, if not altogether get rid of the objections that at present may fairly be urged against the principle of popular elections.[12]

While Parkes and the East Retford Committee lobbied unsuccessfully for the redistribution of one seat, Attwood became convinced of the potential support for both currency reform and limited parliamentary reform that a wider appeal might render. Inspired by the success of the Catholic Association he called the founding meeting of the BPU at Beardsworth's Repository on 25 January 1830. Though it attracted 10–20,000 people it also served to separate Attwood and his middle-class radical supporters from the broader sweep of middle-class opinions.[13] William Redfern, a local lawyer, spoke against the formation of the BPU at the January meeting, drawing attention to the absence of 'the more opulent and influential public characters of the town who usually took part in its public proceedings'.[14] With memories of the 1816–20 period of radicalism still fresh in the public mind there was a good deal of reluctance, on the part of the middle class, to join a popular organization, particularly one modelled openly upon the Catholic Association.[15] William Chance, High Bailiff and a man personally committed to the idea of a redistribution of seats in favour of the urban areas,[16] refused a request to make the January 1830 meeting an official town meeting. *Aris's Gazette* applauded his action and claimed: 'We are satisfied that he carries with him the great majority of the respectable and reflecting part of his townsmen.'[17] John Turner, the button manufacturer, had been a member of the East Retford Committee, but reported to the *Gazette* that his response to Attwood's appeal for support had been 'that he must keep better company before I could go with him, meaning thereby . . . that the mode he was adopting for the formation of the Political Union was calculated to produce not reform but Revolution'.[18]

Attwood's aim, as he expressed it at the 25 January meeting, was to mobilize 'two millions of people to think speak and act as one man'. He need hardly have added that the one man he had in mind was Thomas Attwood. At this stage the political programme of the Union was defined in only the vaguest of terms. The January meeting established the rules of the new organization and indicated a general intention to lobby for some kind of parliamentary reform. Little else was made clear. The next public meeting of significance was called in May 1830 to support the Marquis of Blandford's proposed Reform Bill.[19] There had been a good deal of speculation within the town on the exact nature of the Union's political position and by the May meeting it was clear that universal suffrage, annual parliaments, and the ballot would form no part of this. It was only with great difficulty that George Edmonds gained a hearing to support this limited programme:

> he thought raising objections to a system of reform, by which they should secure the support and influence of a very important and influential part of the country would tend to defeat the objects of the advocates of universal suffrage themselves (cries of no, no!).[20]

The Political Council of the BPU, an exclusively middle-class body, gave eight reasons why universal suffrage, the ballot, and annual parliaments were impractical demands to make. These largely amounted to a recognition of the unwillingness of middle-class opinion to accept the measures in principle, the Council declaring 'the great majority of the middle classes deem them dangerous and the Council cannot find that they have the sanction of experience to prove them safe'. As James Bibb, a mechanic, pointed out from the floor of the meeting, the Council had not yet come anywhere near fulfilling its basic commitment. Despite a political programme tailored to both their needs and their fears the middle classes were still not joining the BPU in numbers.[21] At that point membership stood at only 2,200, five months after Attwood had spoken of the goal of two million.

Through the rest of 1830 Attwood worked hard to stress, to his working-class audience, the continuity between the BPU and the post-war agitation. Sir Francis Burdett, for example, was prevailed upon to share the platform with Attwood at a Union meeting in July.[22] By August membership stood at 6,000 and by January of the following year this had risen to 9,000. By this stage Wellington had made his anti-reform declaration (November 1830) and this had been followed by the formal commitment of Grey's succeeding government to a limited reform measure.[23] These events acted to draw support in the country out into the open. At this point, Attwood, who had a full year of active organizing and agitating behind him, appeared to Place to be 'the most influential man in England'.[24] By December 1830 Attwood had been persuaded by Joseph Parkes and others to add the ballot to the Union's political programme.[25]

This move helped to allay the fears of working-class observers. Besides this, the Whigs had provided a concrete measure for the BPU to back. Debate over the kind of reform desired could be deferred in the face of a need to unify to expedite even this limited proposal. There is evidence that the BPU began to increase both membership and attendance at public meetings from the beginning of 1831. It did not, however, succeed in drawing the wider middle class into its body, even though there was a good deal of support for the Whig government and its stand. In December 1831 Parkes wrote to Francis Place:

> Our Political Union have called a meeting here for tomorrow week on Reform; I wished that the requisition had emanated under present circumstances not from a party . . . because many who differ from the Union, real friends of reform, will not go, and many more will seize the excuse for staying away.[26]

Russell outlined his proposed Bill of Reform in the Commons on 1 March 1831. On 7 March the BPU held a meeting of 15,000 in Beardsworth's to petition parliament in favour of the Bill. Four days later Oliver Mason, the High Bailiff, convened a town's meeting of 2,000 people with a similar object in view.[27] These parallel meetings, with the Union conducting 'popular' support and the town's meetings conducting 'respectable' support, continued throughout the campaign. But Attwood and the BPU council remained central figures in the campaign as a whole. The breadth of their popular support made them the focus of attention. Significantly, Scholefield, Hadley, and Salt, all members of the BPU Council, addressed the town's meeting of March 1831. Similarly, the Union dominated a county reform meeting in April 1831.[28] Here the audience were treated to the hitherto unlikely spectacle of Samuel Tertius Galton appearing and speaking on the same platform as George Edmonds. Galton, a one-time chairman of the Pitt Club and an active member of the Loyal Association in 1819, announced that 'he cordially agreed with those gentlemen who supported "the bill, the whole bill and nothing but the bill"'.[29]

The Whigs' proposed measure of reform acted, therefore, to consolidate opinion within the local middle class. Here the interest lay simply in a readjustment of representation in favour of the urban areas, but the importance of the numerical muscle commanded by the Union in achieving this was widely recognized. Galton's feelings about the county reform meeting of April, for example, were mixed. He described the scene in his diary on the evening of 4 April:

> The day was beautiful and many thousand persons were collected. The flags of the Political Union looked beautiful. Sir George Chetwynd moved the first resolution and was followed by many other able speakers, but it was much regretted that the members of the Political Union took a prominent part in the business and thereby prevented the representatives of ancient county families from moving the principal resolutions. The meeting on the whole was very orderly but not decently courteous to the County representatives and manifestly proved that the House of Commons was one object of contempt in their esteem.[30]

Thus, although before May 1832 the BPU never received unequivocal middle-class support in terms of membership, its central importance to the reform issue was tacitly accepted at all levels. On 6 November 1831 Althorp reminded Parkes that he was the government's vital link with the BPU: 'I shall perhaps again trouble you; for from your position you can give me the best information as to the feelings of the Unionist reformers and I feel great confidence in your judgement.'[31] Within the town some of the most vociferous opponents of the popular movement were publicly declaring for reform. In May 1831, at a dinner at Dee's Hotel to celebrate the return of a reform candidate for Worcester, Joshua Scholefield of the BPU Council proposed the evening's central toast to 'The Constitution, the whole Constitution and nothing but the Constitution'. On the same occasion Paul Moon James spoke out against the corruption of an unreformed parliament.[32] James, of course, had been editor of *Aris's Gazette* during its unceasing war on radicalism after 1815. At a town's meeting on 30 September

1831, John Turner, the button manufacturer who had refused to support Attwood in 1830, made a vigorous defence of the Reform Bill. Edmonds could not resist the temptation to respond:

> He felt assured that the principles which had been expressed (by Turner) had long since been struggling in his heart and only wanted a proper opportunity to avow them and thereby sanction all that he (Mr. E.) had ever said on behalf of the people's rights. He was glad to find that the opinions of many gentlemen present, whom he knew to be attached to Church and State, had so far changed as to warrant the last speaker coming forward with his absolute 'shall'.[33]

THE BPU AND THE WORKING CLASS

Amidst the rush of local dignitaries to declare themselves in favour of the Reform Bill, it is easy to lose sight of the role played by the working class within the reform movement during 1831. It is equally easy to overlook the fact that both inside and outside the BPU the movement brought together groups with vastly different political aspirations. Agreement on the importance of the Reform Bill can at no time be equated with the existence of a political consensus. Nobody was more aware of this than Attwood. By October 1831 the BPU was in a position to hold the first of many open-air meetings at Newhall Hill. The attendance of an estimated 100,000 people indicates that by this time the working class were looking to the Union to provide an initiative. Bronterre O'Brien, editor of the *Midland Representative*, explained this feeling:

> Although a numerous meeting, comprising the wealthier and 'respectable' classes had been held but three days before for a similar purpose, the people were far from satisfied with such a puny and hollow exhibition of public feeling. They considered the High Bailiff's meeting too cold and too aristocratic to speak their genuine zeal especially as that meeting had emanated from men the majority of whom were never remarkable for attachment to popular principles.[34]

Nevertheless, Attwood was aware that he now drew the majority of his direct support from a class with its own political tradition and its own leadership. This awareness fashioned much of his public stance during the campaign and this can be seen in both the dialogue that Attwood continuously engaged in with the membership, and in the organizational structure, of the Union.

The middle-class radicals operating within the BPU were concerned with a good deal more than currency reform. Their political analysis, however, related directly to Attwood's economic theories. His belief that through the medium of a flexible paper currency industrial production could increase to meet potential demand to the full, removed the responsibility for economic ills from the shoulders of the manufacturer and placed it squarely with the government. In economic terms Attwood drew a very firm line between productive and non-productive capital, and through this he arrived at a breakdown of society into the 'productive' or 'industrious classes' and the 'non-productive classes'. In political terms he drew attention to the unrepresented nature of the 'productive classes', which he saw as including 'masters and men in every branch of Agriculture, Manufacture, Commerce and Trade'.[35] Within this concept masters and men were drawn together by a joint interest in the prosperity of industry and by their political exclusion. Economic decline was presented as a function of this exclusion. The founding resolutions of the BPU expressed this as follows:

> The men who have occupied their capital in productive power, in working the great duties upon which the existence of mankind depends – these men have grown poor as the reward of their industry and virtue! But the men who have locked up their capital in a chest have found it daily increasing in value.[36]

Thus the concept of the 'productive' or 'industrious classes' united labour and capital and defined their common interests against a landed and moneyed aristocracy invested with political power through an unrepresentative parliament. In Attwood's own words:

> Ignorance, imbecility, and indifference on the one hand; power, influence and perhaps corruption on the other; all these combine to render the cause of the industrious classes hopeless in England, unless some measure can be derived for restoring to those important classes, that legal control over the legislative functions which the constitution had originally placed in their hands.[37]

The term 'industrious classes' was not coined by Attwood. Rather it was a standard part of the radical vocabulary. Patrick Calquhoun's social analysis published in 1815, for example, divided society on exactly this kind of basis.[38] Attwood, however, in appropriating the term was able to infuse it with a particular class meaning. In this context its strength was that it neatly sidestepped the knotty problems of the social relations of production and the distribution of rewards within the productive classes. Throughout the 1830s Attwood repeated the underlying implication of his analysis like a litany: 'The interests of masters and men are, in fact one. If the masters flourish the men flourish with them; and if the masters suffer difficulties their difficulties must shortly affect the workmen in three-fold degree.'[39] Again, this was a fairly familiar argument. It was the classic defence of individualism by which the entrepreneur justified economic rationalization on the grounds that it benefited the entire workforce in the long run. In this case Attwood and the middle-class radicals gave the argument a political dimension. Their opposition to universal suffrage was fundamental, since the measure was not only dangerous but also unnecessary. If the economic interests of the workforce could be represented by the employer, so too could their political interests.[40] This was a principle embodied in the practical operation of the BPU. All powers of policy-making and strategy were vested in a Political Council drawn almost entirely from the middle-class minority of the Union. The founding resolutions justified this in terms of essential discipline: 'We have given great power to the Political Council. In all organised bodies power must exist somewhere or there can be no order, no discipline, no unity of object.'[41] This was the political facet of the economic argument advanced by small- and large-scale manufacturers to justify their rights over labour in the control of the labour process. The organization of work within the workplace was the right of the employer by virtue of his ownership of the means of production. That same concept of property also validated his control of the world of politics. It was an argument which did much to tie small- and large-scale capitalists together and reinforce Attwood's support among *petit-bourgeois* groups. It did little to convince working people of the need for limited reform.

Attwood was perfectly aware of the distance between the middle-class radical goal of a franchise that would represent productive capital effectively, and the rhetoric of political rights that was, by the 1820s, so central to the working-class programme. Throughout the Reform Bill campaign he was careful to maintain an open debate on the question of universal suffrage and related reforms. As early as 1827 and the East Retford question he suggested that he would support universal suffrage 'if it were practicable'. He was swiftly reminded by Thomas Lakins, ex-treasurer of the Union Society of 1819, that it was 'not only practicable but it might be accomplished not only in Birmingham but all over England'.[42] At the founding meeting of the Union, in 1830, Joshua Scholefield announced that 'he individually felt no objection to universal suffrage, or to annual Parliaments but he thought their advocacy, at the present moment would produce no beneficial effects'.[43] Attwood adopted a position of sympathetic circumspection: 'He did not wish to disparage universal suffrage, annual Parliaments or vote by ballot; it was possible that there was something dangerous in them. All he would say was, that he thought it was not prudent to claim them.'[44]

Once the Union was able to focus on the Whig Reform Bill as a concrete proposal, the crack in the alliance became less obvious. Attwood simply replaced the discussion of universal suffrage with an open commitment to agitate for further reform in the event of the Reform Bill proving to be ineffectual. The alliance, however, remained vulnerable at this point. For example, Henry Hetherington's *Poor Man's Guardian* asked, in December 1831:

> How then can Mr. Attwood talk of doing justice to the working classes till he admits their right to be represented? How can he make them happy and contented till he places them in possession of this important right? . . . To Universal Suffrage, therefore, Mr. Attwood must come if he means to retain the esteem of his fellow countrymen.[45]

Why then was the working class prepared to follow the BPU initiative? Not only was Attwood's political platform far removed from that of post-war radicalism, it was also legitimated by reference to an ideal of workplace unity that was increasingly at odds with the working-class experience. This fundamental point of division, however, was to assume a far greater significance later in the 1830s. For the moment the exact nature of the working-class response was fashioned by the immediate political context. After the defeats of 1815–20 Attwood had stepped forward with what was effectively an offer of alliance working towards limited reform. The eyes of the political leaders of the working community were set far beyond this limited goal, but this in itself did not preclude participation. Through the medium of the *Midland Representative*, Bronterre O'Brien outlined in detail the disadvantages of the proposed Bill to his working-class readership. But even he was prepared to add:

> Notwithstanding that the Bill has these and many other defects, yet with all its faults are we willing to receive it as an instalment, or part payment of the debt of right due to us; for we feel assured that under its provisions, the electoral right will ultimately be capable of expanding and purifying itself into a perfect, representative system.[46]

Men like O'Brien were prepared to go along with Attwood because for the moment he appeared to be a highly effective radical figure. Locally it was clear that, although widely disapproved of for moving toward a popular base for the agitation, he still had the ear of wider middle-class opinion on this vital issue.

This credibility was not limitless and there is much in Attwood's conduct in 1831 and 1832 that suggests his awareness of the delicacy of the alliance within the BPU. Clearly his performance was being monitored by working-class radicals who wished him to go further. This became clear at two important points in the campaign, the arming crisis of November 1831 and the 'Days of May' in 1832.

ARMING THE UNION

The rejection of the Reform Bill by a Lords' majority of forty-one in October 1831 seemed to place the initiative firmly in the hands of the extra-parliamentary movement. Following riots in Nottingham, Derby, and Bristol in November, the BPU announced its plans to reorganize itself on a quasi-military basis. Ostensibly the idea was to create a police force from within the Union to prevent rioting. However, the similarity between the scheme and the National Guards formed during the continental revolutions of the previous year was apparent to most observers. The king, for example, wrote to the Duke of Wellington on 9 November:

> His Majesty believes it to be with the mischievous a plan only advanced on account of its popularity to cover revolutionary designs formed before the change of government and the introduction of the Reform Bill. Designs which had been dormant but were brought into attention by events of revolution in France and Belgium.[47]

Those historians who have chosen to view Attwood's activities during the campaign as an exercise in strategic intimidation and menace, ultimately rooted in bluff, have seen this particular incident as one part of a theatrical show to convince the Whigs to reintroduce the Bill, as swiftly as possible, without amendments.[48] Professor Brock, however, has argued that this move represented an attempt, by Attwood, to retain leadership of the reform movement locally at a time when the Lords' rejection threatened to fragment the alliance. The *Poor Man's Guardian*, Attwood's most persistent critic, had suggested the formation of a National Guard in October. At this point, Brock argues, the BPU Council jumped aboard 'the national guard band-wagon'.[49]

There is a good deal of evidence to substantiate such a view. Throughout the crisis Althorp was informed of developments by Parkes. Following one such report, Althorp wrote to Grey: 'He says as I suspected that the Union is quite out of the control of Attwood.'[50] Certainly the plan of reorganization was aimed at the working class, a point made by 'Truth' in a letter to the Home Secretary: 'it is the lower and not the middling classes that they intend to enrol'.[51] In addition, when the Council debated the plan, Attwood felt it necessary to address the working-class membership in an attempt to prevent them moving into their own agitation, without BPU leadership:

> The working classes must remember that, of themselves, they could do nothing and therefore they ought to suspect those who told them that the Reform Bill would do them no good and exhort them to attempt more. He was not against universal suffrage even; but if he were made Dictator he very much questioned whether he should grant universal suffrage at the present time lest it should prove injurious to the working classes themselves. If this bill did not give liberty and happiness to the great mass of the people he should be quite ready to go for a more extensive reform. He would not be content until he saw

every working man able to obtain bread for honest labour.[52]

Beside this there is Attwood's obvious relief when the intervention of the government, privately through Parkes and publicly through a royal proclamation, enabled him to drop the scheme. The royal proclamation outlawed the plan and, by implication, declared the unions themselves to be illegal.[53] Attwood chose only to recognize the former. The swiftness with which Parliament was reassembled on 6 December and a new bill submitted indicated renewed vigour in the parliamentary campaign. The crisis does, however, emphasize the difficulties faced by the BPU Political Council in affording leadership to an organization that, through its membership, embraced a wider radical vision than they were themselves prepared to accept. To retain control they had moved to the initial threshold of violence from which events had enabled them to withdraw for the moment. At such a point the distinction between leading the movement and being led by it was difficult to determine. The chorus of a popular broadside published during the campaign illustrates this point:

> So join your hands with Attwood boys,
> Unto his wish comply,
> He swears he'll set the nation free
> Or he will nobly die.[54]

Attwood's ultimate obligation to the Union's popular membership is specified clearly in this verse. It left him with less of a margin for manoeuvre than he would, perhaps, have wished for. By the time of the November crisis, Attwood had already been reminded that the working-class membership owed allegiance to a wider movement than that represented by himself. In May 1831 O'Brien's *Midland Representative* carried full coverage of the trial of William Carpenter and in August the Birmingham Co-operative Society began a subscription to assist him.[55] The responsibility for such a fund was taken over a week later by a committee appointed at a meeting, 'composed chiefly of the working classes', held at the Lamp Tavern in Beck Street. This committee included James Guest, a sympathetic bookseller, Timothy Massey, a carpenter, a republican who had been active in the post-war campaign, James Morrison, and the Owenite John Powell.[56]

The following week Morrison and Guest appeared before the

Political Council to lobby support for Carpenter and the repeal of the taxes on knowledge. Morrison reminded them that 'The Council of the Union . . . beckoned the working classes to come on, but unless they helped them to batter down the citadel of taxation they could not follow them.' Eventually a resolution of support was passed, but not before considerable discussion had taken place. Both G.F. Muntz and T.C. Salt spoke out against the new move. The issue re-emerged in January 1832 when the Council was presented with a petition against the taxes on knowledge, for endorsement and support. The matter was deferred for as long as possible until O'Brien goaded the Council into action through the columns of the *Representative* in March.[57] In the light of the continuing passage of the Reform Bill the issue was not serious enough to cause a fracture in the alliance, but it was a reminder of the different political perspectives of the participants.

THE 'DAYS OF MAY'

In some ways the events of May 1832 echoed those of the previous November as the Political Council was taken to the very edge of violent confrontation. In March, the passing of the Reform Bill on its third reading in the House of Commons increased the demand for the creation of peers. April saw a large-scale expansion of provincial political unions. The BPU held a monster rally at Newhall Hill on 7 May which attracted people from towns within a twenty-mile radius of Birmingham. Charles Walters, writing to his business partner the next day, remarked, 'I wish'd to have had room to describe the *Great* meeting here yesterday – Savatard who has been in the artillery at Strasbourg, set the number down at 200,000 men, women and children! colours and bands!'[58]

Two days prior to this rally, Parkes had published his estimate that even if the Bill was passed it would only, under its provisions, enfranchise 5,000 individuals in Birmingham.[59] As a result, feeling was strong within the Union's membership that the wider radical programme had now been compromised quite enough by the Bill itself and that further reduction of its provisions could not be tolerated. Attwood played to the popular image of the broadsides:

> I would rather die than see the great Bill of Reform rejected or mutilated. . . . I see that you are all of one mind upon this

great subject. Answer me then, had you not all rather die than live the slaves of the boroughmongers. (All! All!)[60]

As part of a petition to the Lords the meeting passed a resolution to the effect that if the Bill were not passed, or if the £10 franchise were to be mutilated in any way, the Union would continue to campaign for 'a more extensive restoration of the Constitutional rights of the People than the present Bill of Reform is calculated to give'. Furthermore, the petition warned that the passing of the Reform Bill intact was essential 'for the preservation of peace and order'.[61]

Two days later Grey's government resigned, the king having refused to create the peers necessary to force the measure through the Lords. The crisis that had followed the rejection of the Bill in the previous October had returned in an exacerbated form. If Attwood was to retain control of the movement in Birmingham he had to act decisively. As it was, on 12 May the *Midland Representative* announced:

> The Bill was a mean, jealous, niggardly, aristocratic, Whiggish bill. It was intended not for the relief of the people, but to furnish the means of keeping them down. It was intended by its authors to act as an instrument of compromise between the landed aristocracy, who already possess power, and the middlemen of the towns who want to be taken into the government as partners in the state concern.

With the arrival of the news of Grey's resignation, work stopped in the town and 20–30,000 people gathered around the offices of the BPU waiting for the decisive lead from the Council. Now, for the first time, Attwood was able to speak, directly, for the broad sweep of the middle- and working-class opinion in the town. Around 500 men, 'comprising the professions and mercantile interests of the town', joined the BPU *en bloc* on 10 May.[62] Their names were published and circulated; meanwhile Joseph Russell busied himself handing out window-sized placards that read: 'No taxes paid here till the Reform Bill is passed.' T.H. Ryland remembered the incident clearly when later writing his reminiscences:

> We, that is, our 'set' did not at first take any active part in the Political Union but one morning things looked so bad that my

> father, and his three sons, walked up together to the chief office, entered their names, paid their subscriptions and became members.[63]

Arthur Hill, who had been a member of the Hampden Club in 1816, but had hitherto been uninvolved in the activities of the BPU, was drawn in by the adhesion of so many of the Birmingham notables. He scribbled a hasty note to his wife on 10 May:

> a meeting is just going to be held at Newhall Hill. You are not here but I know what you would advise. I am going to it and I shall imitate W.J. Parks, W. Wills, the Rylands and many others by joining the Union.[64]

The meeting, to which Hill referred, was a spontaneous one, chaired by Attwood, at Newhall Hill and attended by an estimated 100,000 people. A petition drawn up at the meeting exhorted the Commons to withhold supplies in order to force the passing of the Bill. The petition was to be delivered to O'Connell in London by a deputation consisting of Parkes, Scholefield, and John Green. It contained a crucial statement on arming:

> That your petitioners find it declared in the Bill of Rights that the people of England may 'have arms for their defence suitable to their condition, and as allowed by law', and your Petitioners apprehend that this great right will be put into force generally, and that the whole of the people of England will think it necessary to have arms for their defence, in order that they may be prepared for any circumstances that may arise.[65]

This was, of course, only one of a number of meetings held up and down the country at this time. The *Morning Chronicle* and *The Times* carried reports of nearly 200 meetings in support of the Reform Bill, between 9 May and 19 May. Nearly 300 petitions were presented requesting the Commons to refuse supplies.[66] Birmingham's three-man deputation met with others in Francis Place's library on 11 May, where besides a run on the banks, the possibility of armed resistance was discussed.[67] According to Place, resistance was to begin in Birmingham with the erection of barricades. On 13 May Scholefield returned to Birmingham to report on this meeting and also on one with Grey. He had admitted to Scholefield that the Reform Bill was all but lost and that he expected Wellington to form a government and to steal the reformers' clothes by introducing his own bill.[68]

The next day the BPU's Political Council issued a declaration to the effect that it would work against any government Wellington might form. The declaration referred to 'His utter incompetency to govern England by any other means than the sword which has never yet been, and never will be submitted to by the English people'.[69] This outspoken declaration, alongside the invocation of the right to arm in the petition of the previous week, gave rise to the expectation that, in the event of Wellington forming a government, Attwood and members of the Council would be arrested. Frederick Hill wrote to his brother Matthew (who himself purchased a musket during the 'days of May'):[70]

> The middle classes are, I think, rapidly prepared as a whole to refuse the payment of taxes. The general expectation is that the duke will instantly resort to violent measures. An arrest of all the members of the Council is looked upon as a probable measure. I much fear that the people will not be able to restrain themselves in this case.[71]

It is important to remember that at this point the BPU had the support of the full spectrum of reformers, from the most moderate local notary whose aspirations went no further than the representation of urban interests, to the working-class radical with a primary commitment to universal suffrage. Attending church on 13 May, Samuel Tertius Galton was taken to one side by an anxious minister who informed the magistrate that:

> he was much alarmed at having that morning heard that 7,000 persons joined the Political Union within the last week. He said that three soldiers at the barracks had become members of it, and that Lord Plymouth had received notice from every member of the Yeomanry Corps of their intention to resign. He told me that the publicans whose shops bear the sign of the King's Head had reversed it, and altogether he seemed much alarmed at the idea of an immediate rebellion.[72]

The following day, Walters, writing from Birmingham, claimed that 'the name of Wellington is smelt issuing from every jaw'. Large crowds gathered in the Bull Ring to hear the news from London as it arrived; he was also able to pass on the rumour of the moment, 'Many of the Scotch Grays have entered the Political Union – I am told several officers also.'[73]

The BPU Council was offered a 1,500-strong bodyguard from the membership of the Union, and certainly when Attwood retired to bed on the evening of 15 May, after the anti-Wellington declaration had been posted about the town, he fully expected to hear of the issue of a warrant for his arrest on charges of sedition. That night his house in Harborne was guarded by armed men.[74] Parkes, however, arrived from London at 6 a.m. the following morning with news of the recall of Grey. In the ensuing burst of celebration 50,000 people gathered at Newhall Hill to laud Attwood and the Political Council of the BPU.[75]

Any analysis of the 'Days of May' inevitably raises the issue of how close an armed confrontation actually was during the crisis. E.P. Thompson has suggested that 'Britain was within an ace of revolution', but other authorities have disagreed with this view.[76] The centrality of Birmingham within the extra-parliamentary agitation makes an assessment of the local situation crucial to this debate. There are, broadly, two major arguments clouding an accurate assessment: first, the idea of the 'stage-management' of the agitation, and second, the wider question of the relationship between public opinion and political change in this period.

Most authorities have deferred, in some degree at least, to the idea that individuals with the ear of the government exaggerated the degree of support in the country for the Reform Bill. In one sense it is difficult to disagree; any agitation that relies for effect upon the volume of its support defeats its object by understating its strength. However, Joseph Hamburger's analysis, which has Parkes and Place desperately manoeuvring a stage army for the benefit of Whig politicians is barely credible.[77] His claim that 'it is clear there was no real threat of a popular outbreak in Birmingham'[78] is derived from a misunderstanding of the materials with which Attwood was working. Hamburger, for example, accepts Briggs's thesis that the BPU was the political reflection of socially cohesive relations of production.[79] In fact the BPU, as we have seen, was a delicately balanced alliance that pulled in two different directions. Attwood's credibility as a leader was always only one step ahead of the doubts of the working-class leadership as to the viability of the total enterprise upon which they were engaged. When he advocated the use of arms and civil disobedience on

7, 10, and 14 May 1832 he was addressing audiences largely drawn from Birmingham and the Black Country. Many of these people had been campaigning for parliamentary reform for fifteen years. The post-war agitation had also given a fairly clear picture of what a popular reform movement could expect from a Tory ministry. Within this context the room to manoeuvre support and to engage in extravagant bluffs was rather limited.

The second major area of confusion has been the difficulty of reconciling parliamentary considerations with the public agitation. It has been argued convincingly, by a number of historians, that the threat of insurrection, particularly the BPU's petition of 10 May, had little effect upon Wellington's reaching his crucial decision to stand down in favour of Grey.[80] But while, in an immediate sense, the public agitation in general (and the BPU's in particular) cannot be credited with forcing the duke's hand, it is important to separate the threat of revolution from the perception of such a threat by the politicians. The fact that Wellington, in arriving at his political decisions, was unaware of plans for insurrection, and of the general feeling in particular areas, made the situation more revolutionary in potential, rather than less. Parkes wrote to Mrs Grote after the May crisis, 'That to avert revolution always sate most anxiously and weightily on my mind; but if we had been over-reached this week by the Borough-mongers, I and two friends should have made the revolution, whatever the cost'.[81] One can only add that had a Tory administration, under the direction of the Duke of Wellington, been foolish enough to move against the Birmingham Political Union in May 1832, Parkes would scarcely have had any choice in the matter.

AFTER THE ACT

In the wake of the passing of the Reform Bill in June 1832, the question of further reform emerged. As a result of the ensuing dialogue the presence of the two very different radical perspectives on political change is much clearer to the historian than it was during the Reform Bill campaign itself. Working-class political leaders had subsumed both themselves and their programme within the organizational structure of the Union. Now they re-emerged to state their case. In July, following the establishment of a Committee of Non Electors, M.P. Haynes presented the Political Council with a memorial from Union members calling for a declaration in favour of universal suffrage, annual parliaments, and the ballot. Haynes assured them that 'the discontent that prevails amongst some of the working classes' was due 'not to any want of confidence in the Council of the Union, but to the disappointment which had been caused by the crippling of the £10 clause and to the great distress which prevails in the town'.[82] Attwood, who claimed to have fully expected the £10 clause to have enfranchised over 14,000 Birmingham men instead of the actual figure of just under 4,000, explained in reply that the Council was committed to a 'wait and see' attitude to the Act's operation.

This was perhaps the first sign of working-class disillusionment with the Act, although in August the United Trades took to the streets in a parade to celebrate its passing. Continued distress encouraged working-class radicals to maintain the momentum gathered during the Reform Bill campaign. In September a meeting of the unemployed took place at Newhall Hill. Here Thomas Baker, a veteran of the post-war radical agitation, emphasized that the middle class had been latecomers to the reform movement. Working-class support during the Reform Bill campaign had, he claimed, placed the middle-class radicals under an obligation to push for further measures.

> They (the working classes) had borne all sorts of misery and distress and contumely in addition, with the most exemplary patience and resignation because the middle-classes had been made to feel the weight of the burden and had at last joined them in a cry for reform. . . . The working classes had not served them as they had served the working classes; they had not called them revolutionists and anarchists, but had come forward like men in the most magnanimous manner and given up their extended ideas of reform, to obtain the smaller measure called out for by the middle classes.[83]

The meeting's adoption of a programme of universal suffrage, annual parliaments, the ballot, and the repeal of both the taxes on knowledge and the corn laws represented a revitalization of post-war radical aspirations. Six weeks later a meeting took place to form a Midland Union of the Working Classes (MUWC) as a branch of the London-based National Union of the Working Classes (NUWC). The NUWC had been approached by Birmingham radicals for this purpose. Robert Edwards wrote to Henry Hetherington in October asserting that 'The increasing distress of the citizens of this town joined to the growing disaffection manifested by that class to the tardy policy of the "parent Union" induces us to take this step as the only means of efficiently directing the energies of a suffering, disappointed and exasperated people.'[84] Edwards was secretary of the United Committees, a body made up of delegates from the three bodies that now represented working-class feeling: the Committee of Non Electors under the chairmanship of James Larkin, the Committee of the United Trades under Henry Watson, and the Committee of the Unemployed Artisans under Thomas Baker.[85]

The MUWC was formed at a meeting held at Beardsworth's Repository on 29 October 1832.[86] It was addressed by Hetherington, Hunt, and Cleave as well as local leaders. In moving the resolution in favour of universal suffrage Baker pointed out to the audience:

> It must be remembered that the working classes only consented to receive that Bill as part of their rights, and as a step to further and more efficient reforms, which should not leave out any classes but embrace the whole population (cheers).[87]

The significance of the establishment of the MUWC at this point has often been underestimated.[88] This is understandable, since the organization was short-lived and the 5,000 or so that attended its founding meeting compares unfavourably with the BPU's monster demonstrations. It is, however, a reminder that areas of tension existed within the BPU and an indication that the town's working class entered the 1830s with both a leadership and a programme.

The new union sought to exist alongside the BPU and its organizers were at pains to point out that there was no intention to supplant it. Nevertheless its formation indicates the aspirations of some working-class radicals to a share in the leadership so scrupulously denied them within the BPU. Thus the impression registered by General Cambell in a letter to the Home Secretary must have been widely recognized:

> Although it is not mentioned in the placard I have very good information that one grand object of the persons calling the meeting is to do away with the Political Union over which Mr. Attwood presides and to establish a Midland Political Union in its stead – as they say Mr. Attwood is asleep and does not go far enough.[89]

Certainly Attwood himself chose to see the move as a breach of faith: 'If the working classes cannot trust the middle classes', he asked, 'how could the middle classes trust them?'[90] Most of the wrath of the BPU's Political Council was directed at the Revd Arthur Wade, the clergyman from Warwick who had chaired the meeting to form the new Union.[91] Wade, himself a member of the BPU's Political Council, insisted that a working-class union was essential, 'because the leaders in the Unions, being men of property, living upon the rental of land, the interest of money, or the profit of trade, have separate and distinct interests from the working man'.[92]

It would have been foolish in the extreme for working-class radicals to challenge, at this stage, the leadership of the town's popular movement by Attwood's group. The middle-class leadership of the BPU had survived the successive crises of the Reform Bill campaign with their credibility enhanced considerably. They had led the Union in open defiance of the government. Admittedly the government they defied was Wellington's, which was never actually formed, nevertheless they had made the decisive moves. The possibility of revolution, however it might look to historians a century and a half later, had seemed real enough in Birmingham in May 1832. Whatever Attwood's personal reservations may have been, there was little doubt in the popular mind that he would have led such armed resistance. Hence working-class admiration of Attwood for his stand in 1832 was genuine and, whatever his future transgressions might be, the working-class movement was always eager to draw him into any reform agitation.

There is evidence that in the wake of the Reform Bill agitation Attwood's popularity was increasing. By September 1833 membership of the BPU stood at the all-time high figure of 20,000. This was partly because Attwood made public his personal disappointment with the Reform Act. Along with Scholefield, he was elected MP for the newly created borough of Birmingham in 1832, but he was to register nothing but disappointment at the impact of the Reform Act. He informed a meeting in Birmingham in 1834, for example, that the Act 'has given us a House of Commons but little better, I am sorry to acknowledge, than the old concern . . . the House of Commons is not what it ought to be; one half consists of Lawyers, Jews of Change Alley and monks of Oxford – the other half consists of country gentlemen'.[93] The Reform Act had not ensured the representation of productive capital and Attwood was swift to recognize this. The BPU called a mass meeting in May 1833 to call attention to the 'Polandization' of Ireland through the Coercion Bill. Attwood admitted to the audience of 180,000, 'My friends I have been grievously deceived. Almost on the first day of the session I discovered this.'[94] His statement accurately reflected popular feelings on the Reform Act. Lord George Hervey, who attended the same meeting, found the rather more explicit sentiment, 'Damn Earl Grey's bloody head off', chalked on the walls of the town.[95]

The BPU Council remained intransigent over the issue of working-class votes. During the Political Council's debate, which followed the establishment of the MUWC, G.F. Muntz stated his typical position clearly: 'as to universal suffrage, I do not approve of it and I do not believe it would benefit any class'.[96] The Union's commitment to household suffrage could not offset a sense of disillusionment within a working community which had supported the Reform Bill campaign. The debate which ensued took place against a backdrop of increased strike activity and this was reflected in the mode of argument used to contest the ground held by Attwood and the Political Council. Thomas Baker told unemployed workers that Attwood's currency panacea would not raise wages since it was based on an unrealistic appraisal of authority relations within the workplace: 'they must wait till all the hands were brought into full work, and they had in most cases to turn out and get into serious quarrels with their employers before they obtained an advance'.[97] For James Morrison, a devoted advocate of universal suffrage, working-class notions of political form were so close to the issue of workplace authority that he advocated withdrawing agitation for the vote until workplace organizations had been perfected:

Nothing but experience can conduct any system of policy with

> success, and experience of government is better acquired by commencing with the management of a simple business in which we are skilled by partial success, than in launching into an ocean of business without a chart to guide or a gale of wind to lend us an impulse.[98]

This was not a call for the working class to educate themselves to a level of respectability acceptable to their social superiors and thereby earn themselves the vote. Rather it was a call for them to learn to control their immediate environment to the point where they would be able to use the vote in an effective manner once it had been gained. The Political Council, however, stood firmly by the right of employers to take decisions, however difficult these may have been. Joshua Scholefield, borough MP, told a public dinner in his honour in 1834 that 'He despised the master who would lower wages without sufficient cause; but he believed that although there might be some few individuals who would act so, yet, generally speaking they were compelled to reduce from necessity.'[99]

In the face of the day-to-day experience of the workforce Attwood's bland assertions of a unity of interests rang increasingly hollow. The BPU broke up in an atmosphere of mutual recrimination and the role of workplace conflict in the fragmentation of the political initiative goes some way to confirm the closeness of the two areas in the minds of the participants. The resolution of the Political Council, in winding up the Union's affairs in June 1834, pointed out that 'unhappy discords which have latterly broken out in many parts of the kingdom between the lower and middle classes of the people, render any combined operations for their mutual benefit extremely difficult or altogether impossible'.[100] This sentiment was to haunt the BPU in its second phase of life.

5

The early Chartist experience

The town of Birmingham occupies a major place in the many histories of the early Chartist movement. It has often been argued that Chartism grew directly from the revival of the Birmingham Political Union (BPU) in 1837, but that its middle-class leadership, having fashioned the movement's political demands, were then 'frightened off' by the violent rhetoric of 'rabble rousers' like O'Connor and Stephens. As far as Birmingham is concerned it has been widely accepted that these outside influences temporarily destroyed the social harmony of the town and resulted in the Bull Ring riots of July 1839, when the mayor was forced to call in the Metropolitan Police to restore public order.[1] Despite a distinguished pedigree this construction has little to recommend it, since it confuses a contemporary debate over ends with a disagreement over the means of achieving them. The conflict between the middle-class radicals of the BPU and the wider Chartist body (inside and outside Birmingham) cannot be reduced to the issue of strategy, as 'moral force' versus 'physical force'. Rather this was a polarization around the issue of the way authority was mediated through political bodies. An analysis of the break-up of the BPU in its second phase of life will illustrate this point.

The predicament of Birmingham's middle-class radicals, who were present at the birth of Chartism and who subsequently denied paternity, deserves to be placed in a wider context than that afforded by the orthodox interpretation. The inability of the middle-class elements of the BPU to remain within Chartism after March 1839, and the strength of their subsequent reaction to the Chartists in the Bull Ring, highlight a number of general problems created by the participation of an urban middle class in a radical working-class movement. Above all, what became clear during the early Chartist agitation were the different political goals that the middle-class leadership and the working-class membership of the BPU were working towards. This time the working community demanded the right to participate in organizing and running the campaign through membership of the Political Council. Attwood and his colleagues understood this as part of a wider bid for participatory democracy from within a community which recognized the significance of participation through its experience in the workplace. At the same time, the granting of a Charter of Incorporation in 1838 enabled the radical middle class to act out their own concept of political form. This involved the active domination of labour, and the use of the Metropolitan Police in the Bull Ring must be seen within this context.

THE REVIVAL OF THE BPU: THE RELUCTANT UNIVERSAL SUFFRAGISTS

The key to understanding why the BPU was revived in 1837 lies in the issue of local government reform and the concurrency of the agitation for the People's Charter and a Charter of Incorporation. This point has been obscured in the past because the orthodoxy of social cohesion related to economic structure has led to the assumption that the BPU, or radical middle-class elements in other forms, held an unassailed dominance over the town's politics throughout the period. This seems to be confirmed, first, by the regular return of MPs for the borough from the former leaders of the BPU and second, by the way the revived BPU swept the board at the first municipal election in December 1838. In fact, success in the national and local polls, by the Union and its representatives, disguised the highly fluid nature of local politics at this time. In his study of Leeds, Fraser has reminded us that for the large cities the 1832 Reform Act was merely a beginning, providing as it did 'an electoral context in which political rivalries could be resolved'.[2] Throughout the 1830s the radical middle class in Birmingham needed the numerical support of the working community to ensure that this intra-class struggle was resolved in their favour.

Local politics, of course, had always been important in the programme of the BPU and central to its attraction for lower-middle-class groups. This commitment to local reform increased, for Attwood, as his disappointment with the Reform Act grew. The retention of the pre-1832 aristocratic nature of the parliamentary system made all the more necessary the creation of local bodies which accurately represented the interests of productive capital within the urban communities. Throughout his time as a member of parliament, Attwood advocated this view by opposing moves to increase the centralization of local powers and initiatives through the Poor Law Amendment Act, changes in the banking system, and the new police. Such powers should, he felt, always be vested in a body of local men representative of the local ratepayers.

As the study of the Reform Bill campaign in the previous chapter demonstrated, however, Attwood and his followers represented only one section of upper-middle-class opinion, albeit with strong *petit-bourgeois* support. They were consistently opposed in Birmingham by a Tory group with a far greater following and organizational framework than they have ever been really credited with in the past. Acting without let or hindrance from those men later to be active in the BPU, they had been able to break the radical agitation in the post-war years. In December 1834 they re-established the Loyal and Constitutional Association with George Whateley and John B. Hebbert as secretaries.[3] A month later they put forward Richard Spooner as a Tory general election rival to Attwood and Scholefield. This represented something of a turnaround in Spooner's personal political viewpoint and Attwood attributed the fairly high poll for him to his 'half-Liberal, half-Tory character'.[4] The *Birmingham Journal* attacked him as someone who had 'so long and with such admirable mimicry played amongst us as a professor of Whig opinions'.[5] This election represented an attempt to create an alliance between the old warring factions of Whig and Tory within the town's old elite and to unite them in the face of the ratepayer–popular lobby which Attwood and Scholefield represented.

In the 1835 election Spooner polled 915 votes compared with Attwood's 1,780 and Scholefield's 1,660.[6] With Spooner's vote constituting around 21 per cent of the total votes cast the heroes of the Reform Bill campaign were clearly not substantially threatened by him. On the other hand, the amount of support for Spooner was far from derisory and could not be ignored by the successful candidates.

Table 5.1 Percentage of poll gained by Tory candidates, Birmingham parliamentary elections 1835–44[7]

	Total votes cast	*Tory vote as % of total votes cast*
1835	4,355	21
1837	5,305	19
1840	2,375	38
1841	5,963	30
1844	4,176	50

As Table 5.1 demonstrates, the Tories contested elections in the borough of Birmingham five times between 1835 and 1844. At no point did their share of the poll fall below 19 per cent and it was considerably higher in 1840, 1841, and 1844. In the 1844 election, in a contest with William Scholefield, an ex-member of the BPU Political Council, the Tory candidate was elected.[8]

In highlighting the consistent opposition faced by radical candidates in general elections Table 5.1 draws attention to the important role played by the working community at these times.[9] In the 1835 election Spooner's campaign committee ascribed his defeat to two factors. First, even the multifaceted Spooner had been unable to break an alliance between the radicals and the Whigs based upon the issue of church rates. Rather more than this, however, they blamed 'gross and tyrannical intimidation towards those whose daily bread is at the mercy of their customers'. The committee published the text of a handbill which, they claimed, 'appeared in most of the windows of the smaller shops'. This carried a threat to display publicly the names of those who voted for the Tory candidate. 'The licensed victuallers', the committee added, 'are a well known instance of this system of terror.'[10]

Exclusive dealing, and rather more direct forms of intimidation, were common in Birmingham at election time. The 1835 general election in the town was one case investigated by the Select Committee on Bribery at Elections, held in the same year. John Gilbert, a licensed victualler and an active supporter of Spooner, outlined the kinds of intimidation that his trade had experienced at the hands of the crowd:

> I have known instances where they have gone into public-houses and asked whom they were for, and if they said they were for

> Spooner, they have taken their customers out and taken the ale to the door and poured it out into the street and said that it was Tory ale, and they would have some Reform drink.[11]

The crowd was again in action in July 1837 when, as Table 5.1 shows, the Tory A.G. Stapleton took 19 per cent of the votes. The Riot Act was read three times during the process of polling and town missionary Thomas Finigan, intent on saving souls, found that the town's population had more earthly considerations on its mind:

> I set out from my quarters again this morning but found it unwise and perhaps unsafe to persevere in my work in consequence of the commotion the town is in by the election of a member to represent them in Parliament. Wherever I entered the question was asked, 'Who are you for, sir?', 'Are you a Tory or a Radical?' and making such answers as discretion suggested on the occasion I thought it the wisest plan to return home.[12]

Attwood and his followers made the most, in their election campaigns, of the extent of their working-class support. At the nominations in 1835, held in the town hall, Edmonds reminded the audience of Attwood's popular credentials:

> Many of those who were now to be found among the supporters of Mr. Spooner had put themselves under the protection of the Political Union in the year 1832. That Union was but reposing, not sleeping, and was ready to be called into existence at any moment that the 'Political Prospero' at his back should wave his magic wand.[13]

During the 1837 nominations G.F. Muntz explained that the Tories 'never could regain the ascendancy in Birmingham, and there was one circumstance which would for ever prevent them and that was the education of the people'.[14]

By the time of the 1840 election, however, the relationship between the middle-class radicals and the working community had undergone a number of significant changes. In March 1839 the middle-class radical delegates from Birmingham resigned from the Chartist convention. In July 1839 the London police were used to break up Chartist meetings and were directed in this work by a town council dominated by ex-BPU Political Council members.[15] In the 1840 elections, as Table 5.1 shows, the Tory vote doubled to around 38 per cent of the poll.[16] Here G.F. Muntz was elected to replace the retiring, disillusioned, Attwood. At his nomination meeting Muntz was met by a 'storm of hisses, groans and calls of every description', in an attack orchestrated by local Chartists.[17] In the general election of the following year Spooner polled 30 per cent of the votes in a contest against Muntz and Joshua Scholefield. Although elected, Muntz expressed disappointment at the declaration of the poll:

> Who would have thought that any man coming forward at this time of day in Birmingham, in support of the Church, in support of church rates and all the other abuses of which the people had so long and so loudly complained would have received upward of eighteen hundred votes.[18]

Both Muntz and Attwood (who himself endorsed the candidature of Muntz and Scholefield on this occasion) attributed such a situation to the activities of the local Chartists. Attwood claimed that 'these men, my friends, have gone about the country telling the workmen that their masters were their enemies, that they had no sympathy for them, and that they must act and move and effect their object without them'.[19]

Thus the extent to which the middle-class radicals depended upon the active support of the unenfranchised can be seen most clearly when they came to lose that support. In the election of 1844, following the death of Joshua Scholefield, Spooner was at last elected, taking 50 per cent of the votes cast.[20] It is perhaps significant that his opponent, William Scholefield, son of the deceased MP, had been Mayor in 1839 and in this capacity was the official who gave orders to the Metropolitan Police to break up the Bull Ring meeting on 4 July.

The need for broadly based, popular, support applied similarly to local politics, and certainly to the attempts in 1838 and 1839 to introduce a Charter of Incorporation into the town of Birmingham. This point was firmly reflected in Attwood's image of the role that a local council, elected on a ratepayer suffrage, would actually perform. The object of the Municipal Corporations Act, he assured a town's meeting in November 1837, 'was to establish real and legal Political Unions in every borough, which would supersede the necessity of such formidable political bodies as he . . . had the honour of being the head of'.[21] Thus, in Birmingham the move toward the reform of local politics was intricately bound up with the national representation of productive capital. March 1837 saw the first public meeting to lobby for a local Charter. The chair was taken by P.H. Muntz and most of the speeches were by ex-BPU Political Council members.[22] The following month, the Reform Association called a public meeting to consider the declining state of trade.[23] Again, P.H. Muntz took the chair whilst the same ex-BPU Political Council members (notably Salt, Douglas, Hadley, and Edmonds) emphasized the failure of the Reform Bill to shift the nature of representation significantly towards the 'productive classes'. It was agreed that when 4,000 individuals subscribed to the Birmingham Political Union it would be formally reconstituted. Over the next six weeks just over 5,000 individuals joined and the Union was officially re-established on 23 May 1837.[24]

The figure of 4,000 had been suggested because it represented an estimated 10 per cent of the workforce.[25] It was the operatives that the new Union hoped to enlist and although the membership figure had been reached by the end of May, it is clear that the workforce was not joining the Union in anything like the numbers expected. Since 1832 the middle-class veterans of the Reform Bill campaign had taken their wider support rather for granted. They played the popular card relentlessly at election time, often without taking account of the kinds of development within the workplace outlined in Chapter 3. Consequently they overestimated their hold on the town's working community. In November 1834, for example, G.F. Muntz told a public meeting in the town that 'He hoped there would be no necessity for re-establishing the Political Union; but if it were required it could be called into existence in a very few minutes.'[26] Attwood provided a similarly blasé estimate in August 1835. At the time of the parliamentary debate on the Municipal Corporations Bill he told a town's meeting 'that if any attempt had been made to revive the Union he was confident that three fourths of all the men within 20 miles of Birmingham might have been got together in three days'.[27] In fact, by the middle of June 1837, two months after the first moves to revive the Union, membership stood at just over 8,000.[28] At this point the new Union held its first public meeting to announce its new political programme. The audience at Newhall Hill on 19 June, estimated at between 15,000 and 50,000, heard the old leaders declare for household suffrage.[29] By August, membership of the new Union had *dropped* to around 3,000.[30] This occurred despite enormous popular support for Attwood and Scholefield in the general election of July 1837. Clearly, to support the heroes of the Reform Bill against a Tory in a general election was one thing. To join the BPU in a commitment to piecemeal reform was quite another thing entirely.

Birmingham's working community shunned the revived BPU whilst it rejected the principle of universal manhood suffrage and annual parliaments. The Reform Bill campaign and the workplace conflict of the previous years had made political perspectives clearer. G.F. Muntz stated his position in June 1837 with characteristic candour: 'he was said by his enemies to be on the side of the people right or wrong. That was false. Did he not oppose the Trades Union?'[31] On the other hand, the Workingmen's Memorial Committee, established in May 1837 and including Henry Watson, Thomas Baker, and John Collins in its ranks, put the blame for periodic recessions squarely on the shoulders of the employers. As Baker put it in October 1837:

> When the masters found by these fluctuations in trade, their interests were being sacrificed and they could not maintain their prices they turned upon the men and reduced their wages in the hope of being able, by that means, to meet the competition and carry on. Had they, in place of doing so, taken their workmen by the hand and gone to the government and represented their mutual distresses; and insisted upon relief . . . they would, ere that time, have obtained effectual redress, but in place of doing so the masters carried on the murderous system of competition; wages were reduced to the lowest scale of endurance; and general poverty, distrusts, dislikes and combinations were the consequences.[32]

The Memorial Committee organized a series of mass meetings to petition the government over the level of distress in the town. After a frustrating interview with Melbourne the petitioners reported back their lack of success to a large public meeting in November 1837. It was here that the BPU first floated the idea of a massive agitation, lobbying other towns on the basis of a national petition for political reform.[33]

Four weeks later, after extensive discussions, the BPU's Political Council declared, officially, its support of the principle of universal suffrage, with Attwood claiming that his conversion stemmed from shock at the Queen's recent speech, containing as it did no reference to distress at home.[34] This policy decision was endorsed at a meeting of the Political Union at the town hall on 15 January 1838.[35] The next week, on 23 January, the Workingmen's Memorial Committee sent a deputation to the Political Council's meeting. They now formally declared themselves within the orbit of the BPU. Baker explained to Attwood that the reason for the move was the Council's shift in policy:

> The Council (of the BPU) had been agitating for some time past with no great success, and why? Because the great mass of people felt no great interest in their measures; but now they had come forward to advocate the real liberties and inalienable rights and only security for the people, and hence it was that the working men thought it their duty and interest to come forward . . . and stand by . . . the men who were endeavouring to obtain for them substantial relief.[36]

What exactly caused this major change of heart within the Council of the revived BPU? It was, quite simply, that by November 1837 the middle-class radical initiative was floundering on two fronts. The working class refused to join the BPU in large numbers because of its commitment to household suffrage. At the same time, the agitation for a Charter of Incorporation was not going particularly well. On 30 October 1837 a public meeting was held in the town hall on the subject. Although patronized by the Political Council (including Attwood, who made a long speech) this meeting attracted an audience of only 2,500.[37] The petition in favour of incorporation, drawn up by the same meeting, was eventually submitted to the Privy Council with just over 4,000 signatures.[38] Just a week later the BPU announced its plan for a nationwide political campaign. In late December and early January those who opposed incorporation organized themselves, submitting a petition signed by around 2,500 people.[39] This counter-petition appeared to contain the names of more ratepayers, with a greater total rating assessment than the petition in favour of incorporation.[40] By the end of January 1838, however, the BPU had declared for universal suffrage, drawn the organized working class into its orbit, and managed, as a result, to submit a second petition with a total of 8,700 names in favour of incorporation.[41] This second petition made the argument in terms of absolute numbers far more emphatically than the first. Beside this the agitation had drawn in a larger number of small ratepayers such that the second petition now outnumbered the petition against incorporation in terms of ratepayer signatories. As the Tithe Commissioners who carried out the scrutinies put it in a letter to Greville at the Privy Council on 21 September 1838, 'The result showed a nearly equal amount of assessment for the two parties, with a majority in point of numbers in the ratio of three to two in favour of the Charter.'[42]

In fact, the total number of ratepayers and the rating assessment of each petition remained in dispute until September 1838, when a final scrutiny revealed 2,710 ratepayers in favour of incorporation (assessed at a total of £64,586) and 1,892 ratepayers against (assessed at £74,804).[43] Thus the thrust given to the agitation for incorporation in the period November 1837 to February 1838 had been crucial to the success of the campaign. This is not to suggest that Attwood and his followers adopted universal suffrage only in order to revitalize a flagging agitation for local reform. They also had a genuine interest in rectifying the nature of the national representation of urban interests established in 1832. Attwood's disillusionment with the Reform Act has been detailed earlier. Nevertheless, the need to provide a popular base for both the local and the national agitations pushed the middle-class radicals further, in political terms, than they would otherwise have chosen to go.

Attwood's approach to the question of universal suffrage was, at this stage, openly pragmatic. As he said, 'the masses of the people constituted the only engine through which it was possible to obtain reform, and that mighty engine could not be roused into efficient action without the agency of Universal Suffrage'.[44] These sentiments permeated the approach of most of the Political Council. R.K. Douglas, for example, in January 1838 echoed Attwood's words when he claimed that universal suffrage was 'not only right and safe but it was the only proposal by which they could lay hold of the hearts of the masses'.[45] Certainly the shift in policy on the part of the Council, whether occasioned by the Queen's speech, Russell's finality declaration, or the need for a mass base, involved much heart-searching for BPU leaders. Attwood announced in January 1838 that he was 'a thorough convert to Universal Suffrage and if ever I uttered a word against it I now altogether retract it'.[46] G.F. Muntz was a little more guarded in his statements: 'although not originally a friend to universal suffrage he did not regret to find they had adopted the principle'.[47]

This amounted to a considerable achievement for the working-class movement. The lion of the Reform Bill campaign had been drawn into a campaign for the full radical programme including its central, enabling clause of universal manhood suffrage. A good deal of significance was attached to Attwood's conversion. It was seen, as James Epstein has pointed out in his important study of O'Connor, as the final stage in the demystification of the Reform Bill. The greatest advocate of the 1832 measure was now campaigning for the radical franchise. O'Connor prostrated himself in what Epstein refers to as 'hyperbolical humility before the figure of Thomas Attwood'.[48] In July, O'Connor informed readers of the *Northern Star*: 'When he (O'Connor) heard that Mr. Attwood had advanced he said this man would be a more powerful leader than he was – hitherto he had been a leader now he would become a follower – a drummer in the army.'[49]

Such an analysis flattered Attwood and the BPU in terms of their importance in organizing the Chartist movement. This work was already underway, in the north under O'Connor's direction and in the south under the auspices of the London Working Men's Association, by the time the BPU joined the movement. Epstein shows that O'Connor clearly did feel, in 1838, that Chartism could embrace the radical middle class. Only Bronterre O'Brien, among the national leadership, with his close experience of Attwood during the Reform Bill agitation, voiced some disquiet at this sudden conversion to the principle of universal suffrage.[50] The historians of Chartism have undoubtedly put too much emphasis on the role of the BPU in forming the nature and content of Chartism in positive ways.[51] In fact, the actions of the middle-class radicals of the BPU between their miraculous conversion to universal suffrage in December 1837 and their exit from the movement by April 1839 had rather more to do with defining what Chartism was not, rather than what it was.

The conversion to universal suffrage, in fact, involved no deep-seated shift of political perspective within the middle-class radical ideal. Attwood still spoke of the representation of interests; his declaration for universal suffrage included the following statement:

> If they would but send to the House of Commons men born and educated in the thick of the miseries and difficulties of life – men acquainted with the wants and interests of the industrious classes, and sympathising with them – they would get a fair and just representation of the Commons of England; but at present the House of Commons was not a real House of Commons, but rather a house of uncommons, or what he had often called a house consisting of men born in the clouds, living in the clouds and dying in the clouds.[52]

It had taken the Council of the BPU nine months to declare in favour of the wider suffrage simply because in order to represent the industrious classes such a franchise was by no means necessary. In the view of G.F. Muntz, the BPU's second agitation ought to have aimed at 'extending the franchise so as to enable them to return to the House of Commons *a majority of men in business who understood the true interests of the people*, instead of lordlings and scions of nobility'.[53] His brother, P. H. Muntz, a member of the Council and a delegate to the first Chartist Convention, was more frankly utilitarian when he spoke in February 1839:

> He would acknowledge no abstract right of suffrage in either rich or poor. Prove to him that the good of the community at large could be promoted by the destruction of the right he possessed and most cheerfully he would resign it tomorrow. The suffrage that would produce the greatest happiness for the greatest number of his fellow men was the suffrage he would look for.[54]

The hierarchical social model that was so central to the middle-class radical ideal was not abnegated when the Political Council accepted universal suffrage.[55] In some ways, given O'Connor's stage humility before Attwood as leader, it may even have been reinforced. The right to lead and represent the interests of the productive sector of society fell logically, the middle-class radical argued, to those who led that sector economically. This theory of a 'virtual representation' of working-class interests by middle-class men, was always presented and justified within an ethos of social mobility by which master manufacturers could be seen simply as successful working men. At a public meeting on 15 January 1838, to discuss the sending of deputations to other towns, Henry Watson reminded the audience of the discreteness of the working-class claim:

> Labour was not only the mine of real wealth, but that mine was the sole property of those who toiled. No man had a right to another man's labour without an equivalent; not even a king upon his throne any more than that more useful man who delves in the mine, ploughs the field or throws the shuttle.[56]

Listening in Birmingham Town Hall there can have been few members of the audience who had ever delved a mine, ploughed a field, or thrown a shuttle. Watson was using the universal imagery of a collective consciousness. For Attwood and his followers the economic dominance of the manufacturer, merchant, and banker over the 'productive class' best fitted them to represent the whole of that class. By the late 1830s it was exactly this economic dominance that working-class radicals hoped to break by achieving the right of representation.

This difference of interpretation became clear in 1838 and 1839 during disputes over the distribution of authority, within the BPU in particular, and within the Chartist movement as a whole. The middle-class radicals' concept of democratic form was enshrined in the organizational structure of the Union. In Attwood's own nomenclature the working class were generally referred to as the 'masses', but with the addition of the productive element of the middle class they became the 'people'. He informed his wife, in a letter of June 1839: 'Salt writes me word that 8,000 men have now re-enrolled their names and paid up their subscriptions to the Union and that the Council is better and stronger than ever.'[57] The Political Council that he referred to contained no working men, its thirty-five members being composed of one banker, five merchants, three factors, eighteen manufacturers (generally large scale), five professionals, two shopkeepers, and one gentleman of some means. The emphasis on property was quite deliberate. Looking back on the period from 1841 Attwood claimed: 'There is no instance in history in which political movements have been successful without leaders and in almost every instance those leaders have been men of wealth and influence.'[58] Given its social composition, the Political Council was to be invested with absolute control of the movement. As Attwood again remembered:

> The very essence of the Birmingham Union, under the law, was unlimited obedience to their leaders who formed the Political Council. . . . Who would ever think of building a railroad without a committee or of sending, even a disciplined army into the field without officers.[59]

BREAK-UP OF THE ALLIANCE

As the work of agitation went on throughout the country in the spring and summer of 1838 it became clear that the working-class leadership was unwilling to accept an alliance on these terms. The climax of the agitation was the mass meeting at Holloway Head in August 1838, designated by Mark Hovell as 'the official beginning of the Chartist movement'.[60] Whatever the accuracy of that statement it was certainly a gala occasion, with both O'Connor and Attwood addressing the enormous crowd.[61] Seven of the Political Council were elected delegates to the Convention: T.C. Salt, Benjamin Hadley, John Pierce, George Edmonds, R.K. Douglas, and G.F and P.H. Muntz. At this meeting, however, the membership demanded the election of seven working men to the BPU's Political Council and the adoption of John Collins as one of the Chartist delegates.[62]

Tension began to mount within the BPU from this point on as the working-class councillors reported back to section meetings throughout the town on the way the BPU operated. In November, Henry Watson, for example, remarked upon 'a tendency to an aristocratic feeling amongst them that when a wealthy man moved they generally carried those resolutions'.[63] The final rift between the middle-class radicals and the broader movement, resulting in the resignation of the BPU delegates (with the exception of Collins) in March and April 1839, cannot be adequately explained as the clash between physical and moral force that it has been portrayed as in the past. In the wake of the resignations, Feargus O'Connor asked rhetorically, 'Had none of the Birmingham leaders ever used strong words?'[64] Arguably the whole tenor of the BPU's approach was one of physical force. One member of the Political Council said of the government at the start of the campaign that 'The terrors of a few Newhall Hill meetings would induce them to relax the screw.'[65] Although the Political Council liked to draw a distinction between this approach, which it referred to as 'wholesome terror', and actually advocating the use of force, in the first half of 1838 they went much further. At the main meeting of August 1838 Attwood revived memories of May 1832 by claiming that: 'If our enemies shed blood – if they attack the people – they must take the consequences upon their own heads.'[66]

Nor can the tensions be contained adequately within an explanation reliant upon the clash of personalities between O'Connor and the BPU leadership. Certainly the question of the control of the movement was central, but it actually revolved around the level of participation allowed to the working-class element. This was the crucial issue. Edward Brown's comment on middle-class participation, made after the resignations of March 1839, was characteristic of working-class feeling: 'Did they think they were going to lead the working men by the nose any longer?'[67] Above all, this related not only to participation within Chartism, the movement, but also to the question of working-class participation in any democratic form that might emerge in the event of its exertions being successful. This was surely in O'Connor's mind when he claimed of the BPU radicals that 'It was always their intention to stop universal suffrage morally, if they could.'[68] The middle-class and working-class elements within the BPU had arrived at Chartism via two different routes. Though they shared the same political programme their concept of the emergent democratic form was essentially different. Working-class aspirations within Chartism lay not only in obtaining political rights, but in using them effectively. Any social programme, implicit in the six points, was dependent upon the full exercise of those rights at all levels of political life. Thus the pragmatism of the middle-class radicals of the BPU robbed the working man of his first demand, for 'égalité: equality of citizenship'.[69]

Once again the concurrent chronology of the Chartist agitation and the reform of local government in Birmingham gives a penetrating insight into the confrontation of the two radical ideals. In December 1838, at the town's first municipal election, the radical middle class swept the board. The Tories contested every ward and every one was defeated.[70] The election made town councillors of thirteen of the BPU's Political Council as it stood in June 1837. Two further Political Councillors, R.K. Douglas and George Edmonds, found posts within the newly formed Corporation.[71] All the Birmingham Chartist delegates, with the exception of Collins, were now involved in some official capacity with the town council. It would be far too simplistic to suggest that the middle-class radicals now pulled out of Chartism because they had achieved their primary objective in the reform of local institutions. The middle-class radicals also had genuine objectives within the national movement, but by 1839 they were less ambitious than perhaps they had previously been.

Tension increased within the BPU in the second half of 1838. The differences between Salt and O'Connor over violence of language were settled amicably at a public meeting in November, but they seemed to point to a more fundamental division.[72] The Political Council met every Tuesday evening, the Working Men's Committee met on Thursdays as did working-class sectional groups throughout the town. By January 1839 there was obviously disagreement between the two since Edward Brown, of the Working Men's Committee, felt constrained to explain: 'It had been said of them they wished to dictate to the council. That was not the case.'[73] In the same month some of the Political Council, Edmonds in particular, were barracked by the Chartists at a public meeting designed to initiate a local movement for Corn Law repeal. At the same meeting Thomas Weston, a member of both the Political Council and the town council, betrayed a crucial doubt on the possible immediacy of universal suffrage. 'I don't think we shall get it this week', he told a hostile audience, 'It may take years.'[74]

Nevertheless, the stand taken by most of the Political Union against the move to start a separate anti-Corn-Law campaign, enabled it to weather this particular storm with its credibility intact. But the full attendance of middle-class radicals at the dinner at the end of February 1839 to celebrate incorporation contrasted noticeably with the dwindling attendance of Political Councillors at the Tuesday BPU sessions.[75] These sometimes had to be abandoned as they were inquorate. In March 1839 Watson complained that: 'It appeared some of them must be forced on, that the people must take the lead.'[76] A week later the Council attempted to disband the National Rent Committee, alleging misappropriation of funds by the working-class leadership. The Committee had been established to raise funds for the Convention and had emerged as the focus of the working-class element within the Union.[77] The abortive attempt to disband it represents a last-ditch attempt by the middle-class radicals of the BPU to snatch back the leadership of the movement. On 19 March, the Working Men's Committee submitted a resolution deprecating the non-attendance of Councillors and censuring Hadley, Salt, Muntz, and Douglas for not agitating the locality in accordance with a Convention direction.[78] Salt, Hadley, Douglas, and Pierce resigned as delegates to the Convention at the end of March.[79] A week later the BPU, now with a membership of less than 300, was disbanded.[80]

The resignations from the Convention of the two Muntzes and Edmonds followed shortly. A Holloway Head meeting at the end of April elected working men, Edward Brown, John Powell, and John Donaldson to take their places at the Convention.[81] It has often been suggested that it was the flagging interest of the Union's middle-class radicals that created a local working-class leadership in the early months of 1839.[82] But this is to confuse cause and effect. For it was the strength and articulacy of the working-class leadership in both its local and national forms that convinced the middle-class radicals that Chartism would not provide the platform for the kind of democratic form they envisaged. Locally the working-class leadership drew on its own tradition of political radicalism, particularly that of the post-war period. The sectional meeting of the Cross Guns, Lancaster Street, declared in February 1839, 'that with nothing short of Liberty and Prosperity will we be content! or we will die in the attempt!' It also published the following verse:

> Britons arise and yet be free
> Demand your rights and liberty,
> Tyrants long have shared the spoil,
> The Working Class share all the toil,
> Now! or never! strike the blow!
> Exert yourselves and crush the foe![83]

It was for the publication of this verse that Charles Whitworth, as Chairman of the Union Society, had been imprisoned for six months in 1819.[84] In the same vein John Fussell told a meeting at Holloway Head in April 1839, after the delegates had resigned, that: 'First they must petition; secondly demand; and while they demanded they must adopt and act upon the advice of Major Cartwright and Wooller and demand with arms in their hands and then they should have some attention paid to them.'[85] With the failure of the alliance the rhetoric of the working-class radicals drew strength from an earlier period of agitation, when the movement had been purer.

By the end of 1838, however, through the reform of local government, the middle-class leadership of the BPU had achieved locally the kind of democratic form that they had hoped the Chartist movement might produce nationally. A painfully small municipal electorate (a mere 3 per cent of the population, less even than the 1832 roll of voters for the parliamentary elections)[86] returned a radical middle-class council in December 1838, charged with the task of defending the interests of the ratepayer against a range of non-elected bodies representing those local vested interests which had hitherto dominated local government. The middle-class leadership of the BPU had hoped that parliamentary reform would produce a similar effect upon the state, with the interests of the church, the aristocracy, and all non-producing capital, subordinated to those of the 'productive classes' whom they hoped to represent. Admittedly the new corporation was the middle-class radical dream writ small. Nevertheless, most were prepared to settle for this given the alternative which Chartism by now so obviously offered, that is, a fuller democracy with the working class as the dominant element. To the Chartists there was an inescapable correlation between the success of the middle-class radicals at the municipal elections of 1838 and their gradual withdrawal from the Chartist movement. Speaking to the Convention in April 1839, Dr Taylor claimed that as far as Birmingham was concerned incorporation had proved to be 'the grave of Radicalism'.[87]

At the same time, success in the local elections for key figures on the BPU Political Council transformed a mass-based agitation, in which they were participants, into a problem of law and order. In no issue was this metamorphosis exemplified more completely than in the question of the meetings in the Bull Ring. During the Reform Bill agitation the BPU middle-class leadership had fostered these meetings to maintain momentum within the movement.

Their revival in January 1839 under working-class direction, however, was a manifestation of the tension between the working-class and middle-class leadership within the BPU. In April, after the resignations of the Birmingham delegates, these meetings grew in attendance. By the first week in May, just prior to the Convention's move from London to Birmingham, they were being held twice a day. On 10 May they were declared illegal by the magistrates, who, since incorporation, included among their number three ex-Political Councillors.[88] One of these, P.H. Muntz, had himself been elected as a delegate to the Convention. On 16 May, three days after the arrival of the Convention, Fussell and Brown were arrested for holding meetings and using violent language.[89] On 17 and 29 June Henry Wilkes, Joseph Nisbett, a gun-maker, and William Smallwood were prosecuted before a bench of magistrates which included P.H. Muntz. They were charged with obstruction whilst holding Bull Ring meetings. Nisbett and Smallwood were unable to pay a fine and were imprisoned. The irony of Muntz's position as poacher turned gamekeeper was not lost on the Chartists. A defiant Henry Wilkes made the point: 'It appears to me very strange that the working classes should now be prosecuted. In the year 1832 when I took an active part, there was no such interruptions or prosecutions. The influential gentlemen then took part with the people and there was no such objections raised.'[90]

THE BULL RING RIOTS: JULY 1839

Unlike almost every other aspect of working-class history in Birmingham the disturbances in the Bull Ring in July 1839 generated a plethora of documentation. Newspaper reports at the time were extensive and there is a considerable correspondence preserved in the Home Office papers. The disturbances were also the subject of two separate enquiries following complaints that magistrates had not acted quickly or decisively enough.[91] Nevertheless, the disturbances have never been systematically examined either for their events or significance. One suspects that this is because within the accepted history of social relations in the town they have been seen as an aberration brought about by national rather than local conditions. They appear to be the inevitable consequence of the influence of O'Connor and a Chartist rhetoric heavily laced with the threat of violence.[92] In any analysis of class relationships during the early Chartist period, however, the Bull Ring riots deserve fairly close attention. They followed closely on the departure from Chartism of the BPU's middle-class radicals and showed these same individuals attempting to demonstrate, as forcefully as possible, that they had broken with the past. For the Chartists the introduction of the Metropolitan Police in July appeared to verify their own rhetorical statements about the possibility of a violent intervention by the state. The action was a forceful reminder that through incorporation those who exercised authority in the workplace had been provided with an extension of those powers outside work.

The disturbances should be seen as a sequence of events taking place over the period of a fortnight, rather than one or two serious incidents.[93] At 8 o'clock on the evening of Thursday 4 July 1839 a detachment of sixty Metropolitan Police officers arrived in Birmingham accompanied by William Scholefield, ex-member of the BPU Political Council and now Mayor and magistrate of the newly incorporated borough. Also in the party were two other magistrates, Dr J.K. Booth and William Chance, one of the town's leading glass manufacturers.[94] The London police were sworn in as special constables at the railway station and, leaving their side-arms behind, they proceeded to the Bull Ring armed only with staffs.[95] Here a large crowd had gathered, as they had done daily over the previous six months, to listen to Chartist speakers and newspaper readings. George Martin, Inspector of Police, had been given his orders on the journey from London. He was to arrest the main speakers at any meeting he might find and similarly arrest any individual obstructing him in this purpose.[96] The appearance of the magistrates and their party was met, by the crowd in the Bull Ring, by a stunned and rather eerie silence. This was followed by groans, hisses, and a hail of stones directed at the police.[97] At the command of Dr Booth, Martin and his men attempted to arrest the main speaker (whose identity remains unknown).[98]

During a fight which lasted twenty minutes the police were decimated. They retreated in considerable disorder and, lacking any knowledge of the geography of the town, took refuge in any building which appeared to offer shelter. Martin, having lost his hat, a tooth, his staff, and most of his coat, sheltered in the Grand

Turk public house with three other officers, one of them badly wounded.[99] Others sought the sanctum of Peter's liquor store and the Public Office in Moor Street.[100] The military were called out and the Riot Act read in the Bull Ring.[101] The army remained in the centre of town and succeeded in dispersing a crowd of around 2,000 people who moved down from a meeting at Holloway Head. They gathered outside the Golden Lion in Aston Street, where the Convention had been meeting, and were addressed by Dr Taylor, he and Peter McDouall being the only delegates still on the premises. After the fight with the police earlier in the evening, Taylor had been warned by John Fussell that 'it was the object of the magistrates to excite the people into an outbreak, by the introduction of the London police, rather than to protect the peace of the town'.[102] He now advised the crowd to return to their homes peacefully. During the course of the evening there were nine arrests made including that of Dr Taylor.[103]

The following morning, Friday 5 July, at the request of a large body of Birmingham Chartists, William Lovett issued a handbill, on behalf of the Convention, condemning the action of the police and the magistrates.[104] During the day forty more police officers arrived from London and the Warwickshire Yeomanry were collected and held in readiness, on the outskirts of the town.[105] That evening the Riot Act was read at a large meeting at Holloway Head by W.C. Alston, a magistrate, accompanied by a detachment of the Fourth Irish Dragoons with a large artillery piece.[106] The streets around the Bull Ring were cleared by a combination of police and army units and there were a large number of scuffles and arrests. On Saturday 6 July Lovett was arrested at the Convention rooms for having composed the handbill of the previous day. John Collins, implicated in this incident by virtue of having published the handbill, surrendered himself to the authorities upon hearing that a warrant had been issued for his arrest. At 9 p.m. both men were brought before the magistrates and committed. Towards the end of their examination the large crowd that had gathered outside the Public Office grew restive and a number of shop fronts were pushed in. Once again the cavalry was used to restore order.[107]

Feargus O'Connor, who had gone to Warwick to stand bail for Dr Taylor, arrived back in the town at 1.30 a.m. on Sunday 7 July. He was greeted peacefully by a large crowd and left immediately for Manchester. At 7 a.m. the Birmingham Owenites held a well-attended secular service at Holloway Head, which roundly condemned the actions of the police. The rest of Sunday passed off reasonably peacefully. Only the congregation of St Martin's were disturbed when a woman announced during morning service that 'This day Salvation is come to the House of Israel.' She was hastily bundled outside by William Chance, the magistrate, a member of the same congregation. The military were not needed during Sunday and there appears to have been only one further incident when an off-duty soldier made the mistake of visiting a public house and was beaten senseless by the regular customers.[108] Following this incident the police were instructed never to move about the town in groups of less than four and even then they had 'strict orders not to enter public houses'.[109]

On Monday 8 July it was widely rumoured that 200 colliers were on their way from West Bromwich. Although this remained only a rumour large crowds gathered again in the Bull Ring and were dispersed with the by now familiar scuffles.[110] On 9 July George Julian Harney was brought into the town under arrest. His announcement at a Holloway Head meeting on 14 May that he would campaign with a 'musket in one hand and a petition in the other' had brought a warrant for his arrest.[111] Finally tracked down in Newcastle he was brought to Birmingham and swiftly dispatched to Warwick for trial.

The town remained fairly quiet for the rest of the week with the streets regularly patrolled by the police and the army. By Wednesday 10 July forty of the police returned to London and William Scholefield's daily reports to the Home Office reveal that the town was 'perfectly quiet' by Sunday 14 July.[112] On Monday 15 July the magistrates felt the situation sufficiently in hand for them to cease their daily vigil at the Public Office. At two o'clock in the afternoon Colonel Chatterton, commanding the Dragoons, was informed by the Mayor that there would be no need for his men to 'stand to' that evening. Chatterton protested that he had 'heard several people say there was an impression in the town that there might be disturbances that night'. He was, however, reassured by Scholefield and the men were given the order to 'stand down'. The Colonel dined at home that evening for the first time since the disturbances began.[113] At three o'clock the Mayor saw Inspector May and informed him that since the town was 'peaceable and quiet and had been for some days past', he might return to London with some of his men. May was instructed 'not to place any men as patrols in the Bull Ring as heretofore, but keep them in the yard of the Public Office as this being Monday and kept a holiday there would be a great many idle persons about the streets'. If all remained calm May was to take half the fifty remaining policemen back to London on the midnight train.[114]

For the Chartists, however, the day was marked by the growth of tension and rumour. The Chartist petition had been discussed in parliament the previous Friday. It was widely expected that both Attwood and, possibly, Feargus O'Connor would be in the town on Monday 15 July to report the rejection of the petition and the start of the 'Sacred Month'. The Chartists employed a bellman to ring supporters to a Holloway Head meeting at two o'clock in the afternoon, but in the absence of the expected speakers this was adjourned until six o'clock.[115]

The meeting drew a crowd of 2,000 people and was addressed by a number of speakers including Henry Wilkes. He drew the lesson of the previous week by pointing out that the people were not yet strong enough to confront the troops. He added, however, according to one witness at his subsequent trial, 'that if the sheds were barricaded and the railroad destroyed, they would have nothing to fear from them. He said there were 200,000 men completely armed in the North, ready to march at a moment's notice and join them, at Birmingham.'[116] Shortly before 8 p.m., at Wilkes' suggestion the crowd moved off, via the Bull Ring and on to Digbeth, to greet John Collins, who had been bailed out from Warwick gaol that evening and was expected back in the town. While most of the crowd moved down the Stratford Road large groups remained in the Bull Ring, spreading into the adjacent Moor Street, where the Public Office stood.

Between 8 p.m. and 8.30 p.m. there was an incident involving police officers in Moor Street, when two individuals refusing to be 'moved on' were beaten.[117] Word of this passed to the crowd moving to greet Collins, which by this time had reached Camp Hill. Five or six hundred of this group, mostly young men, now returned to the Bull Ring, pulling up fencing for weapons on the way.[118] During the week that followed 4 July the police had rarely been seen on the streets without military support and they had been guilty of a number of unprovoked acts of aggression.[119]

Now, with the troops in their barracks, the police, or so it must have appeared, were eager for a confrontation with the population that had humiliated them the week before.

Inspector May, who had already changed into his civilian clothes in preparation for returning home, had no such intention.[120] He and his men locked themselves in the Public Office and refused to be drawn out despite the crowd's systematic destruction of the eighty-seven panes of glass in the front of the building.[121] Such was the noise and commotion that May at this point estimated the crowd to be 'five to eight thousand armed men'.[122] He took some solace from the fact that his orders prevented him from acting without direct authorization from a magistrate and there was none in attendance. Tory groups in the town later claimed that had there been a magistrate present to authorize immediate police action the disturbance could have been quelled at this early stage. But even though the crowd was shown to be about one-tenth the size May at first thought it to be, the Inspector consistently claimed, throughout the subsequent investigations, that police action at this point would have involved 'a loss of life and limb on both sides'.[123]

Unable to draw the police from the Public Office the crowd retired to the Bull Ring and broke into two shops, a grocer's and a bedding merchant's. A bonfire was made of their contents in front of the Nelson statue. The fire was later transferred to the two shops themselves and there was also a certain amount of thieving from some of the jewellers in the area. Much was made after the events of the fact that young boys were responsible for firing the shops and also for the thefts.[124] The two elements should not, however, be confused. There was no interference from the crowd in the activities of those burning the contents of the shops. Indeed, Enos Edwards and his son were actively prevented, by the crowd, from driving the two fire engines of the Birmingham Fire Office to the scene of destruction.[125] There was, on the other hand, a good deal of disapproval displayed towards the thieves who took advantage of the situation to pocket goods from the shops in the area. Thomas Baker, law stationer, reported later:

> I saw a boy come out of one of the shops, I think Savages, with his pockets stuffed out. I heard a person standing near me, who was looking on say to the boy, 'what have you got there, that

is not what we want, we are too brave for that, and if I find anyone stealing, I will be the first to strike a dagger through his heart'.[126]

It was not until 9.40 p.m. that the troops and police arrived to clear the area.[127] The crowd had controlled the streets for one hour and forty minutes from the time of their first appearance in the Bull Ring. News that the military were on their way spread rapidly and, as Chatterton later admitted, 'in fact there was nobody to disperse'.[128]

In the wake of 15 July the number of special constables was increased, bringing the total number to around 4,000. They were now systematically organized on a ward basis and began regular patrols through the day and night.[129] These, alongside patrols by the London police, the Dragoons, and the Warwickshire Yeomanry, kept the streets clear and ensured that meetings were broken up before they could start.[130] May reported later that seventy prisoners were taken on 15 July and several more the following evening.[131] A large meeting was dispersed on the evening of 21 July and the last incident appears to have occurred on 22 July. That night the shop-and-warehouse of Whittal, a master builder, was burned to the ground. Whether this was the work of an incendiary or an accident is impossible to judge. What is certain is that the crowd that gathered in Lancaster Street to watch the conflagration enjoyed the spectacle and steadfastly refused to co-operate with attempts to douse the flames.[132]

The report from the enquiry into the riots, appointed by the town council, exonerated the magistrates and the army from any accusations of neglect. It just as emphatically condemned the London police for their provocative actions on 4 July and during their subsequent stay in the town. This was by no means an unexpected verdict. The committee of enquiry was chaired by Joseph Sturge, who also led the campaign to prevent the imposition of a Home-Office-controlled police force on Birmingham following the riots.[133] It was convenient to place the blame for the disturbances squarely on the shoulders of the London police since they had few friends in any quarter. The inclination of contemporaries has been shared by historians. Dr Tholfsen comments on the incidents of 4 July that 'Although Scholefield had instructed the police to avoid provocation they paid no attention. Their provocative behaviour was directly responsible for the riot.'[134] A complementary argument is that the actual introduction of the London police was unavoidable given the disruptive nature of the Bull Ring meetings between January and July. This point is certainly implicit in most accounts. J.T. Ward, for example, sets the scene thus: 'Mayor Scholefield arrived in the town that evening with 60 policemen to find a rowdy and illegal meeting in progress in the Bull Ring.'[135] Tholfsen adds soberly, 'the first responsibility of public officials is the maintenance of public order, and the magistrates were understandably alarmed at the proceedings in the Bull Ring'.[136]

The sympathy of historians for the position of the magistracy has been reinforced by the evidence of their apparent contrition after the event. During the week following 4 July, William Scholefield informed the town council that 'The magistrates had acted solely with a view to preserve the peace of the town; and if, in the course they pursued they had acted wrong, it was an error of judgement. Their sole object was to save loss of life.'[137] Five years later Scholefield was to reject sole responsibility for the use of the police: 'He looked upon their introduction as an unfortunate step marked by impolicy and error, but as the majority of magistrates resolved that they should be introduced he had no choice but to act ministerially, as Mayor, and introduce them.'[138]

The use of the London police deserves closer examination. During the 1830s feeling about the new police had been something of a unifying factor between working-class and middle-class radicals in London and the provinces. In 1834, at a public dinner in honour of the borough members, Attwood had described Peel's force as 'that fearful engine of Bourbon tyranny'. He also added, rather ironically in view of later events, 'I told the House of Commons that the men of Birmingham would fight but they would never submit to the new Police.'[139] Middle-class radicals had long cited the police force as the creation of an unrepresentative government. It is therefore pertinent to repeat the question put by Fussell, the Chartist, to a town's meeting on the Birmingham Police Bill in November 1839: 'If the Mayor considered it an unconstitutional force why did he use it to disperse a peaceable meeting?'[140]

As far as the Chartists in the town were concerned such a decision could only be seen as a deliberate act of provocation. The unstamped press circulated widely in Birmingham and details of the Calthorpe Street affair must have been well known. When Fussell rushed from the Bull Ring on the evening of 4 July to inform Dr Taylor of what was happening, it was this thought that was uppermost in his mind. When one remembers the involvement of the town in the Oliver affair a quarter of a century earlier, this must have appeared perfectly credible.[141] The Bull Ring meetings had been reasonably peaceful, as a number of witnesses were prepared to testify to both investigations.[142] Military strength in the area was known to be good. Chatterton commanded about 150 mounted troops and two rifle companies.[143] In addition, by the end of May, 2,500 special constables had been sworn in when the Convention moved to Birmingham.[144] Besides these forces the Warwickshire Yeomanry was available (although there might well have been a disinclination on the part of the town council to use a county force in a borough affair). These elements together appeared to comprise a reasonably sufficient force to deal with any local disturbances. Certainly on 1 July the magistrates decided to use a combination of troops and special constables to disperse a Bull Ring meeting. In the event the Convention got to know the plan and, on the recommendation of O'Connor, adjourned the meeting to Gosta Green.[145]

It is difficult to estimate accurately the size of the crowd in the Bull Ring on the evening of 4 July. After the disturbance the Chartists, anxious to stress the peaceful nature of the meeting, cast its estimate of numbers uncharacteristically low. Fussell claimed that there had been between 300 and 700 people present.[146] Inspector George Martin, on the other hand, anxious to explain and justify the rout of his men, felt constrained to put the number closer to 5,000.[147] Estimating on the basis of the meetings on previous nights it seems unlikely that there were less than 800 present. The figure could have been as high as 1,000 since Thursday was market day.[148]

What did the magistrates really hope to achieve with sixty policemen, on foot, armed only with staffs, against such a crowd? It is revealing in this respect to look more closely at Scholefield's orders to Martin. Certainly these requested that his men act 'quietly and temperately; but firmly and decidedly'. The object in view was clearly spelt out however:

Should the meeting be addressed by one or more persons, you

will endeavour to arrest the speakers or leaders of the assembly. If you fail in this, owing to the obstructions offered by any parties, you will forthwith arrest such parties, and any other whom you may find breaking the law, either by impeding the road, or in any other way.[149]

Effectively Martin was given the task of doing what the Manchester Yeomanry attempted in St Peter's Fields, Manchester, in August 1819: the arrest of a speaker during a mass meeting. The sequence of events is also of interest. After their arrival at the station, Dr Booth left the party and went to his home to pick up his horse. He returned to the station by way of the Bull Ring, where his appearance was greeted with groans and hisses from the crowd. At the station he reported the nature of the meeting and the police were instructed to move off, armed only with their wooden staffs.[150] Thus the magistrates knew the size of the meeting and accepted the possibility of a fight if the police attempted to carry out their orders. Despite this no attempt was made to reinforce the small police detachment at this point. The army was not approached until after the fight in the Bull Ring had begun.

This remarkable incident can be explained in one of three different ways. First, it could be seen as the result of an error of judgement on the part of an inexperienced official (Scholefield, acting for the body of the magistrates). Possibly he felt that sixty lightly armed men would be sufficient to suppress the crowd. If he was mistaken in this he was at least motivated by the perfectly laudable desire to preserve public order in the face of what he saw as mounting Chartist violence. This as has already been suggested, is the most popular explanation with Scholefield's honest admissions of collective error lending apparent authenticity to this point. Apart from the Bull Ring meetings themselves, where the language was often inflammatory, there was other evidence to suggest that the Chartists were arming themselves. In May, for example, just before the arrival of the Convention, Lancashire delegates Peter McDouall and James Duke placed an order with a Birmingham gun-maker for 500–1,000 muskets with bayonets.[151]

Despite this, the evidence suggests that Scholefield himself was never really worried by the Bull Ring meetings. They were declared illegal by the town council on 8 May.[152] Four days later he wrote to the Home Secretary: 'Many of the wealthier families and larger shopkeepers are in a state of considerable excitement – but I cannot see anything to warrant the excessive fears entertained by them.'[153] On 13 May, after nearly 20,000 people turned out to greet the arrival of the Convention, he reported, 'The excitement today has been very much less than anticipated.'[154] His father, Joshua Scholefield, drew similar conclusions from the event and informed Lord John Russell of his view that 'the risk is small indeed of any riotous proceedings whatever occurring here'.[155] The evidence that points to the predominantly peaceful nature of the Bull Ring meetings has already been touched upon. Ultimately the explanation that by early July the meetings had reached such a tumultuous pitch that intervention of some sort became necessary relies almost entirely upon the self-fulfilling argument that force will never be used by public officials unless it is absolutely necessary.

A second, and rather more plausible, explanation is that the ex-BPU middle-class radicals sought a public demonstration of their recent severance from the popular movement. This was far more than a simple disavowal of 'physical force' tactics; it was a rejection of the entire working-class movement and its political aspirations. A radical town council had been elected in December 1838 with extensive popular support, but following the break-up of the BPU that popular base was gone. The town council was only one of a range of administrative bodies in the town in 1839. If, at some point in the future, the council was to absorb the functions of the street commissioners and extend its own powers, its authority had to be at least credible. In this respect the long-established links with the popular movements were an enormous embarrassment. This was particularly so in the case of the Bull Ring meetings, since the BPU had sanctioned these in the earlier agitation for the Reform Bill. The street commissioners made the most of this when Scholefield applied to them at the end of June, to allow the Chartist meetings to take place in the town hall. In the discussion that ensued Francis Lloyd reminded his fellow commissioners:

> Meet the people would and nothing could prevent them. The Political Union had taught them lessons and they were too apt scholars to forget them at any man's command. Let the Commissioners attend to their own duty, and not be dragged

through the dirt to save other people from the consequences of their folly and wickedness.[156]

It was evident that what was needed was a swift and decisive act of control that would vindicate the authority of the council and the dominance of ex-BPU elements within it. William Scholefield favoured the arrest of the Convention leaders whilst they were in Birmingham, a suggestion that he made to the Home Secretary on 13 May.[157] In order for ex-BPU elements to dominate middle-class politics they needed to make just such an overt act of aggression against the organized working-class movement. The army was unsuitable for such a task, since they had been successfully mopping up disturbances in the town for years, irrespective of who dominated local politics. The use of the London police would represent the 'new' men acting in a 'new' way. Besides this, the London police, sworn in as special constables, and acting under direct orders from the magistracy, would demonstrate how a town-council-controlled police force might operate and would make the case powerfully for the establishment of such a force in the area. Scholefield therefore chose the Bull Ring meetings not because he saw them as a real threat to public order but rather the reverse. The considerations in his mind on 4 July were not those of the public official, of public order or Chartist anarchy. Rather his intervention was a means of deciding a political question, that is, whether or not middle-class politics in Birmingham would continue to be dominated by the radical middle class. For Scholefield the Bull Ring meetings were ideal. There had already been a number of successful prosecutions of speakers in June. On the face of it, sixty London policemen would have little difficulty in arresting the speakers at a peaceful meeting. The radical middle class would have acted against their old allies, thus justifying their leadership of middle-class politics. Scholefield's error was not that he misunderstood the nature of crowd control, but rather that, forgetting the lessons of May 1832, he misunderstood the working-class movement.

The third explanation of the incident, and that favoured by the Chartists themselves, was that the introduction of the London police was a simple act of provocation designed to draw Chartist violence into the open. If this is unlikely to provide the full explanation it is worth examining from the Chartist point of view.

The movement had always existed in the expectation of such an attack from the government and the advocacy of defensive violence was a positive and unifying force within early Chartism. The authorization for use of the London police was given by the Home Secretary and thus the Birmingham Town Council was seen to be acting as an arm of corrupt government. There was no sleight of hand involved, therefore, in Edward Brown's claim after the event that 'The government had made an unjustifiable attack on the people.'[158] The size of the force involved must have appeared significant in Chartist eyes. As events were to prove, a party of sixty men was too small to deal with an angry crowd of 1,000, but large enough to provoke them into retaliation. In addition, the Riot Act was not read until after the attack, and thus the crowd had not been presented with the customary opportunity to disperse peacefully.

Because of this analysis of the events, in the Chartist mind, the disturbance of 4 July served to unify the movement in the town of Birmingham and throughout the country. It is therefore rather odd that historians should use the incident as a vehicle for the condemnation of the 'physicals'. J.T. Ward (following Hovell closely) draws attention to 'Lovett's noble self sacrifice and the general cowardice of the verbal militants', along with what he calls 'the brave loyalty of the "moral force" leader, as opposed to the actual timidity of the wordy "physicals"'.[159] This analysis, it must be said, misses the point altogether. Far from emphasizing and extending any polarization of the movement into two tactical camps, 'moral force' and 'physical force', the attack of 4 July demonstrated how close these two groups were at this point. Lovett and Collins, who had both advised local Chartists to meet elsewhere to avoid conflict with the authorities, both now vociferously defended the right of the people to meet in the Bull Ring. Taylor and McDouall, two 'physicals', convinced that the attack was an 'Oliver'-style act of provocation, counselled the kind of calmness which Lovett had preached for some time. Both groups agreed that the state had made an unconstitutional attack upon the people, and that they, in their turn, had every right to defend themselves.

In assessing long-term strategies for achieving the franchise the 'physical–moral' force dichotomy may be of some use. In evaluating a series of events such as the Bull Ring disturbances, particularly that of 4 July, it could impede a full understanding. The examination of trade society activity presented in Chapter 2 of this study emphasized the important, and universally accepted, role of collective violence within the working community. Such violence, particularly where it was defensive, was clearly compatible with artisan concepts of what constituted respectable behaviour. The twenty-seven local men prosecuted for their part in the disturbances were in the main neither 'criminal types' nor high-spirited youths. The majority were young men of some education (see Table 5.2). Eleazer Hughes, for example, a journeyman button-maker with Hammond, Turner, and Sons, was sentenced to 18 months' hard labour for attacking the police with a cutlass on 4 July.[160] Like John Collins he was an active member of Lady Huntingdon's Chapel.[161] Frederick Mason, a journeyman gun-maker found with stones about his person on 4 July and sentenced to six months in prison, was given an excellent character reference by his employer Charles Swinburne. William Eades, slipper-maker, who was similarly charged and received an 18 months' sentence, was steward of a local sick benefit club.[162]

The question of the involvement of young boys in the riot of 15 July should not be allowed to cloud the issue of involvement of the wider community. It is often difficult to differentiate within the statements of witnesses, between a subjective judgement on behaviour and an objective assessment of age. What, for example, does one make of Inspector May's claim that the individuals involved on the night of 6 July were mostly 'grown up boys'?[163] There is much in the attack on Bourne's and Leggett's shops on the night of 15 July that is reminiscent of the kind of rough justice meted out through folk violence by the working community over a variety of matters. The bonfire of the contents was a clear statement that the object was something other than straight plunder. The motivation for attacking these two shops is unclear, but there are clues. First, stones had been thrown at the crowd during Bull Ring meetings towards the end of June from the rooftops in the general area of the two shops. Second, it was strongly rumoured that Bourne had made a large financial contribution toward the introduction of the London police.[164] Third, Bourne clearly expected trouble. On the evening of 15 July, when neither the military nor the special constables were on the alert, when the magistrates left the Public Office and Colonel Chatterton dined at

Table 5.2 Local individuals committed in connection with the Bull Ring disturbances, July 1839[165]

Name	*Age*	*Level of education**	*Occupation (where this can be determined)*	*Nature of charge*	*Findings of court*
Thomas King	18	IMP		Riotous assembly on 4 July	Discharged
John Neale	30	IMP	Shoemaker	Riotous assembly on 4 July	18 months' hard labour
John Drinkworth	21	IMP		Riotous assembly on 4 July	12 months' hard labour
James Rhodes	18	N		Riotous assembly on 4 July	9 months' hard labour
William Eades	21	IMP	Slipper-maker	Riotous assembly on 4 July	18 months' hard labour
John Storey	21	IMP		Riotous assembly on 4 July	6 months' hard labour
Thomas Salter	25	IMP	Brass-worker	Riotous assembly on 4 July	6 months' hard labour
John Smith	21	IMP		Riotous assembly on 4 July	Discharged
William Clift	21	N		Riotous assembly on 4 July	Discharged
Frederick Mason	21	IMP	Gun-maker	Riotous assembly on 4 July	6 months's hard labour
William Shears	23	N		Assault on police on 4 July	18 months' hard labour
Eleazer Hughes	22	IMP	Button-maker	Assault on police on 4 July	18 months' hard labour
George Best	21	IMP		Riotous assembly on 5 July	Acquitted
James Pomeroy	19	IMP	Gun-maker	Riotous assembly on 5 July	18 months' hard labour
George Baker	50	WELL		Riotous assembly on 5 July	Acquitted
John Tatlow	30	IMP		Riotous assembly on 5 July	1 month's hard labour
William James	20	IMP		Riotous assembly on 5 July	Acquitted
John Collins	36	WELL	Tool-maker and fitter	Seditious libel on 5 July	1 year in goal
Thomas Cooper	19	IMP		Riotous assembly on 8 July	Acquitted
John Gavin	12	N		Theft	Acquitted
Thomas Aston	15	N		Theft, and demolishing a house	Death recorded – transported 10 years

Table 5.2 contd.

Name	*Age*	*Level of education**	*Occupation (where this can be determined)*	*Nature of charge*	*Findings of court*
Francis Roberts	26	IMP		(i) Riotous assembly on 15 July (ii) Demolishing a house	Death. Later commuted to transportation for life
John Jones	21	IMP			
Jeremiah Howell	34	N			
John Bird	24	N		Riotous assembly on 15 July	Acquitted
Henry Wilkes	21	IMP		Riotous assembly on 15 July	Discharged
John Ingram	14	IMP		Riotous assembly on 15 July	Acquitted

*Levels of education are given as they appear on the calendar of Warwickshire Summer Assizes: 'N' signifies that the prisoner could neither read nor write; 'IMP' that he could read or read and write imperfectly; 'WELL' that he could read and write well; 'SUP' that he had a superior education.
Note: As members of the Convention, rather than local men, Lovett and Taylor have been omitted from the list.

home, Bourne took the precaution of guarding his premises with sixteen to eighteen young men.[166]

If the effect of the disturbance of 4 July was to unite the movement, that of 15 July returned the initiative to the authorities. The destruction of property was a capital offence, and Jeremiah Howell, Francis Roberts, and John Jones were sentenced to death for their part in the proceedings. The establishment press now found it easy to portray Chartists as levellers. The universal condemnation of the London police turned into a similar condemnation of the Chartists. The effect was partially achieved through an enormous exaggeration of the extent of the destruction. Even Dr Taylor, a sympathetic observer, writing to the Secretary of the Convention from Birmingham the day after the riot, claimed that 'seven or eight houses were . . . set fire to and gutted'.[167] The Duke of Wellington informed parliament that 'he had never known a town taken by storm, so treated as the accounts from Birmingham stated that town had been treated'.[168] Lady Charlotte Guest, who deplored the decision to commute the death sentence on Howell, Roberts, and Jones to transportation for life, registered enormous surprise when she subsequently visited the scene of destruction: 'We walked to the Bull Ring to see the damage done there in the late riot by the Chartists. Two very small houses, the whole frontage of which would not occupy, I should think, as much as forty feet were all that was burnt.'[169]

The 15 July disturbance, therefore, raised some serious tactical questions for the Chartists, for whom public opinion was a significant factor to be considered. It was clearly one thing to justify violence within the movement by reference to a shared perspective, and another to take account of the way the outside world would read those same events. The issues on 4 July were clear-cut, and if 15 July was seen as part of a continuum of events then it was explicable in the same terms. But the destruction of property on 15 July, when the roles of attacker and attacked were apparently reversed from those of 4 July, meant that the latter riot was always likely to be quoted out of context.

AFTER THE BULL RING

The events of July 1839, followed by the trial and imprisonment of many of the local leaders, clearly formed only one small part of a wider attack on the movement. The rejection of the Charter, the break-up of the Convention, and the abortive uprising in November at Newport, all posed fundamental problems of strategy which had not been fully confronted previously. Godfrey calculates that nearly 500 people served prison terms between 1839 and 1841 for offences related to Chartist activity.[170] In Birmingham the local council continued to demonstrate that liberal-democracy involved a close control of labour and its wider cultural context. A local Police Act in August 1839 established a force of 340 men.[171] That its primary concern was to extend its authority into working-class areas is perhaps demonstrated by the fact that during 1840 (it first full year of operation) a total of 190 individuals were arrested for assaults on policemen. Political meetings, both public and private, were infiltrated, with Police Commissioner Burgess even employing spies to report on his spies. In 1843 the new mayor was James James, the screw manufacturer whose rationalization of work within his 'model' factory had so impressed Grainger the year before. He assured the Home Secretary that all meetings were being 'closely watched'.[172]

Despite this the Chartist organizational framework was extended and consolidated in this period. By the end of 1841 there were seven branches of the National Chartist Association operational in the town.[173] Seventy thousand people turned out to greet John Collins on his release from Warwick gaol in 1840 and a similar number were present when O'Connor appeared the following year.[174] There were 43,000 Birmingham signatures on the 1842 Chartist petition.[175] A wide range of political activity was evident in this period, from the groups who drilled after dark in November 1839 to the congregation of Arthur O'Neill's Jerusalem Chapel, opened in December 1840.[176] Epstein's work on Nottingham draws attention to the ways in which Chartist activity, at grass-roots level, reflected and expressed the nature of working-class culture.[177] A similar point might be made about branch life in Birmingham. Town missionary Jackson found Chartist affiliation to follow localized community structure: 'Most of the people hereabouts . . . are "Christian Chartists"', he noted of Floodgate Street, 'and generally flock after Arthur O'Neill.'[178] After 1839, middle-class attempts to draw in local workers as foot-soldiers in any radical initiative were likely to be met by a community-rooted, politically articulate response. Within this industrial organization clearly underpinned the political, as William Smith Lindon's speech at an Anti-Corn-Law meeting in 1842 demonstrated. Lindon was a member of the National Chartist Association and worked in a fender-making manufactory:

> He said that he had been delegated by his shopmates to attend that meeting and he thought that he should not be doing his duty if he neglected to state their views of the subject. They admitted that the Corn Laws were unjust but they also knew that the imports on tea, coffee and other articles of consumption were equally unjust. . . . They were of opinion that the democratic axe must be laid to the root of the tree of monopoly before any good results could accrue to the sons of industry, for if the people had the power of voting they would soon get rid of the Corn Laws and other bad laws.[179]

The debate over new initiatives revolved around the issue of authority within, and through, democratic structures. John Collins took heart from the failure of the Leeds Reform Association, having been delegated to attend its inaugural meeting: 'he felt that what he there witnessed proved that the day was gone by when any middle class man could again dictate what was to be done'.[180] The Complete Suffrage Union (CSU) of Joseph Sturge and Edward Miall was conceived within the context of authority, leadership, and levels of working-class participation. As Miall put it in 1841, 'If they (the CSU) do not teach them to wrestle for rights by peaceful means, those who have not the gospel of peace in their hands will lay hold on them and war or violence instead of peaceful firmness will be resorted to.'[181] John Mason, the trade unionist, warned his fellow-Chartists that the agenda for the CSU conferences had been set by the experiences of the previous years: 'if there were to be a union between the middle and working classes he hoped the working men would take care to have their share of representation'.[182]

In fact the Chartists met the CSU with a united front at its second national conference in Birmingham in December 1842. The determination of the Chartists to stand by the Charter, 'name and all', however, is often presented as an almost sentimental approach born of the movement's martyred past. Hovell's history, for example, suggests that it was a 'point of honour' to retain the name at the December 1842 conference. Echoing Hovell, J.T. Ward adds, 'To Chartists there was something sacred in the old cause and the old styles; and there was a blasphemy, a sacrilege in the proposed change.'[183] Our earlier examination of the break-up of the BPU would suggest that it was something much more than this. In fact, the CSU raised all the old problems of authority and democratic form which made the BPU so unacceptable to its working-class adherents in its second phase of life. The 'People's Charter' was not simply six political demands. It also represented a vision of an active and participatory form of democracy, of the sort working people were familiar with in their own institutions, which would involve the working class at all levels of political life. This was vital for the realization of the social programme which lay behind the Charter. The social philosophy of the BPU, enshrined in its structure and its political aspirations, enabled it to offer only the virtual representation of working-class interests by men of wealth to a movement which claimed the inclusion of that class on the basis of equality. Since the 'People's Charter' was not only a political programme, but also an approach within a programme, its acceptance became the acid-test of any middle-class initiative.

By May 1843 the *Birmingham Journal*, by now hardly a supporter of Chartism, reported the CSU to be gaining few converts: 'The Chartists – that is those who stand out for "the name and all" – are a numerous body and a powerful one; . . . They have a strong hold on the people. The popular sympathies are strong in their favour.'[184]

Despite this, Thomas Attwood stepped forward again, in what was for him a last attempt to unite the 'productive classes'. In August 1843 he floated the idea of a National Union or General Confederation of All Classes, which aimed to present a united front to the government, and draw its attention to prevalent distress.[185] Having failed in previous attempts to combine unity with practical policies he now planned an organization without policies: 'the movement which I have in view has no reference whatsoever to any reform of Parliament, nor the currency, or the Corn Laws, nor to any other subject which has yet been brought before the public mind'.[186] John Follows, of the National Chartist Association, was deputed as a spokesman by a public meeting to discuss the nature of the new union with Attwood. The point made at the December 1842 CSU meeting, was re-stated, Follows explaining:

> that if it is your design again to stand forth as an advocate of those great and inviolable principles of political justice embodied in the People's Charter, with a clear recognition of that *Sacred Document* as the only basis of just and legitimate government we shall hail your return to public life with enthusiasm. . . . But if you have excluded that measure from your plans, you have excluded us.[187]

Attwood's response, that 'if I interfered at all in any public movement it would be my duty to teach and guide and not to be taught and guided',[188] can have done little to allay working-class fears that the union would be run by an exclusively middle-class leadership.

All this is not to deny the very real differences of approach, style, and strategy that existed, in the early 1840s, between the various sectors of the Chartist movement in Birmingham. But among local Chartists there was a common awareness, drawn from the bitter experience of early Chartism, that working-class interests would not be served by an alliance established on middle-class terms. Take, for example, John Collins. As a Birmingham delegate to the conference of the Leeds Reform Association in 1841 and the CSU in 1842, a pastor of the Christian Chartist church and co-author of the founding text for Lovett's 'new move', he probably had a finger in more 'moderate' pies than did anyone else. Yet, as he emphasized in March 1841, his view was implacably that 'If ever the middle classes united with them again it must be upon the principle of equality.' That the point had to be reiterated by Chartists again and again during the early 1840s bears testimony to the myopic nature of those middle-class radicals who attempted to harness the energies of Chartism. The failure of such initiatives suggests that the point was at least clear to the working community.

Conclusion

It has been argued in this study that historians have, in the past, been rather too preoccupied with centres of small-scale production as survivals or extensions of early industrial forms of economic organization. A concentration upon the elements of continuity represented by the prevalence of small workshops in towns such as Birmingham as late as 1850 has distracted attention from the profound changes that the economies of these towns underwent, particularly in the 1830s and 1840s. Here intensified competition increasingly placed a greater economic emphasis upon capital's dominance of credit and market facilities within production. This involved a fundamental reorganization of work through which production at all levels was affected. Accelerated industrialization did not signal the end of the small workshop but it did alter both its nature and its function.

By 1850 the small producer was far from being the small master who had figured so prominently in artisan aspirations for generations. He had been replaced, in the main, by the small manufacturer, himself a mirror-image of his large-scale counterpart. Servicing the needs of the larger concerns, the smaller firms adopted the same modes of reorganization and discipline in order to come to terms with similar, if often more pressing, problems of market viability. Judged purely upon economic criteria, such as personal wealth or the size of the concern, the small manufacturer may well have been closer to the traditional artisan–small master than to the factory-owner. In terms of consciousness, however, the reorganization of production drew a firmer line between the employer of labour and the workforce than had existed previously. The small manufacturer could only survive in an economic universe characterized by the rarefied atmosphere of intense competition by rejecting the values of the working community. By the 1830s the conflict over work control was being fought at all levels of industry, in workshop and factory alike. Whereas we may expect to find small producers active within the plebeian radicalism of the immediate post-war period we should not be surprised to find them less evident in the overtly working-class Chartist movement. Even though they had formed part of the audience which Paine addressed, by the 1840s, following the extensions of municipal reform, the politics of the small producer were more concerned with economism in local administration than with the debate over political rights.

The argument that Birmingham was the scene of class confrontation in these years hinges, to a great extent, on a demonstration that the workforce recognized the nature of change as a process with implications that went beyond the particular workplace in which they may have encountered it. The case must be made strongly for a consideration of trade-based organization, in the 1830s and 1840s particularly, as representing class consciousness rather than the fragmentary sectionalism that it is all too often held to be. What is of importance is less the question of whether or not trade unions, as distinct entities, supported this or that political movement, or even the fact that the period saw real attempts to establish general unions (although we would not wish to deny these factors their importance as manifestations of class awareness). More significant is the way in which the trade-based organizations which underwent growth, demise, and rebirth many times in this period clearly embraced a set of values and beliefs that was endorsed by the wider working community as a whole.

In the contest over authority at the point of production we may see the clash of different definitions of politics, morality, and social order. Defending the labour process in a period of intense economic change involved realignment within the working community and the construction of both formal and informal modes of organization. The six points may have been drawn from an older social framework but the experience of work gave them a new class-specific relevance in the 1830s and 1840s. Similarly, the agitation for bourgeois democracy in the image of industrial capital, endorsed, and later enhanced, the employer's claim to control production by right. Before this analysis is condemned as a piece of Marxist determinism it is as well to bear in mind that in the liberal interpretation, which continues to dominate historical analysis, the worlds of work and politics have *always* been seen as interlocked in a causal relationship. The liberal interpretation assumes that a consensus society grew from the recognized common benefits of a high-wage–high-profit economy; workplace conflict is an aberration, and 'human progress' can be crudely equated with increased production. The Birmingham case, however, reminds us that this interpretation mistakes reality for what was only one view of social relations at the time. Nineteenth-century estimates of social consensus were invariably exercises in wish-fulfilment on the part of those who were forcing the pace of change. They were linked to radical political demands because capitalism required a new political context in which to achieve full development.

Thus we must relate radical political ideals, both middle-class and working-class, to the experience of the workplace in order to understand the view of the world that lay behind them. If capitalism required a congruent system of morality as an underpinning, so too did opposition to the changes that were taking place. Where the liberal ethic claimed to offer freedom of choice to 'free agents' in the marketplace, the morality of work stressed the obligations of the individual to the group. It was for this reason that outsiders to the working community condemned workplace organizations as 'democratic'. They feared not only the demands that were being made but also the structure of assumptions which lay behind them. Chartism embraced the same concept of democratic form, with the political process being at once participatory and continuous.

It has always been difficult to view Chartism in this way because it failed. Its failure has been equated with a weakness of organization and ideology. On the other hand, the twentieth-century acceptance of five of the six points has been seen as a demonstration that peaceful evolution and consensus can deliver the goods where conflict and opposition only hold back significant change. There is today, for example, no lobby for the achievement of the one outstanding point of the Charter, annual parliaments. The measure is inconceivable in a modern democracy to the extent that it is perhaps difficult to see how it might ever have been rationally defended. Yet the Chartists were not children of a liberal democracy and they saw politics differently, as both inclusive and active. Thomas Winters explained the electoral structure of the Leicester glovers' union in 1845:

> They are constituted as one general body in Leicester and they meet on the first Monday of the month to elect a committee. That committee consists of five. Three of them go out one month and two the other. There is also a secretary who is elected every month. We have likewise two auditors, one of whom goes out one month and one the other so that they serve two months then we have a fresh one.[1]

Considered in the context of this monthly turnover of public officials the idea of annual elections appears quite restrained. To understand Chartism we must enter a world where the represented surrendered none of their authority to the representative.

By 1850, however, the failure of the workforce to constrain the labour process within their own image was also reflected in political defeat. The ruling class had, in both the local and the national spheres, annexed politics and defined democracy in terms relevant to themselves. Municipal and national politics, for all their trenchant in-fighting, took place around a series of commonly held assumptions. Citizenship was validated by property ownership and morality defined accordingly. This is not to say that alternative visions of the world died at the mid-century. Mid-Victorian workers were far less compliant than many historians would have us believe. After Chartism, however, it was always easier to define opposition to dominant values as the aberration of deviant groups in the workplace or in the street.

Notes

INTRODUCTION

1. J. H. Clapham, *An Economic History of Great Britain*, vol. II, *Free Trade and Steel 1850–1886* (Cambridge 1963), 22–46. This volume first appeared in 1932. For timely reminders of the point referred to see R. Samuel, 'The workshop of the world: steam power and hand technology in mid-Victorian Britain', *History Workshop*, 3 (Spring 1977); A. E. Musson, *The Growth of British Industry* (London 1978), 139–42; R. Gray, *The Aristocracy of Labour in Nineteenth Century Britain c1850–1914* (London 1981), 20–1.
2. On the continuing and changing role of the small unit within an industrial economy see G. Crossick, 'La petite bourgeoisie britannique au xix siècle', *Mouvement Social*, 108 (juillet–septembre, 1976). See also D. Ward, 'Victorian cities: how modern?', *Journal of Historical Geography*, 1:2 (1975), 141–3, where the author stresses that the persistence of workshop quarters in many Victorian cities in the second half of the century is perfectly consistent with the concept of accelerating industrialization.
3. See particularly A. Soboul, *The Parisian Sans-Culottes and the French Revolution 1793–4* (Oxford 1964); T. S. Hamerow, *Restoration, Revolution, Reaction, Economics and Politics in Germany, 1815–1871* (Princeton, NJ 1958); P. H. Noyes, *Organisation and Revolution: Working Class Associations in the German Revolutions of 1848–1849* (Princeton, NJ 1966). Noyes notes that 'Artisans, and not industrial workers, were the major source of mass revolutionary unrest in mid-nineteenth century Europe'; ibid., 3. Among many recent distinguished studies reiterating this point particular mention should be made of R. Bezucha, *The Lyon Uprising of 1834: Social and Political Conflict in the Early July Monarchy* (Cambridge, Mass. 1974); B. H. Moss, *The Origins of the French Labour Movement 1830–1914: The Socialism of Skilled Workers* (Berkeley, Cal. 1976); C. H. Johnson, *Utopian Communism in France: Cabet and the Icarians, 1839–1851* (New York 1974). Johnson suggests: 'Few historians today would contest

the thesis that conscious militance in the early industrial revolution was to be found largely among artisans'; ibid., 159.

4. E. P. Thompson, *The Making of the English Working Class* (London 1963; all references to 1968 edn); I. J. Prothero, *Artisans and Politics in Early Nineteenth Century London: John Gast and His Times* (London 1979). Prothero notes: 'Nineteenth century European artisans are now at last receiving proper attention and this study is intended as a contribution to the process'; ibid., 3; J. Rule, 'The property of skill in the period of manufacture', in P. Joyce (ed.), *The Historical Meanings of Work* (Cambridge 1987).
5. The available literature of these and other areas is usefully drawn together and assessed in D. Geary, *European Labour Protest 1848–1939* (London 1981).
6. W. H. Oliver comments, on the involvement of the London trades in the GNCTU, 'London and the other towns in which the Consolidated acquired a following of any consequence were characterised by small scale industry . . . the greater number of workers associated with the union were craft workers. . . . Compared with textile workers, particularly cotton textile workers, they were pre-Industrial Revolution', 'The Consolidated Trades' Union of 1834', *Economic History Review*, 2nd ser., XVII:1 (1964). For an analysis of the tailors' involvement in the GNCTU, which related directly to the experience of industrial change, see T. N. Parssinen and I. J. Prothero, 'The London tailors' strike of 1834 and the collapse of the GNCTU: a police spy's report', *International Review of Social History*, XXVII (1977); Bythell argues the non-politicization of handloom weavers as a rebuttal of Thompson, op. cit., 297–346; D. Bythell, *The Handloom Weavers* (Cambridge 1969). Foster uses the Northampton workforce as a counterpoint to Oldham's revolutionary working class. Differences of consciousness are, he suggests, related, among other factors, to differences in economic structure – Northampton retaining a workshop system; J. Foster, *Class Struggle and the Industrial Revolution: Early Industrial Capitalism in Three English Towns* (London 1977). This has brought a strong defence of the class consciousness of the Northampton shoemakers in this period in M. J. Haynes, 'Class and class conflict in the early nineteenth century: Northampton shoemakers and the GNCTU', *Literature and History*, V (Spring 1977). Ironically the case has been made that the Oldham workforce could not have been as class conscious as Foster suggests since the average size of the unit of production in that town was actually smaller than he thought; D. S. Gadian, 'Class consciousness in Oldham and other north-west industrial towns 1830–1850', *Historical Journal*, XII:1 (1970), 42. For a defence of Foster which highlights the importance of smaller firms and workshops in the development of political movements, see R. A. Sykes, 'Some aspects of working class consciousness in Oldham, 1830–1842', *Historical Journal*, XXIII:1 (1980), 169–71. Pollard argues that a degree of class cohesion was possible in the cutlery trades of Sheffield; S. Pollard, *A History of Labour in Sheffield* (Liverpool 1959), 41–2.

The point is extended to cover working-class absorption of middle-class values in C. Reid, 'Middle-class values and working-class culture in nineteenth century Sheffield – the pursuit of respectability', in S. Pollard and C. Holmes (eds), *Essays in the Economic and Social History of South Yorkshire* (Sheffield 1976). A fierce case for a class-conscious workforce in the region is however made in J. Baxter, 'The origins of the social war in South Yorkshire: a study of capitalist evolution and labour class realization in one industrial region c1750–1855' (unpub. Ph.D. thesis, Sheffield University 1976). For a view of social cohesion in the Birmingham trades derived from the workshop structure see the work of Briggs, Tholfsen, and Fox as discussed on p. 13.

7. Among others, Thompson, op. cit., 259–97, 781–887; E. J. Hobsbawn, *Labouring Men* (London 1964), 147; R. Harrison, *Before the Socialists* (London 1956), 25; Foster, op. cit., 8–46.
8. Contrast, for example, Thompson, op. cit., 546, with the view expressed in M. Thomis, *The Luddites* (Newton Abbot 1970), 23. Thompson's position is reinforced by J. Dinwiddy, 'Luddism and politics in the Northern counties', *Social History*, 4:1 (Jan 1979).
9. A. E. Musson, *British Trade Unions 1800–1875* (London 1972), 19, 52; 'Class struggle and the labour aristocracy 1830–1860', *Social History*, 3 (Oct 1976), 336–7.
10. Musson 'Class struggle', 337.
11. Musson, *British Trade Unions*, 37–8, 52; M. I. Thomis, *The Town Labourer and the Industrial Revolution* (London 1974), 146.
12. Musson, 'Class struggle', 356. The reluctance of employers to use the Combinations Acts in the face of open wage bargaining is sometimes seen to give substance to this view.
13. I. Prothero, 'London Chartism and the trades', *Economic History Review*, 2nd ser., XXIV (May 1971); Musson, *British Trade Unions*, 47. Musson's view is broadly supported by D. J. Rowe, 'The failure of London Chartism', *Historical Journal*, XI (1968). For further work which relates structural changes in London trades to political protest see D. Goodway, *London Chartism 1838–1848* (Cambridge 1982).
14. S. and B. Webb, *The History of Trade Unionism* (London 1920), 46.
15. This approach to the role of custom and tradition in establishing continuities between the eighteenth- and nineteenth-century workplace is well demonstrated by J. Rule, *The Experience of Labour in Eighteenth Century Industry*, London (1981) 194–216. See also my review, in *Social History*, 8:1 (Jan 1983).
16. W. H. Sewell, Jr, *Work and Revolution in France: The Language of Labor from the Old Regime to 1848* (Cambridge 1980). Sewell draws attention to the shift in emphasis, within ostensibly similar forms, between the 1790s and the 1840s: 'It soon became clear that the corporate content of the workers' ideology in 1848 had not been delivered intact from the old regime but had been reshaped by the vast historical change in the intervening years'; ibid., 4. A similar point is raised in W. M. Reddy, 'The textile trade and the language of

the crowd at Rouen 1752–1871', *Past and Present*, 74 (Feb 1977).

17. See, for example, the case for 'traditional' restrictions in framework knitting, G. Henson, *History of the Framework Knitters* (Newton Abbot 1970; first published 1831); see particularly 231–4.
18. H. J. Habakkuk, *American and British Technology in the Nineteenth Century* (Cambridge 1962); D. S. Landes, *The Unbound Prometheus* (Cambridge 1972), 74; G. N. Von Tunzelman, *Steam Power and British Industrialisation to 1860* (Oxford 1978), 212; R. C. O. Matthews, *A Study in Trade Cycle History: Economic Fluctuations in Great Britain 1833–42* (Cambridge 1954), 129–36; A. D. Gayer, W. W. Rostow, and A. J. Schwartz, *The Growth and Fluctuation of the British Economy 1780–1850* (Oxford 1953), 173, 211–41, 622; P. Hudson, 'Proto-industrialisation: the case of the West Riding', *History Workshop*, 12 (Autumn 1981), 49.
19. M. Berg, *The Machinery Question and the Making of Political Economy 1815–1848* (Cambridge 1980), 144.
20. This point is dealt with in more depth on p. 108.
21. R. Price's *Masters, Unions and Men: Work Control in Building and the Rise of Labour 1830–1914* (Cambridge 1980), on the building trade is the most thorough analysis of attempts at 'autonomous regulation'. See also Prothero, *Artisans and Politics*, 329. In the French context the question of work control is taken up in M. P. Hanagan, *The Logic of Solidarity: Artisans and Industrial Workers in Three French Towns 1871–1914* (Chicago 1980).
22. S. Pollard, 'The ethics of the Sheffield Outrages', *Transactions of the Hunter Archaeological Society*, VII:3 (1954), 121. G. Crossick, *An Artisan Elite in Victorian Society: Kentish London 1840–1880* (London 1978), 114–19.
23. 'Report on combinations by Nassau Senior Esq. and Thomas Tomlinson Esq. presented to the Rt. Hon. Lord Viscount Melbourne Secretary of State for the Home Department on 21 August 1832', HO 44/56.
24. *Pioneer*, 7 Sept 1833.
25. F. Bechhofer and B. Elliott, 'Persistence and change: the petite bourgeoisie in industrial society', *Archives Européennes de Sociologie*, XVII (1976), 78; Crossick, 'La petite bourgeoisie britannique', 37–51; R.Q. Gray, 'Religion, culture and social class in late nineteenth and early twentieth century Edinburgh', in G. Crossick (ed.), *The Lower Middle Class in Britain 1870–1914* (London 1977), 149–51.
26. Geary, op. cit., 38; the author notes a similar division in Germany emerging at the same time.
27. This ambiguity has been noted many times in the past, see for example Thompson, op. cit., 819; R. Q. Gray, *The Labour Aristocracy in Victorian Edinburgh* (Oxford 1976), 110–11, 131–75; R. S. Neale, *Class and Ideology in the Nineteenth Century* (London 1972); Crossick, *Artisan Elite*, 47–53, 114, 134; 'La petite bourgeoisie britannique', 28–9, 33–4, 41, 54; I. J. Prothero, *Artisans and Politics in Early Nineteenth Century London: John Gast and His Times* (London 1979), 5.

28. S. Volkov, *The Rise of Popular Anti-modernism in Germany: The Urban Master Artisans 1873–1896* (Princeton, NJ 1978). This work notes the growing division between journeymen and small producers as industrialization progressed in Germany. She uses the British example as a counterpoint, noting that among historians of nineteenth century Britain 'It is almost impossible to find any statement in which the two are distinguished or in which their mingling appears to require an explanation'; ibid., 99.
29. D. Blackbourn, 'Between resignation and volatility, the German petite bourgeoisie in the nineteenth century', in G. Crossick and H. G. Haupt (eds), *Shopkeepers and Master Artisans in Nineteenth Century Europe* (London 1984).
30. H. G. Haupt, 'The petite bourgeoisie in France 1850–1914: in search of the *juste milieu*?', in Crossick and Haupt, op. cit., 103–4.
31. J. Vincent, *Pollbooks: How Victorians Voted* (Cambridge 1968), 6. For an example of this approach using census material see W. A. Armstrong, *Stability and Change in an English County Town: A Study of York 1801–51* (Cambridge 1971).
32. This point is argued in C. Behagg, 'Controlling the product: work, time and the early industrial workforce in Britain 1800–1850', in G. Cross (ed.), *Worktime and Industrialisation* (Philadelphia, Temple University Press 1989).
33. *British Parliamentary Papers, Report from the Committee Appointed to Enquire into the State of the Copper Mines and Copper Trade of this Kingdom* (x), 1799, 663.
34. J. Lord, *Capital and Steam Power 1750–1800* (London 1966); E. Robinson, 'Boulton and Fothergill, 1762–1782, and the Birmingham export of hardware', *University of Birmingham Historical Journal*, VII:1 (1959).
35. S. Timmins (ed.), *The Resources, Products and Industrial History of Birmingham and the Midland Hardware District* (London 1866; reprinted 1967), 223.
36. C. Erickson, *British Industrialists: Steel and Hosiery 1850–1950* (Cambridge 1959), 177–87; S. D. Chapman, *The Early Factory Masters* (Newton Abbot 1967); F. J. Kaijage, 'Labouring Barnsley 1816–1856' (unpub. Ph.D. thesis, Warwick University 1975), 150–1; Foster, op. cit., 7–22.
37. V. A. C. Gatrell, 'Labour, power and the size of firms in Lancashire cotton in the second quarter of the nineteenth century', *Economic History Review*, 2nd ser., XXX:1 (1977), 124.
38. See, for example, H. G. Gutman, 'The reality of the rags to riches "myth": the case of Paterson, New Jersey, locomotive, iron and machinery manufacturers 1830–1880', in S. Thermstrom and R. Sennett (eds), *Nineteenth Century Cities: Essays in the New Urban History* (London 1969).
39. Crossick, *Artisan Elite*, 47, 53, 114, 119.
40. Quoted in N. McCord, 'Some difficulties of Parliamentary reform', *Historical Journal*, X:4 (1967), 378.

41. *Birmingham Journal*, 10 July 1841.
42. C. Flick, 'Muntz metal and ships' bottoms: the industrial career of G. F. Muntz', *Transactions of the Birmingham and Warwickshire Archaeological Society*, LXXXVII (1975).
43. G. C. Allen, *The Industrial Development of Birmingham and the Black Country* (London 1929), 170.
44. See, for example, A. W. Coats (ed.), *The Classical Economists and Economic Policy* (Bungay 1971), 3–17, 144–79.
45. The 'new paternalism' involved the development of a more finely formalized structure of relationships within the workplace, with a very specific hierarchy of authority defined within 'consensus' interests; see particularly, P. Joyce, *Work, Society and Politics: The Culture of the Factory in Later Victorian England* (Brighton 1980), 134–200.
46. A. Briggs, 'Thomas Attwood and the economic background of the Birmingham Political Union', *Cambridge Historical Journal*, IX:2 (1948); 'The background of the parliamentary reform movement in three English cities (1830–2)', *Cambridge Historical Journal*, X:3 (1952); 'The social structure of Birmingham and Lyons', *British Journal of Sociology*, I (1950); *Victorian Cities* (Harmondsworth 1968), 184–8. For the closeness of Briggs and Allen on this point compare for example, Allen, op. cit., 119, with Briggs, *Victorian Cities*, 186.
47. T. R. Tholfsen, 'The Chartist crisis in Birmingham', *International Review of Social History*, III (1958); 'The artisan and the culture of early Victorian Birmingham', *University of Birmingham Historical Journal*, IV (1953–4); A. Briggs, *Chartist Studies* (London 1959), 7, 17–28.
48. T. R. Tholfsen, 'Origins of the Birmingham caucus', *Historical Journal*, II:2 (1959). The idea of continuity between the character of earlier movements for reform and Chamberlain's Birmingham is also drawn in D. Judd, *Radical Joe* (London 1977), 23–34.
49. J. Money, *Experience and Identity: Birmingham and the West Midlands 1760–1800* (Manchester 1977), 279–82.
50. A. Fox, 'Industrial relations in Birmingham and the Black Country 1860–1914' (unpub. D.Phil. thesis, Oxford University 1954); 'Industrial relations in nineteenth century Birmingham', *Oxford Economic Papers*, new ser., VII (1955). For a similar view of unions in the town see also E. P. Duggan, 'The impact of industrialisation on an urban labour market: Birmingham 1770–1860' (unpub. Ph.D. thesis, Wisconsin University 1972), 163–71.
51. Pollard, *Labour in Sheffield*, 41–2; Reid, op. cit., 279; D. J. Rowe, 'Class and political radicalism in London, 1831–2', *Historical Journal*, XII:1 (1970), 42; Gadian, op. cit., 162, 171–2.
52. Rowe, 'Class and political radicalism', 42, 32.
53. Gadian, op. cit., 171–2.
54. R. B. Rose, 'The origins of working class radicalism in Birmingham', *Labour History*, IX (Nov 1965).
55. M. Frost, 'The development of provided schooling for working class

children in Birmingham 1781–1851' (unpub. M.Litt. thesis, Birmingham University 1978), 125–9, 362–78.

56. A. Hooper, 'Mid-Victorian radicalism: community and class in Birmingham 1850–1880' (unpub. Ph.D. thesis, London University 1978); W. M. Bramwell, *Pubs and Localised Communities in Mid-Victorian Birmingham*, Occasional Paper no. 22, Department of Geography and Earth Science, Queen Mary College (London 1984).
57. D. A. Reid, 'Labour, leisure and politics in Birmingham c1800–1875' (unpub. Ph.D. thesis, University of Birmingham 1985).
58. Bramwell, op. cit., 5.
59. For example, Rowe notes: 'The alternatives were not only middle class ideology . . . or Chartism and Republicanism. There were many stages in between as the London Radical Club and the Complete Suffrage Movement show'; Rowe, 'Class and political radicalism', 32.
60. D. J. Rowe, 'The London Working Men's Association and the "People's Charter"', *Past and Present*, 36 (Apr 1967), 74. Here Rowe contends that Chartism 'may be seen as originating less from any new working class consciousness than from a radical middle class element'; ibid., 74.
61. Thomis combines these points in his analysis of Chartism: 'The failure of Chartism exemplified all the weaknesses of the working class as a political force, a basic lack of interest in politics, fragmentation, and a pre-occupation with sectional economic interests'; M. I. Thomis, *The Town Labourer and the Industrial Revolution* (London 1974), 191.
62. A point most recently raised in G. Stedman-Jones, 'The language of Chartism', in J. Epstein and D. Thompson (eds), *The Chartist Experience* (London 1982). The issues highlighted by this important essay are discussed more fully in Chapter 3.

1 INDUSTRIALIZATION AND THE TRANSFORMATION OF THE SMALL PRODUCER

1. *BPP, Children's Employment Commission, Second Report of the Commissioners (Trades and Manufactures)*, pt 1, Reports and Evidence from Sub-Commissioners, 1843 (431), xiv. For a fuller analysis of the inadequacies of this report as a comprehensive overview see p. 41.
2. G. C. Allen, *Industrial Development of Birmingham and the Black Country* (London 1929), 32, 113–15, 125, 151, 170.
3. J. R. Immer, 'The development of production methods in Birmingham, 1760–1851' (unpub. B.Litt. thesis, Oxford University 1954), 296.
4. The probate documentation used in this study is located at Lichfield Record Office (Diocesan records) and the Public Record Office (Prerogative Court of Canterbury). For use of probates see W. D. Rubinstein and Daniel H. Duncan, 'Probate valuations: a tool for the historian', *Local Historian*, 11:2 (May 1974).

5. S. T. Galton to C. Ingleby, 30 June 1832, Galton Papers.
6. According to the reports published in 1837 by the Birmingham Philosophical Institution, of 5,009 deaths in the borough in 1836, 2,453 were of children under the age of five. Robert Rawlinson in 1849 reported that 24.6 per cent of deaths in the borough were of children under the age of one. Sir R. Rawlinson, *Report to the General Board of Health on a Preliminary Inquiry into the Sewerage, Drainage and Supply of Water and the Sanitary Conditions of the Inhabitants of the Borough of Birmingham* (London 1849).
7. *Birmingham Chronicle*, 17 Nov 1825.
8. S. Timmins (ed.), *The Resources, Products and Industrial History of Birmingham and the Midland Hardware District* (London 1866; reprinted 1967), 439.
9. ibid., 480.
10. ibid., 605.
11. Compare, for example, Timmins, op. cit., 223, 688, with Allen, op. cit., 170.
12. Order to Martineau, 10 Feb 1852, Martineau Papers 713, University of Birmingham.
13. *Children's Employment Commission* 1843.
14. Letter to G. J. Holyoake, 12 July 1846, Holyoake Papers 179, Cooperative Union, Manchester.
15. G. J. Holyoake, *Sixty Years of an Agitator's Life* (London 1906), 21.
16. Timmins, op. cit., 223.
17. *BPP, Census of 1851, Population Tables II, Ages, Civil Condition, Occupation and Birthplace of the People*, 1852–3 (1691), lxxxviii.
18. *BPP, Report from His Majesty's Commissioner on the Administration and Practical Operation of the Poor Laws in England and Wales*, 1834 (44), xxiv, app. A, pt II, 32a.
19. *Birmingham Journal*, 22 Sept 1832.
20. *BPP, Fourth Report from Select Committee on Artisans and Machinery*, 1824 (51), v, 319.
21. ibid., 319.
22. Revd J. H. Spry to Home Secretary, 17 Aug 1824, HO 40/18.
23. Often those who lived through the experience of rapid industrialization sought to explain qualitative changes in production by reference to a recent decline in craftsman-retailing; see for example, W. Hutton, *History of Birmingham* (Birmingham 1781), 98; W. Hawkes-Smith, *Birmingham and its Vicinity as a Manufacturing District* (Birmingham 1836), 20; H. H. Horton, *Birmingham: A Poem in Two Parts with Appendix* (Birmingham 1853); E. Edwards, *Old Taverns of Birmingham* (Birmingham 1873).
24. M. J. Wise, 'Birmingham and its trade relations in the early eighteenth century', *University of Birmingham Historical Journal*, II:1 (1949); Court, *The Rise of the Midland Industries 1600–1838* (London 1938), 74.
25. D. Landes, *The Unbound Prometheus* (Cambridge 1972), 54.
26. *BPP, Minutes of Evidence taken before the Committee of the whole House . . .*

to consider the several petitions . . . against the Orders in Council, 1812 (210), iii.

27. A. W. Keep, *Sixty Years in Business: A Birmingham Merchant's Recollections*, reprinted in the *Birmingham Mail Scrapbook*, Birmingham Reference Library.
28. *Chapman's Birmingham Directory* (Birmingham 1803); *Wrighton and Thompson's Directory of Birmingham* (Birmingham 1812); *Wrighton and Webb's Directory of Birmingham* (Birmingham 1833); *Wrighton and Webb's Directory of Birmingham* (Birmingham 1839).
29. Immer, op. cit. Immer stresses growth of all forms of factory by 1850; even the firm of over 500 employees was a common feature.
30. *Children's Employment Commission*, 1843 (431), xiv, f17; quoted in A. Briggs, *Victorian Cities* (Harmondsworth 1968), 186; T. R. Tholfsen, 'The artisan and the culture of early Victorian Birmingham', *University of Birmingham Historical Journal*, IV (1953–4), 151.
31. *Children's Employment Commission*, 1843, f20.
32. ibid., f20.
33. ibid., f142.
34. Will of James Boyce, Prerogative Court of Canterbury, 1831.
35. *Journal of the Statistical Society*, II (Jan 1840), 440.
36. W. West, *Topography of Warwickshire* (Birmingham 1830), 208.
37. *BPP, Report from Select Committee on Manufactures, Commerce and Shipping in the United Kingdom*, 1833 (690), vi.1, Q4556.
38. Holyoake, op. cit., 19–25; for details of the Eagle Foundry see evidence of John Brunton in *BPP, Select Committee on Artisans and Machinery*, 1824, 322–33.
39. L. Simond, *Journal of a Tour and Residence in Great Britain During the Years 1810 and 1811* (Edinburgh 1817), 120–4.
40. *Journal of the Statistical Society*, II (Jan 1840), 440.
41. ibid., 440.
42. The list is quoted in A. Briggs, 'Thomas Attwood and the economic background of the Birmingham Political Union', *Cambridge Historical Journal*, IX:2 (1948), 198; *Midland Representative*, 24 Sept 1831; the list also appeared in *Poor Man's Guardian*, 29 Oct 1831, and *Lancashire and Yorkshire Co-operator*, June 1832.
43. *Birmingham Journal*, 5 Dec 1835.
44. *BPP, Third Report from the Select Committee Appointed to inquire into the State of Agriculture*, 1836 (465), viii, pt ii, Q16560.
45. *Select Committee on Manufactures, Commerce and Shipping*, 1833, Q4644–Q4645. See also Salt's comments on prosperity of 1825, *First Report from the Secret Committee of House of Lords on Commercial Distress*, 1847–8 (395), viii, 1, Q1149.
46. *Report from the Committee of Secrecy on the Bank of England Charter*, 1832 (722), vi, Q5692.
47. *Select Committee on Manufactures, Commerce and Shipping*, 1833, Q4688.
48. Muntz, *Select Committee on Agricultural Distress*, 1836, Q16528, Q16530.
49. R. C. O. Matthews, *A Study in Trade Cycle History: Economic Fluctuations*

in Great Britain 1833–42 (Cambridge 1954), 129–36; A. D. Gayer, W. W. Rostow, and A. J. Schwartz, *The Growth and Fluctuation of the British Economy 1780–1850* (Oxford 1953), 173, 211–41, 622.

50. Matthews, op. cit., 129–34, 143–5; G. N. von Tunzelman, *Steam Power and British Industrialisation to 1860* (Oxford 1978), 212, 290; Gayer *et al.*, op. cit., 172–4, 212, 646–54. The broader analysis of these authorities would suggest that what was happening in Birmingham in the first half of the nineteenth century was fairly characteristic of most areas. H. J. Habakkuk has suggested in *American and British Technology in the Nineteenth Century: The Search for Labour Saving Inventions* (Cambridge 1962), 162, that 'the need to avoid a falling rate of profit is a more powerful incentive to devise new methods than the possibility of increasing the rate of profit'. See also Landes, op. cit., 74, for the same point. As Matthews points out, where decline in prices was due to increased output such efforts offered only a short-term solution, eventually exacerbating the problem; Matthews, op. cit., 133.
51. C. Erickson, *British Industrialists: Steel and Hosiery 1850–1950* (Cambridge 1959), 183.
52. *Midland Representative*, 23 Apr 1831.
53. *Birmingham Journal*, 20 Jan 1838.
54. *Monthly Argus and Public Censor*, Sept 1829.
55. *Birmingham Journal*, 22 Oct 1831, speech of M. P. Haynes to town's meeting.
56. *Select Committee on Manufactures, Commerce and Shipping*, 1833, Q4564, Q4565.
57. *Children's Employment Commission*, 1843, f167. See also evidence of William Clark, whip manufacturer, ibid., f160–f161. The same point was put to the Factory Commissioners in 1862 by J. S. Wright, a large-scale button manufacturer (and later to be one of the contributors to the Timmins volume of 1866): 'it is of the highest importance, if we would retain any considerable part of this trade, that adult male labour should be supplemented by that of children and young persons'; *BPP, Children's Employment Commission, 1862. Third Report of the Commissioners*, 1864 (3414–1), xxii, 96–7.
58. See M. Drake, 'The census 1801–1891', in E. A. Wrigley, *Nineteenth Century Society: Essays in the Use of Quantitative Methods for the Study of Social Data* (Cambridge 1972), 7–46. On this point I can only endorse the qualifications made by Gareth Stedman-Jones comparing the 1861 and 1891 censuses for London in *Outcast London* (Oxford 1971; 1976 edn), 350. With earlier censuses, as used here, the results will, necessarily, be even more approximate.
59. *BPP, Abstract of the Answers and Returns, Occupation Abstract, 1841 Census*, 1844 (587), xxvii, 1; *Census of Great Britain*, 1851.
60. Fluctuations, or seasonality of demand, provided the workforce in these trades with some leverage against restructuring. For the struggle to preserve small-master status in the gun trade see pp. 66–70; for growth of contracting in the building trade see D. B. Viles, 'The building trade workers of London 1835–1860' (unpub. M.Phil.

thesis, London University 1976), 104–17; R. Price, *Masters, Unions and Men: Work Control in Building and the Rise of Labour 1830–1914* (Cambridge 1980), 19–55.

61. R. Samuel, 'The workshop of the world: steam power and hand technology in mid-Victorian Britain', *History Workshop*, 3 (Spring 1977), 8, 17–20, 27–32, 34–9, 53–6. E. P. Thompson, *The Making of the English Working Class* (London 1963; all references to 1968 edn), 259–96. For structural reorganization without extensive resource to the machine or the factory in a number of trades, see the following discussions: hosiery in Nottingham area—S. A. Taylor, 'The political implications of urbanisation with specific reference to the working-class housing market in Nottingham 1830–1855' (unpub. M.A. thesis, Essex University 1976), 104–17; shoemaking—P. G. Hall, 'The east London footwear industry: an industrial quarter in decline', *East London Papers*, V:1 (1962); M. J. Haynes, 'Class and class conflict in the early nineteenth century: Northampton shoemakers and the Grand National Consolidated Trades' Union', *Literature and History*, V (Spring 1977), 75–8; tailoring—E. Yeo and E. P. Thompson, *The Unknown Mayhew* (London 1973), 137–273; T. N. Parssinen and I. Prothero, 'The London tailors' strike of 1834 and the collapse of the GNCTU: a police spy's report', *International Review of Social History*, XXVII (1977).
62. See, for example, Oliver on support for the GNCTU in 1834: 'London and the other towns in which the Consolidated acquired a following of any consequence were characterised by small scale industry. . . . Compared with textile workers, especially cotton textile workers, they were pre-Industrial Revolution'; W. H. Oliver, 'The Consolidated Trades Union of 1834', *Economic History Review*, 2nd ser., XVII:1 (1964), 77; see also reactions to E. P. Thompson's work as analysed in F. K. Donnelly, 'Ideology and early working class history: Edward Thompson and his critics', *Social History*, 2 (May 1976), 220–3.
63. *Pioneer*, 8 Feb 1834.
64. *Birmingham Journal*, 8 Mar 1845.
65. Landes, op. cit., 118–19; D. Bythell, *The Sweated Trade Outwork in Victorian England* (London 1978), 143; C. Lis and H. Soly, *Poverty and Capitalism in Pre-Industrial Europe* (Bristol 1979), 159–61. For particular areas see W. H. B. Court, 'Industrial organisation and economic progress in the eighteenth century West Midlands', *Transactions of the Royal Historical Society*, 4th ser., XXVIII (1946), 87, 93. W. G. Rimmer, 'The Industrial Profile of Leeds, 1740–1840', Thoresby Society publications 113, *Miscellany* 14, pt 2 (1967), 147; Erickson, op. cit., 187; F. Bedarida, 'Urban growth and social structure in nineteenth century Poplar', *London Journal*, 1:2 (Nov 1975), 177–80; in describing the relationship between the factory and the workshop in the Coventry ribbon trade by 1830 Searby has said: 'the structure of the industry was rather like that of a large estate with a core of constantly cultivated fertile soil and concentric circles

of increasingly marginal land round it'; P. Searby, 'Weavers and freemen in Coventry 1820–1861: social and political traditionalism in an early Victorian town' (unpub. Ph.D. thesis, Warwick University 1972), 108–9.

66. *First Report to the Commissioners for Inquiring into the Employment of Children in Factories*, 1833 (450), xx. B1,6.
67. *Children's Employment Commission*, 1843, f129.
68. Timmins, op. cit., 441 (my italics).
69. *Children's Employment Commission*, 1843, f135.
70. F. Mendels, 'Proto-industrialisation: the first phase of the industrialisation process', *Journal of Economic History*, 32 (1972), 255–6; H. Medick, 'The proto-industrial family economy: the structural function of household and family during the transition from peasant society to industrial capitalism', *Social History*, 3 (Oct 1976), 296; see also Landes, op. cit., 43.
71. M. B. Rowlands, *Masters and Men in the West Midland Trades Before the Industrial Revolution* (Manchester 1975), 52; D. Hey, *The Rural Metal-Workers of the Sheffield Region: A Study of Rural Industry Before the Industrial Revolution* (Leicester 1972).
72. On the theme of work rhythms, see E. P. Thompson, 'Time, work discipline and industrial capitalism', *Past and Present*, XXXVIII (Dec 1967).
73. Landes, op. cit., 117–19; W. H. B. Court, *Rise of the Midland Industries*, 73.
74. R. Tangye, *'One and All': The Autobiography of Richard Tangye of the Cornwall Works, Birmingham* (Birmingham 1889), 97.
75. ibid., 107.
76. J. Luckock, *A Sequel to Memoirs in Humble Life* (Birmingham 1825), 20.
77. V. A. C. Gatrell, 'Labour, power and the size of firms in Lancashire cotton in the second quarter of the nineteenth century', *Economic History Review*, 2nd ser., XXX:1 (1977), 124. In this article the author refers to firms of a comparable size to Luckock's as 'small'. Obviously this kind of measurement is a relative one and Gatrell has the giant concerns of the 'cotton kings' in mind. However, the application of the term 'small' to these concerns is confusing when we turn our attention to the concerns of the small producer proper. In this study producers who are able to escape the net of dependency, in the way that Luckock could, have been designated 'large' although it is recognized that there will be enormous variations within this group.
78. *Select Committee on Manufactures, Commerce and Shipping*, 1833, Q4539, Q4628.
79. ibid., Q4539, Q4628.
80. See letters to *Aris's Gazette*, 22 Nov 1830, 4 Nov 1833; *Select Committee on Copper and Copper Trade*, 1799; S. Pollard, *The Genesis of Modern Management* (London 1965), 83–4.
81. See case of 'Baldwin v. Lawrence', *Aris's Gazette*, 18 Mar 1824.

82. *Aris's Gazette*, 26 Feb 1821.
83. Articles of Birmingham Brass Company, Birmingham Reference Library.
84. 'A Struggling Man', *The Three Social Evils of Manufacturing Towns and the Remedy Considered* (Birmingham 1858), 10.
85. *Select Committee on Manufactures, Commerce and Shipping*, Q4662.
86. Rimmer, op. cit., 151.
87. HO 40/20.
88. *Morning Chronicle*, 4 Nov 1850.
89. Bythell, op. cit., 145, 163.
90. K. Marx, *Capital*, vol. 1, chs xiv and xv. The distinctive nature of the shift between the two is explored in M. Berg, 'The machinery question: conceptions of technical change in political economy during the industrial revolution c1820 to 1840' (unpub. D.Phil. thesis, Oxford University 1976), 71–8. The phase of 'manufactures' is defined by Marx as one dominated by a division of labour and by capitalist social relations.
91. *Select Committee on Manufactures, Commerce and Shipping*, 1833, Q4668.
92. ibid., Q4654.
93. This distinction has been highlighted in a study of the emergent German middle class in the nineteenth century; J. Schlumbohm, '"Traditional" collectivity and "modern" individuality: some questions and suggestions for the historical study of socialisation. The examples of the German lower and upper bourgeoisies around 1800', *Social History*, 5:1 (Jan 1980). As the author suggests, 'The collective mode of behaviour comes most clearly to light in conflict situations', 76.
94. *Children's Employment Commission*, 1843, f153.
95. ibid., f154–f156.
96. W. H. Ryland (ed.), *Reminiscences of Thomas Henry Ryland* (Birmingham 1904).
97. Walters to Musgrave, 10 Jan 1832. (The letters are deposited at Gloucester Record Office.)
98. ibid., 14 Feb 1832.
99. ibid., 22 May 1832.
100. ibid., 22 May 1832.
101. *Select Committee on Manufactures, Commerce and Shipping*, 1833, Q4707.
102. Walters to Musgrave, 14 Feb 1832.
103. ibid., 28 Mar 1832.
104. ibid., 28 Mar 1832.
105. *Select Committee on the State of Agriculture*, 1836, Q16657–Q16660.
106. Walters to Musgrave, 7 Feb 1832.
107. ibid., 24 Jan 1832.
108. ibid., 13 Mar 1832.
109. ibid., 25 Apr 1832.
110. ibid., 1 May 1832.
111. ibid., 7 Feb 1832.
112. ibid., 13 Mar 1832.

113. ibid., 14 Feb 1832.
114. ibid., 1 May 1832.
115. Berg, op. cit., 213. The author also emphasizes the importance of the 1830s for the extension of this process; ibid., 104–8.
116. S. Pollard, 'Factory discipline in the Industrial Revolution', *Economic History Review*, 2nd ser., XVI (1963).
117. D. A. Reid, 'The decline of Saint Monday', *Past and Present*, 71 (May 1976), 84–6.
118. R. Harrison, *Before the Socialists* (London 1956), 37–9.
119. *Children's Employment Commission, 3rd Report*, 1864, offers many good examples of the 'new model' employers at work. See particularly interviews with Thomas Beckett, 84, J. Matthews, 104, Charles Ile, 106, and J. Hawkins, 111. A. Hooper, 'Mid-Victorian radicalism: community and class in Birmingham 1850–1880' (unpub. Ph.D. thesis, London University 1978), 28–30, stresses Chamberlain's commitment, as an employer, to a 'high wage, high productivity, high profit economy'. For the way in which owners of textile factories created 'deference communities', see P. Joyce, 'The factory politics of Lancashire in the later nineteenth century', *Historical Journal*, XVIII:3 (1975), 525–33.
120. *Birmingham Journal*, 7 Oct 1837.
121. *Children's Employment Commission*, 1864, 102–3.
122. *BPP, Report of Select Committee on the Manufacture of Small Arms*, 1854 (236), xviii, Q2653.
123. The contrast with the highly mechanized gun trade in the USA is striking; see E. Ames and N. Rosenberg, 'The Enfield Arsenal in theory and history', in S. B. Saul (ed.), *Technological Change: The United States and Britain in the Nineteenth Century* (London 1970).
124. 'Enquiry by Board of Officers ordered by the Duke of Wellington into charges of corruption and neglect in the receipt and examination of arms sent to the small arms inspection department during the late war 1824', War Office Papers 44/519 (my italics).
125. *Select Committee on the Manufacture of Small Arms*, 1854, Q1674.
126. ibid., Q336. This is not, of course, to say that the gun trade retained its craft basis. The distance between the trade in Birmingham and London, where the craft trade was based, can perhaps be seen in the reluctance of London contractors to hire Birmingham men. A gun-lock filer interviewed by Mayhew in 1851, had moved to London in the 1830s, and found work difficult to obtain: 'I fancy that the London masters don't like the Birmingham hands'; H. Mayhew, *London Labour and the London Poor*, vol. II (London 1968), 378.
127. *Select Committee on the Manufacture of Small Arms*, 1854, Q3473.
128. *Birmingham Journal*, 8 Aug, 24 Oct 1840.

2 POLITICS AND SMALL-SCALE PRODUCTION

1. H. Cunningham, *Leisure and the Industrial Revolution, 1780–1880* (London 1980); R. W. Malcolmson, *Popular Recreations in English Society 1700–1850* (Cambridge 1973); P. Bailey, *Leisure and Class in Victorian England* (London 1978).
2. S. Timmins (ed.), *The Resources, Products and Industrial History of Birmingham and the Midland Hardware District* (London 1866; reprinted 1967), 223.
3. *Northern Star*, 1 Mar 1845.
4. See, for example, the industrialists interviewed by the *Morning Chronicle* investigator in 1850–1: *Morning Chronicle*, 6 Jan 1851, 17 Feb 1851.
5. *Birmingham Journal*, 8 Mar 1845.
6. *Pioneer*, 19 Oct 1833.
7. *Aris's Gazette*, 11 July 1831.
8. D. A. Reid, 'Labour, leisure and politics in Birmingham c1800–1875' (unpub. Ph.D. thesis, University of Birmingham 1985).
9. ibid., viii.
10. ibid., 241, 229.
11. T. K. Hareven, *Family Time and Industrial Time* (Cambridge 1982), 135; P. Bailey, '"Will the real Bill Banks please stand up?" Towards a role analysis of mid-Victorian respectability', *Journal of Social History*, 12:3 (Spring 1979).
12. *Pioneer*, 21 Sept 1833.
13. B. Elbaum, W. Lazonick, F. Wilkinson, and J. Zeitlin, 'The labour process, market structure and Marxist theory', *Cambridge Journal of Economics*, 3:3 (1979); W. Lazonick, 'Production relations, labor productivity and choice of technique: British and United States cotton spinning', *Journal of Economic History*, XLI:3 (Sept 1981); C. Sabel and J. Zeitlin, 'Historical alternatives to mass production', *Past and Present*, 108 (Aug 1985).
14. P. Joyce, 'Work', in F. M. L. Thompson (ed.), *Cambridge Social History of Great Britain 1750–1850* (forthcoming); 'Labour, capital and compromise: a response to Richard Price', *Social History*, 9:1 (Jan 1984). This whole area of debate is examined in more detail in Chapter 3.
15. *Birmingham Journal*, 1 Mar 1834; *Birmingham Advertiser*, 20 Feb 1834.
16. *Birmingham Journal*, 14 Mar 1846.
17. *Aris's Gazette*, 8 Aug 1825.
18. ibid., 27 Apr 1835.
19. Timmins, op. cit., 454.
20. *Birmingham Journal*, 22 Sept 1849.
21. *Morning Chronicle*, 4 Nov 1851.
22. *Sam Sly's Birmingham Budget*, 30 Sept 1850.
23. *Monthly Argus and Public Censor*, May 1830.
24. *Morning Chronicle*, 6 Jan 1851.
25. *Birmingham Labour Exchange Gazette*, 26 Jan 1833.

26. Parkes to Abercromby, 12 Jan 1834, 2nd Earl Grey Papers, University of Durham.
27. R. A. Sykes, 'Popular politics and trade unionism in south east Lancashire, 1829–1842' (unpub. Ph.D. thesis, University of Manchester 1982).
28. For example, Elbaum *et al.*, op. cit.
29. C. Hibbs, 'Trade Societies, Their Past Present and Future; Address to the Members of the Birmingham United Goldsmiths, Jewellers and Silversmiths Mutual Aid and Protection Society', 11 Feb 1873 (Birmingham 1873).
30. W. H. Oliver, 'The labour exchange phase of the Co-operative movement', *Oxford Economic Papers*, new ser., X (Oct 1958); I. J. Prothero, *Artisans and Politics in Early Nineteenth Century London: John Gast and His Times* (London 1979), 245–64. Prothero points out that the Owenite scheme for a labour exchange was simply an extension of existing practice amongst groups of London artisans.
31. *Crisis*, 24 Nov 1832; *Birmingham Journal*, 17 Nov 1832.
32. Pare to Owen, 24 Oct 1832, Owen Documents 575.
33. *Crisis*, 15 Dec 1832.
34. *Crisis*, 8 Dec 1832.
35. Attwood to Owen, 16 Nov 1832, Owen Documents 579. A number of historians have accepted that Attwood supported the scheme: J. F. C. Harrison, *Robert Owen and the Owenites in Britain and America* (London 1969), 205; Prothero, op. cit., 247; Oliver, op. cit., 355–7, 362–3.
36. Scholefield to Owen, 25 Nov 1832, Owen Documents 583. Scholefield pleaded the pressure of his 'multifarious occupations' as the reason for withdrawal.
37. *Birmingham Journal*, 1 Dec 1832; *Aris's Gazette*, 3 Dec 1832; *Crisis*, 8, 15 Dec 1832. Oliver claims erroneously that Attwood chaired the meeting and that this reflected his enthusiasm for the scheme; Oliver, op. cit., 363.
38. *Crisis*, 15 Dec 1832.
39. *Crisis*, 8 Dec 1832.
40. *Crisis*, 15 Dec 1832.
41. *Birmingham Labour Exchange Gazette*, 26 Jan 1833.
42. *Aris's Gazette*, 25 Mar 1833; *Birmingham Journal*, 23 Mar 1833.
43. Hawkes-Smith to Owen, 23 Oct 1832, Owen Documents 574. A list of the many trades attracted to the Exchange as depositors can be found in the *Birmingham Labour Exchange Gazette*, 19 Jan 1833 and *Crisis*, 9 Feb 1833.
44. *Birmingham Labour Exchange Gazette*, 2 Feb 1833.
45. *Crisis*, 15 Dec 1833.
46. *Crisis*, 3 Aug 1833.
47. *Crisis*, 27 Apr 1833.
48. See Chapter 4 p. 179.
49. *Birmingham Co-operative Herald*, 1 May 1829.
50. O'Brien to Owen, 27 May 1832, Owen Documents 546.

51. Pare to Owen, 2 Sept 1833, Owen Documents 575.
52. Morrison to Owen, 2 Sept 1833, Owen Documents 659.
53. Welch to Owen, 6 Sept 1833, Owen Documents 657.
54. *Birmingham Journal*, 17 Aug 1833.
55. *Aris's Gazette*, 5 Aug 1833.
56. *Birmingham Journal*, 9 Nov 1833.
57. *Pioneer*, 25 Jan 1834.
58. *Birmingham Journal*, 1 July 1837.
59. ibid., 20 Sept 1834.
60. R. B. Rose, 'The Priestley riots of 1791', *Past and Present*, 18 (Nov 1960); J. Money, *Experience and Identity: Birmingham and the West Midlands 1760–1800* (Manchester 1977), 214.
61. *Birmingham Journal*, 6 Feb 1836.
62. Clearly a local manifestation of a broader phenomenon; see E. P. Thompson, *The Making of the English Working Class* (London 1963; all references to 1968 edn), 57–8.
63. R. B. Rose, 'The origins of working class radicalism in Birmingham', *Labour History*, IX (Nov 1965).
64. See C. Behagg, 'Radical politics and conflict at the point of production: Birmingham 1815–1845. A study in the relationship between the classes' (unpub. Ph.D thesis, University of Birmingham 1982), 301–45 for a more detailed analysis of the radical movement 1816–20.
65. F. Bechhofer and B. Elliott, 'Persistence and change: the petite bourgeoisie in industrial society', *Archives Européennes de Sociologie*, XVII (1976).
66. G. Crossick, 'La petite bourgeoisie brittanique du xixe siècle', *Mouvement Social*, n° 108, (July–Sept 1979); 'Urban society and the petty bourgeoisie in nineteenth century Britain', in D. Fraser and A. Sutcliffe (eds), *The Pursuit of Urban History* (London 1983); 'The petite bourgeoisie in nineteenth century Britain: the urban and liberal care', in G. Crossick and H. G. Haupt (eds), *Shopkeepers and Master Artisans in Nineteenth Century Europe* (London 1984).
67. Evidence of William Payn, Chief Constable of Hundred of Helmingford, HO 42/155; Askew and his son were both later to be prominent members of the Birmingham Paine Club. In 1823 he declared himself to be one 'who has a better opinion of the devil than he has of the priest'; *Republican*, 21, 28 Feb 1823.
68. Evidence of Gideon Taylor, HO 42/155: *Warwickshire Advertiser*, 2 Nov 1816, 19 Apr 1817.
69. HO 30/3(ii).
70. *Birmingham Inspector*, 25 Jan 1817.
71. *The Addresser Addressed* (Birmingham 1816).
72. *Black Dwarf*, 3 Mar, 2, 30 June 1819; *Edmonds' Weekly Recorder*, 10 July 1819.
73. F. D. Cartwright (ed.), *Life and Correspondence of Major Cartwright* (London 1826), vol. II, 165.
74. T. M. Parssinen, 'Association, convention and anti-parliament in

British radical politics, 1771–1848', *English Historical Review*, LXXXVIII (July 1973), 515–17.

75. T. B. Howell (ed.), *Reports of State Trials*, vol. 1 (London 1826); A Correct Report of the Proceedings of a Meeting Held at Newhall Hill Birmingham on Monday July 12 1819; *Aris's Gazette*, 19 July 1819; Treasury Solicitors' Papers 11/695/2206.
76. Spooner to Home Secretary, 27 May 1817, HO 40/5(i).
77. *Resolutions, declarations and rules of the Birmingham Union Society* (Birmingham 1819); *Edmonds' Weekly Register*, 6 Nov 1819.
78. Hamper to Sidmouth, 7 Oct 1819, HO 42/197.
79. *An Address From the Members of the Birmingham Union Society*, HO 40/11.
80. *Aris's Gazette*, 25 Oct, 8, 15 Nov 1815.
81. *Edmonds' Weekly Recorder*, 24 July 1819.
82. Price to Sidmouth, 26 Feb 1829, HO 52/1.
83. *Resolutions of the Birmingham Hampden Club* (Birmingham 1816).
84. *Birmingham Inspector*, 19 July 1817.
85. *Black Dwarf*, 7 Aug 1822.
86. Money, op. cit., 214; J. Walvin, 'English democratic societies and popular radicalism 1791–1800' (unpub. Ph.D. thesis, University of York 1969), 175–8, 244–5.
87. J. Luckock, *A Sequel to Memoirs in Humble Life* (Birmingham 1825).
88. ibid., 35.
89. ibid., 35.
90. J. L. Dobson, 'The Hill family and educational change in the early nineteenth century. I. Thomas Wright Hill and the school at Hill Top Birmingham', *Durham Research Review*, 10 (Sept 1959); 'Hazelwood School: the achievement of Rowland Hill and his brothers', *Durham Research Review*, 11 (Sept 1960). See also D. Gorham, 'Victorian reform as a family business: the Hill family', in A. Wohl (ed.), *The Victorian Family* (London 1978).
91. MS journal of Rowland Hill, vol. II, 1816, 143, Bruce Castle Museum Tottenham. Rowland's brother, Matthew Davenport Hill, a lawyer, sometimes addressed the members of the Club but was never a member. MS diary of Matthew Davenport Hill (10 Mar 1817, 8 Mar 1818), Bodleian Library, MS Eng. misc. 188 - see entry for 19 Apr 1817.
92. *Black Dwarf*, 7 Aug 1822. For similar events on the release of other local radicals, see *Black Dwarf*, 28 Nov 1821, 30 Oct 1822, 22 Jan 1823.
93. *Black Dwarf*, 7 Aug 1822.
94. The King against George Ragg, Treasury Solicitors' Papers 11/90/272.
95. *Black Dwarf*, 7 Aug 1822.
96. *Edmonds' Weekly Recorder*, 14 Aug 1819.
97. Sidmouth to Bedford, 18 Aug 1819, HO 42/198.
98. King v. Russell, Treasury Solicitors' Papers 11/45/169.
99. *Black Dwarf*, 22 Jan 1823.
100. *Birmingham Journal*, 23 Feb 1839.

101. ibid., 29 May 1830 (my italics).
102. *Birmingham Independent*, 3 June 1828.
103. ibid., 2 Feb 1828.
104. ibid., 3 June 1828.
105. ibid., 1 Sept 1827.
106. *Monthly Argus and Public Censor*, Jan 1830.
107. ibid., Feb 1830.
108. ibid., Dec 1829.
109. ibid., Feb 1830.
110. ibid., Nov 1830.
111. ibid., Aug 1830.
112. Founding resolutions, *Birmingham Journal*, 30 Jan 1830.
113. *BPP, Report from the Commissioners . . . Inquiring into the Administration and Practical Operation of the Poor Laws*, 1834, xxix, app. A, pt II.
114. *Birmingham Journal*, 3 June 1837.
115. ibid., 18 Mar 1837.
116. Journal of Thomas Finigan, 6 Feb 1838.
117. *Birmingham Journal*, 17 Feb 1838.
118. See ch. 5.
119. *Birmingham Journal*, 17 Feb 1838.
120. ibid., 7 Oct 1838.
121. Minute-book of Duddeston-cum-Nechells Reform Association, 4 Nov 1839, Birmingham Reference Library.
122. *Birmingham Journal*, 11 Feb 1843.
123. E. P. Hennock, *Fit and Proper Persons: Ideal and Reality in Nineteenth Century Urban Government* (London 1973).
124. L. Davidoff and C. Hall, 'The architecture of public and private life: English middle class society in a provincial town 1780–1850', in D. Fraser and A. Sutcliffe, *The Pursuit of Urban History* (London 1983). The argument is powerfully extended for the middle class as a whole in L. Davidoff and C. Hall, *Family Fortunes: Men and Women of the English Middle Class* (London 1987).

3 'THE WORST OF DEMOCRACIES': THE INTERNAL LIFE OF THE WORKPLACE

1. E. P. Thompson, *The Making of the English Working Class* (London 1963; all references to 1968 edn); see also F. K. Donnelly, 'Ideology and early working class history: Edward Thompson and his critics', *Social History*, 2 (May 1976).
2. I. J. Prothero, *Artisans and Politics in Early Nineteenth Century London: John Gast and His Times* (London 1979); 'London Chartism and the trades', *Economic History Review*, 2nd ser., XXIV (May 1971); R. A. Sykes, 'Early Chartism and trade unionism in south-east Lancashire', in J. Epstein and D. Thompson (eds), *The Chartist Experience* (London 1982).
3. Sykes, 'Early Chartism', 152. On the compartmentalist approach see p. 3.

4. See works referred to on p. 74; also W. Lazonick, 'Industrial relations and technical change: the case of the self-acting mule', *Cambridge Journal of Economics*, 3:3 (1979); R. Penn, 'Trade union organisation and skill in the cotton and engineering industries in Britain 1850–1960', *Social History*, 8:1 (Jan 1983); C. More, *Skill and the English Working Class* (London 1980).
5. J. Zeitlin and C. Sabel, 'Historical alternatives to mass production: politics, markets and technology in nineteenth century industrialisation', *Past and Present*, 108 (Aug 1985); D. Reid, 'Labour, leisure and politics in Birmingham *c.*1800–1875' (unpub. Ph.D. thesis, University of Birmingham 1985), 167.
6. P. Joyce, 'Labour, capital and compromise: a response to Richard Price', *Social History*, 9:1 (Jan 1984), 69–71; 'Languages of reciprocity and conflict', *Social History*, 9:2 (May 1984); *The Historical Meanings of Work* (Cambridge 1987), 6–8.
7. P. Anderson, 'Origins of the present crisis', *New Left Review*, 23, 1964.
8. P. Anderson, '*Arguments Within English Marxism*', (London 1980), 46.
9. G. Stedman-Jones, 'The language of Chartism', in J. Epstein and D. Thompson (eds), *The Chartist Experience* (London 1982); an extended version of the argument is presented in G. Stedman-Jones, *The Languages of Class* (Cambridge 1983). This argument is contested in N. Kirk, 'In defence of class: a critique of recent revisionist writing upon the nineteenth century English working class', *International Review of Social History*, XXXII (1987).
10. P. Joyce, Review of *The Chartist Experience*, *Social History*, 9:2 (May 1984).
11. Prothero, *Artisans and Politics*, 3.
12. For a review article raising such points about the work of Prothero and myself, see G. Eley, 'Re-thinking the political: social history and political culture in 18th and 19th century Britain', *Archiv für Socialgeschichte*, XXI (1981).
13. Prothero, *Artisans and Politics*, 337.
14. It is to avoid such a narrowing process that Price rejects the term 'craft control' in favour of the broader 'work control'; R. Price, *Masters, Unions and Men: Work Control in Building and the Rise of Labour 1830–1914* (Cambridge 1980), 9–12.
15. See G. Eley and K. Neild, 'Why does social history ignore politics?', *Social History*, 5:2 (May 1980).
16. P. Linebaugh, 'Labour history without the labour process: a note on John Gast and his times', *Social History*, 7:3 (Oct 1982).
17. *Select Committee on Manufacture, Commerce and Shipping*, Q4564, Q4565.
18. *Birmingham Journal*, 3 June 1837.
19. E. J. Hobsbawm, 'Economic fluctuations and some social movements since 1800', *Labouring Men* (London 1964), 126–57. Trades in Birmingham engaged in strike activity in 1820–50 were: basket-makers; bellows-makers; blank-tray-makers; boot- and shoemakers; brass-candlestick-makers; brass-cock-founders; braziers;

bricklayers; Britannia-metal-makers; brush-makers; builders' labourers; button-burnishers; cabinet-makers; cabinet-case-makers; carpenters; chair-makers; cordwainers; edge-tool-makers; fender-makers; fire-iron-makers; glass-workers; gun-finishers; barrel-makers; stockers and lockmakers; heavy-steel-toymakers; horn-button-makers; iron-founders; japanners; locksmiths; malt-mill-makers; metal-button-makers; moulders; pearl-button-makers; pin-makers; platers; plasterers; rule-makers; sawyers; silk-hatters; silver-platers; stonemasons; tailors; tin-platers; weighing-machine-makers; wire-drawers; and wireworkers. C. Behagg, 'Radical politics and conflict at the point of production: Birmingham 1815–1845. A study in the relationship between the classes' (unpub. Ph.D. thesis, University of Birmingham 1982), app. 1, 494–7.

20. See, for example, A. E. Musson, *British Trade Unions 1800–1875* (London 1972), 18–20, 36–48.
21. *Operative Stone Masons (OSM): Fortnightly Returns*, 22 Apr–6 May 1841.
22. S. J. Pratt, *Harvest Home* (London 1805), 417. For eighteenth-century artisan debating societies see J. Money, 'Taverns, coffee houses and clubs: local politics and popular articulacy in the Birmingham area in the Age of the American Revolution', *Historical Journal*, XIV:1 (1971).
23. A list of Friendly Societies in the County of Warwick, 21 June 1793 – 31 Dec 1855, QS.83, Warwick Record Office. This table is also quoted in J. W. Nicholas, 'Trade clubs and societies in Birmingham 1790–1826' (unpub. B.A. dissertation, Birmingham University 1949), 29.
24. For disputes in the cabinet trade see *Aris's Gazette*, 27 July 1807; 25 June 1808; 30 Oct 1809; 27 Nov 1809.
25. ibid., 2 July 1810.
26. *Morning Chronicle*, 21 Oct 1850.
27. R. B. Rose, 'The Priestley riots of 1791', *Past and Present*, 18 (Nov 1960); J. Money, *Experience and Identity: Birmingham and the West Midlands 1760–1800* (Manchester 1977), 219–74.
28. Calquhoun calculated in 1797 that, with regard to London, of 1,600 friendly societies in existence, only around 853 had registered; P. Calquhoun, *A Treatise on the Police of the Metropolis* (London 1797), as quoted in L. D. Schwarz, 'Conditions of life and work in London *c.*1770–1820, with special reference to East London' (unpub. D.Phil. thesis, Oxford University 1976), 192.
29. R. B. Rose, 'The origins of working class radicalism in Birmingham', *Labour History*, IX (Nov 1965).
30. HO 40/18.
31. *Birmingham Mercury*, 28 Aug 1852.
32. Walters to Musgrave, 15 May 1832.
33. *Birmingham Journal*, 25 Aug 1832; G. D. H. Cole, *Attempts at a General Union 1818–1834* (London 1953), 22.
34. *Poor Man's Guardian*, 20, 27 Oct 1832.

35. These were: wireworkers and weavers, pearl-button-makers, fire-iron-makers, rule-makers, clock-makers, japanners, steel-toymakers, glass-cutters, smiths, coopers and boxmakers, locksmiths, brick-makers, sawyers, carpenters and joiners, plasterers; *Pioneer*, 4, 25 Jan, 1, 8, 22 Feb, 1, 29 Mar 1834.
36. *Pioneer*, 21 Dec 1833; *Birmingham Journal*, 5 Apr 1833.
37. R. Postgate, *The Builders' History* (London 1923).
38. *Pioneer*, 21 Dec 1833.
39. Postgate, op. cit., 77–114.
40. Hansom to Owen, 23 Feb 1834, Owen Documents.
41. *Pioneer*, 7 Dec 1833.
42. ibid., 7 Dec 1833.
43. *Rules of the GNCTU* (1834), Webb Trade Union Collection, section C, vol. 109, rule 46.
44. ibid., rule 28.
45. Parkes to Abercromby, 12 Jan 1834, Grey Papers, University of Durham.
46. *Pioneer*, 25 Jan 1834; *Birmingham Journal*, 9 Mar 1839, 22 Sept 1849.
47. *Aris's Gazette*, 8 Dec 1828; *Pioneer*, 25 Jan 1834; *Birmingham Journal*, 23 Mar 1839; *OSM: Fortnightly Returns*, 30 Jan 1840 (the stonemasons supported the strike financially).
48. For tailors see p. 50; for cabinet-makers, see *Northern Star*, 2 May 1846.
49. Prothero, 'London Chartism and the trades', 213.
50. T. Cooper, *Life* (Leicester 1971), 135.
51. *Northern Star*, 25 Jan 1845.
52. Prothero, 'London Chartism and the trades', 212.
53. *Northern Star*, 22 Mar 1845.
54. *Birmingham Journal*, 13 Dec 1845; *OSM: Fortnightly Returns*, 12–26 Nov 1846. Clearly the 'United Fire Iron Makers' had not survived the 1830s; *Pioneer*, 25 Jan 1834.
55. *Northern Star*, 16 Nov 1844, 8 Feb 1845; *Birmingham Journal*, 13 June 1846.
56. Prothero, 'London Chartism and the trades'; *Artisans and Politics*, 300–27.
57. *Birmingham Journal*, 1 Mar 1845; *Northern Star*, 1 Mar 1845.
58. *Birmingham Journal*, 13 Sept, 18 Oct 1845.
59. ibid., 2 May 1846.
60. *Northern Star*, 26 Sept 1846.
61. *Birmingham Journal*, 29 July 1848.
62. Sir A. Alison, *Some Account of My Life and Writings* (Edinburgh 1883), 350.
63. E. C. Tufnell, *The Character, Objects and Effects of Trades Unions: with some remarks on the laws concerning them* (London 1834), 125.
64. *Birmingham Advertiser*, 20 Feb 1834.
65. *Blackwood's Magazine*, Mar 1834.
66. ibid., Mar 1834.
67. ibid., Mar 1838.

68. *Birmingham Journal*, 24 June 1848.
69. E. Burke, *Reflections on the Revolution in France* (Harmondsworth 1983), 128–9.
70. *Rules and Orders to be observed by a Society called the United Brethren of Wire Workers and Weavers, Nov 12 1833* (Birmingham 1833), rule 3.
71. P. H. J. H. Gosden, *Friendly Societies in England 1815–1875* (Manchester 1961), 7; T. Matsumura, 'The flint glass makers in the classic age of the labour aristocracy, 1850–1880, with special reference to Stourbridge' (Ph.D. thesis, University of Warwick 1976).
72. H. A. Turner, *Trade Union Growth, Structure and Policy: A Comparative Study of the Cotton Unions* (London 1962), 87–9.
73. Tufnell, op. cit., 23, 59.
74. 'Byelaws to be strictly observed by the Operative Stone Masons', MSS, Modern Records Centre, University of Warwick.
75. *Bye-laws for the Government of the Operative Carpenters and Joiners Society of Birmingham* (Birmingham 1833).
76. The spinners of Manchester, for example, had an elaborate jury system whereby the defendant retained the right to object to jurors. *BPP, First and Second Reports from the Select Committee on Combinations of Workmen* (1837–8), app. 3, 304–5.
77. *BPP, Report from Select Committee on Masters and Operatives (Equitable Councils of Conciliation)*, 1856, (343), xiii, 498. See also A. Little, 'Thomas Winters: Chartist and trade unionist', *Bulletin of the Society for the Study of Labour History*, 49 (Autumn 1984), 23.
78. 30 Nov 1845, Holyoake Papers, letter 146.
79. G. J. Holyoake, *Sixty Years of an Agitator's Life* (London 1906), 21.
80. V. L. Allen, 'A methodological criticism of the Webbs as trade union historians', *Bulletin of the Society for the Study of Labour History*, IV (Spring 1962); see also his *Sociology of Industrial Relations* (London 1971), 25–36.
81. *BPP, Royal Commission on Trades Unions 1867–9, 10th Report* (3952), xxxii, Q18654.
82. *Birmingham Journal*, 23 Nov 1844.
83. 'Report on Combinations by Nassau Senior Esq. and Thomas Tomlinson Esq.', HO 49/56.
84. J. Rule, *The Experience of Labour in the Eighteenth Century Workplace* (London 1981), 151.
85. Price, *Masters, Unions and Men*, 54–79.
86. D. Wilson, 'Government dock-yard workers in Portsmouth' (unpub. Ph.D. thesis, University of Warwick 1975), 314–17.
87. *Royal Commission on Trades Unions*, 1867–9, Q18706.
88. ibid., Q18713.
89. S. Pollard, *The Sheffield Outrages* (Bath 1971), xxii.
90. *Aris's Gazette*, 14 May 1810.
91. *Birmingham Journal*, 23 Nov 1833.
92. *Morning Chronicle*, 20 Jan 1851.
93. An earlier version of the following section appeared as 'Secrecy,

ritual and folk violence: the opacity of the workplace in the first half of the nineteenth century', in R. D. Storch (ed.), *Popular Culture and Custom in Nineteenth Century England* (London 1982).

94. Price, *Masters, Unions and Men*, 74–93. The work of Richard Price is central in the debate over work control; see particularly 'The labour process and labour history', *Social History*, 8:1 (Jan 1983); 'Conflict and co-operation: a reply to Patrick Joyce', *Social History*, 9:2 (May 1984); 'Theories of labour process formation', *Journal of Social History* (Fall 1984).
95. Journal of E. Derrington, 14 July 1839, Carrs Lane Town Mission Records, Birmingham Reference Library.
96. ibid., 12 Dec 1839.
97. Journal of P. Sibree, 12 Dec 1838, Carrs Lane Town Mission Records. In this context the term 'infidel' is invariably another term for 'Owenite'.
98. Journal of William Jackson, 11 Dec 1846, Carrs Lane Town Mission Records.
99. ibid., 26 Aug 1846.
100. ibid., 21 Aug 1843.
101. Derrington, 11 Sept 1843.
102. Sibree, 6 July 1838.
103. Derrington, 20 Apr 1838.
104. Sibree, 8 Apr 1839.
105. Derrington, 19 Oct 1843.
106. ibid., 23 Feb 1843.
107. D. Wilkinson, *Rough Roads: Reminiscences of a Wasted Life* (London 1912), 30.
108. ibid., 18.
109. K. Marx, *Capital*, vol. 1 (Harmondsworth 1976), 490. The meaning behind this statement is explored in J. Rules's excellent essay, 'The property of skill in the period of manufacture', in P. Joyce (ed.), *The Historical Meanings of Work* (Cambridge 1987).
110. *Birmingham Journal*, 10, 17, 24 Mar 1838. Corbett referred to the rules of the society as 'traditionary laws'.
111. *Morning Chronicle*, 5 Feb 1851.
112. ibid., 3 Jan 1851.
113. Webb Trade Union Collection, section A, f70–f71.
114. *Rules to be Observed by the Members of the United Orders of Smiths* (Derby 1839), in K. Carpenter (ed.), *Rebirth of the Trade Union Movement* (New York 1972).
115. *Bye-laws . . . for the Government of the Operative Carpenters and Joiners Society*.
116. *Pioneer*, 9 Nov 1833.
117. Cole, op. cit., 70–5; Thompson op. cit., 557–61; T. N. Parssinen and I. Prothero, 'The London tailors' strike of 1834 and the collapse of the GNCTU: a police spy's report', *International Review of Social History*, XXVII (1977), 81–3; Postgate, op. cit., 63–7; A. J. Randall, 'Labour and the industrial revolution in the west of

England woollen industry 1756–1840' (unpub. Ph.D thesis, University of Birmingham 1979). Randall traces the activities of the secret societies of Gloucestershire, Wiltshire, and Somerset, formed in late 1828, and notes that 'The ceremonial facet of the secret society was far more elaborate than that of previous unions', 584; L. Smith, 'The carpet weavers of Kidderminster 1800–1850' (unpub. Ph.D. thesis, University of Birmingham 1982) 291–3; J. Marlow, *The Tolpuddle Martyrs* (London 1971), 47.

118. As late as 1843 Edward Derrington reported from his district in Birmingham that 'The case is thus, at some of these iniquitous places where such societies are held they have what they call a lecture delivered – the lecturer stands behind the form of a coffin on which is placed a skullbone – the lecture is delivered in a kind of theatrical style the lecturer occasionally exhibiting the skull and illustrating part of what he advances'; Derrington, 19 Oct 1843.

119. *Select Committee on Combinations of Workmen*, Q3359; R. G. Kirkby and A. E. Musson, *Voice of the People: John Doherty 1798–1854* (Manchester 1975), 36–7, 88, 111, 176, 191, 291–2, 310.

120. For the debate between Morrison and Carlile over ceremonial see *Gauntlet*, 9, 16, 23, 30 Mar 1834; *Pioneer*, 15 Mar 1834: 'No man of sense', Morrison claimed in this edition of the *Pioneer*, 'could raise objections to any form which we embrace.'

121. Morrison to Owen, 2 Sept 1833, Owen Documents. Owen took Morrison's advice to heart and rule 31 of the GNCTU made provision for an initiation ceremony; *Rules and Regulations of the GNCTU of Great Britain and Ireland* (London 1834), Webb Trade Union Collection, section C, vol. 109.

122. *Gauntlet*, 23 Mar 1834.

123. *Birmingham Advertiser*, 20 Mar 1834.

124. *Pioneer*, 15 Mar 1834.

125. Parssinen and Prothero, op. cit., 81; *The Initiating Parts of the Friendly Society of Operative Stone Masons* (Birmingham 1834), Modern Records Centre, University of Warwick.

126. *Pioneer*, 1 Feb 1834, 29 Mar 1834, 7 June 1834. For similar ceremonies among Northampton shoemakers see M. J. Haynes, 'Class and class conflict in the early nineteenth century: Northampton shoemakers and the GNCTU', *Literature and History*, 5 (Spring 1977), 85–8.

127. D. Thompson, 'Women and nineteenth century radical politics', in J. Mitchell and A. Oakley (eds), *The Rights and Wrongs of Women* (Harmondsworth 1976).

128. S. O. Rose, 'Gender at work: sex, class and industrial capitalism', *History Workshop Journal*, 21 (Spring 1986); 'Gender antagonism and class conflict: exclusionary strategies of male trade unionists in nineteenth century Britain', *Social History*, 13:2 (May 1988); *Pioneer*, 1 Mar 1834, 7 Dec 1834.

129. *Birmingham Journal*, 25 Aug 1832. Trades participating were: carpenters and joiners; sawyers; brush-makers; pin-makers;

masons; farriers; plumbers, painters, and glaziers; bricklayers; jewellers; gilt-toymakers; stampers and piercers; tailors; silk-hatters; plasterers.

130. *Pioneer*, 7 Dec 1833.
131. ibid., 7 Dec 1833.
132. Pratt, op. cit., vol. 1, 385n.
133. *Birmingham Journal*, 23 Nov 1833.
134. ibid., 23 Nov 1833.
135. Evidence of J. Gilbert, *BPP, Report from Select Committee on Bribery at Elections*, 1835 (viii), Q4101–Q4125.
136. *Birmingham Journal*, 10 Mar 1838. In 1843 Corbett recommended the replacement, through government intervention, of public houses with 'other recreative resources, as for instance gymnastic exercises, quoits, cricket, etc.; public gardens, walks, baths, reading rooms etc'; *BPP, Children's Employment Commission, Appendix to the Second Report of the Commissioners*, pt I, 1843 (432), xv, f132.
137. *Birmingham Journal*, 17 Mar 1838.
138. *Aris's Gazette*, 29 Mar 1830.
139. ibid., 27 Apr 1835.
140. *Morning Chronicle*, 6 Jan 1851.
141. ibid., 13 Jan 1851.
142. T. Laqueur, *Religion and Respectability: Sunday School and Working Class Culture, 1780–1850* (London 1976), 239; C. Reid, 'Middle class values and working class culture in nineteenth century Sheffield – the pursuit of respectability', in S. Pollard and C. Holmes (eds), *Essays in the Economic and Social History of South Yorkshire* (Sheffield 1976), 279; D. Reid, 'Labour, leisure and politics'.
143. P. Bailey, '"Will the real Bill Banks please stand up?" Towards a role analysis of mid-Victorian respectability', *Journal of Social History*, 12:3 (Spring 1979).
144. *Morning Chronicle*, 27 Jan 1851.
145. W. M. Bramwell, *Pubs and Localised Communities in Mid-Victorian Birmingham*, Occasional Paper no. 22, Department of Geography and Earth Science, Queen Mary College (London 1984), 5.
146. *Birmingham Journal*, 14 Mar 1846.
147. *Birmingham Mercury*, 31 Jan 1852.
148. *Birmingham Journal*, 10 Aug 1839; HO 20/10.
149. Musson, op. cit., 14–15; see also D. E. Brewster and N. McCord, 'Some labour troubles of the 1790s in north-east England', *International Review of Social History*, XIII (1968), pt 3.
150. *OSM: Fortnightly Returns*, 2 Sept 1836.
151. Martineau letters 1322, n.d.
152. ibid., 7 Aug 1859.
153. *Birmingham Chronicle*, 21 July 1825.
154. *Warwickshire General Advertiser*, 22 Oct 1831.
155. *Reformer*, 7 May 1835; *Birmingham Advertiser*, 7 May 1835.
156. See Chapter 1 pp. 69–70.
157. *Birmingham Journal*, 23 Nov 1844.

158. ibid., 22 July 1848.
159. Parkes to Abercrombie, 12 Jan 1834, Papers of 2nd Earl Grey, Department of Palaeography and Diplomatic, University of Durham.
160. *Birmingham Journal*, 1 Mar 1834.
161. ibid., 4 Apr 1841.
162. ibid., 4 Mar 1843.
163. *Pioneer*, 8 Feb 1834.
164. See Linebaugh, op. cit., 322.
165. F. J. Kaijage, 'Labouring Barnsley 1816–1856' (unpub. Ph.D. thesis, Warwick University 1975), 317–20.
166. *Pioneer*, 8 Feb 1834.
167. *Birmingham Journal*, 14 Feb 1846.
168. ibid., 24 June 1848.
169. See R. Price, 'Theories of labour process formation', *Journal of Social History* (Fall 1984), 94; C. Behagg, 'Evaluation and action: small scale producers and the economic crisis of the late 1840s in Birmingham', unpub. paper presented to the European Round Table on the Petite Bourgeoisie, University of Nanterre, Paris 1984. A brief summary of this paper appears in D. Blackbourn, 'Economic crisis and the petite bourgeoisie in Europe during the nineteenth and twentieth centuries', *Social History*, 10:1 (Jan 1985).
170. See p. 46.
171. *Birmingham Advertiser*, 28 Oct 1847.
172. W. H. Ryland (ed.), *Reminiscences of Thomas Henry Ryland* (Birmingham 1904).
173. *Birmingham Journal*, 6 Mar 1847.
174. *Birmingham Mercury*, 28 Aug 1852.
175. It was this which gave this notion of property a class-specific context to operate in; a point perhaps not fully taken into account in Stedman-Jones, 'Language of Chartism', 23.
176. *Morning Chronicle*, 21 Oct 1850. For similar organization in textiles, carpet-weaving, and glass-making see Lazonick, op. cit., Smith, op. cit., and Matsumura, op. cit. respectively.
177. *Morning Chronicle*, 21 Oct 1850.
178. W. Lazonick, 'Production relations, labor productivity and choice of technique: British and U.S. cotton spinning', *Journal of Economic History*, XLI:3 (Sept 1981), 500.
179. *Morning Chronicle*, 16 Dec 1850.
180. ibid., 16 Dec 1850.
181. In addition, as Price points out, the continuity of sub-contract has been overestimated. In this respect he particularly singles out the work of Littler; Price, 'Theories of the labor process', 101.
182. *Morning Chronicle*, 23 Dec 1850.
183. ibid., 21 Oct 1850.
184. ibid., 6 Jan 1851.
185. ibid., 6 Jan 1851.
186. *BPP, First and Second Reports from the Secret Committee of the House of*

Lords on Commercial Distress, VIII (i) 1847–8, Q1097.
187. *Morning Chronicle*, 3 Jan 1851.
188. ibid., 3 Jan 1851.
189. ibid., 17 Feb 1851.
190. ibid., 13 Jan 1851.
191. ibid., 3 Feb 1851.
192. ibid., 13 Jan 1851.
193. ibid., 17 Feb 1851.
194. *Aris's Gazette*, 11 Oct 1824.
195. ibid., 29 Mar 1830; *Birmingham Journal*, 27 Mar 1830.
196. *Aris's Gazette*, 20 Dec 1824; *Birmingham Journal*, 11, 25 Oct 1845.
197. *Birmingham Journal*, 30 May 1846.
198. *Aris's Gazette*, 8 Dec 1828.
199. *Birmingham Journal*, 8, 15 Mar 1845; *Morning Chronicle*, 13 Jan 1851.
200. *Birmingham Journal*, 23 Nov 1833; *Morning Chronicle*, 20 Jan 1851.
201. *Birmingham Journal*, 1 Mar 1845.
202. *Northern Star*, 1 Mar 1845.
203. *Morning Chronicle*, 3 Feb 1851.
204. *Northern Star*, 1 Mar 1845.
205. P. Joyce, *Work, Society and Politics: The Culture of the Factory in Later Victorian England* (Brighton 1980), 71.
206. A. Hooper, 'Mid-Victorian radicalism: community and class in Birmingham 1850–1880' (unpub. Ph.D. thesis, London University 1978), 74–169.
207. Price, *Masters, Unions and Men*, 94–163, raises exactly this point.
208. ibid., 64–5, 71.
209. In 1878, for example, factory legislation ws extended to workshops.
210. R. F. to H. Martineau, 7 Aug 1859, Martineau Papers.
211. ibid., 15 Aug 1859.
212. R. Price, 'Structures of subordination in nineteenth century British industry', in P. Thane, G. Crossick, and R. Floud, *The Power of the Past* (Cambridge 1984), 119.
213. Bailey, op. cit.; Laqueur, op. cit.
214. *Morning Chronicle*, 16 Dec 1850.
215. Reid, op. cit. In his later work Reid, however, stresses the existence of a moral consensus in the workplace.
216. *Morning Chronicle*, 27 Jan 1851.
217. ibid., 13 Jan 1851.
218. ibid., 13 Jan 1851. For similar developments in the tin-plate trade, see ibid., 3 Feb 1851.
219. Stedman-Jones, 'Language of Chartism', 39–42.
220. *Birmingham Journal*, 2, 16, 23 Feb, 2, 25 Mar 1839.
221. See B. Taylor, *Eve and the New Jerusalem* (Tiptree 1983), 83–117.

4 'RIDING THE TIGER': MIDDLE-CLASS AND WORKING-CLASS RADICALISM IN THE REFORM BILL CAMPAIGN

1. A. Briggs, *Victorian Cities* (Harmondsworth 1968), 189.
2. A. Briggs, *The Collected Essays of Asa Briggs*, vol. 1, *Words, Numbers, Places, People* (Brighton 1985), 230; *Chartist Studies* (London 1959), 26–8.
3. T. R. Tholfsen, 'The Chartist crisis in Birmingham', *International Review of Social History*, III (1958), 465.
4. C. Flick, *The Birmingham Political Union and the Movement for Reform in Britain 1830–1839* (Folkestone 1978).
5. Briggs, *History of Birmingham*, II (Oxford 1952), 6.
6. B. Elbaum, W. Lazonick, F. Wilkinson, and J. Zeitlin, 'Symposium: The labour process, market structure and Marxist theory', *Cambridge Journal of Economics*, III (1979).
7. D. Cannadine, 'The Calthorpe family and Birmingham 1810–1910: "Conservative interest" examined', *Historical Journal*, XVIII (1975); see also 'The aristocracy and the town in the nineteenth century: a case study of the Calthorpes and Birmingham 1807–1910' (unpub. D.Phil. thesis, University of Oxford 1975).
8. G. Stedman-Jones, 'Language of Chartism', in J. Epstein and D. Thompson (eds), *The Chartist Experience* (London 1982).
9. E. Yeo, 'Some practices and problems of Chartist democracy', in Epstein and Thompson, op. cit.
10. For similar movements in Manchester around the Penryn seat see J. Cannon, *Parliamentary Reform 1640–1832* (Cambridge 1972).
11. *Aris's Gazette*, 18 June 1827. Parkes made five visits to London to lobby MPs in favour of a transfer of seats; J. K. Buckley, *Joseph Parkes of Birmingham* (London 1926), 37–40.
12. *Aris's Gazette*, 29 Feb 1828.
13. *Birmingham Journal*, 30 Jan 1830.
14. ibid., 30 Jan 1830; see also letter of 'X', ibid., 13 Feb 1830, where same point is made.
15. At the meeting Edmonds, in his speech, asked: 'Had not the Duke of Wellington conferred the power and force of public opinion as concentrated in the Catholic Association?', ibid., 30 Jan 1830.
16. See, for example, his speech of thanks to Tennyson, the MP that had brought forward the East Retford issue, at the High Bailiff's dinner: *Aris's Gazette*, 27 Sept 1830.
17. ibid., 11 Jan 1830.
18. ibid., 1 Feb 1830.
19. The bill is analysed in Cannon, op. cit., 192–5.
20. *Birmingham Journal*, 29 May 1830. Edmonds' analysis of the failure of the 1815–20 agitation in terms of a lack of middle-class support, was strongly expressed: Edmonds now claimed that 'the remonstrances of 1,000 men with £1,000 in their pockets, were far more influential with

their present government, than the just complaints of 10,000 men not possessed of a farthing'.

21. ibid., 29 May 1830. Feeling was strong for any form of political reform, however, and a petition, submitted by the meeting, for limited reform and various currency proposals, received 25,000 signatures; *Aris's Gazette*, 24 May 1830.
22. *Birmingham Journal*, 31 July 1830.
23. ibid., 13 Nov 1830.
24. British Museum, Add. MSS 35, 148, f67–f70; quoted in D. J. Rowe (ed.), *London Radicalism: A Selection from the Papers of Francis Place* (London 1970).
25. *Birmingham Journal*, 18 Dec 1830.
26. British Museum, Add. MSS 35, 145, f77.
27. *Birmingham Journal*, 14 Mar 1831.
28. *Aris's Gazette*, 11 Apr 1831.
29. ibid., 11 Apr 1831. A number of the most vociferous opponents of radicalism in the 1815–20 period were attracted to this limited measure of reform. Theodore Price recalled in 1834 that 'I was a sincere promoter of the Reform Bill'; ibid., 29 Dec 1834.
30. Diary of S. T. Galton, 4 Apr 1831, Galton Papers, University College, London, item 30. In view of this evidence it is clear that Flick underplays Attwood's central role in the agitation at this time; his assessment of the meeting is as follows: 'In April, Attwood and several lieutenants participated in the large Warwickshire reform meeting . . . but he displayed the proper deference and made no attempt to interfere with its proceedings, having already learned that the county meetings were the preserve of the gentry and aristocracy not easily poached upon by townsmen'; Flick, op. cit., 56.
31. Althorp to Parkes, 6 Nov 1831, Parkes Papers, University College, London.
32. *Midland Representative*, 28 May 1831.
33. ibid., 1 Oct 1831.
34. ibid., 8 Oct 1831; *Aris's Gazette*, 3 Oct 1831; *Birmingham Journal*, 1 Oct 1831.
35. C. M. Wakefield, *Life of Thomas Attwood* (London 1885), 389.
36. *Birmingham Journal*, 30 Jan 1830.
37. ibid., 30 Jan 1830.
38. P. Calquhoun, *Treatise on Population, Wealth, Power and Resources of the British Empire* (London 1815), 102–28. Attwood met Calquhoun in 1818 during a visit to London and the similarity of their views must have been apparent to both. Attwood reported to his wife, 'The old man was quite delighted with me, and could hardly be prevailed upon to part with me. Of course, you will say, I thought him a very clever man, he really is so'; quoted in D. J. Moss, *Thomas Attwood: The Biography of a Radical* (unpub. D.Phil. thesis, University of Oxford 1973), 109.
39. *Birmingham Journal*, 18 Dec 1830.
40. A similar point was made by the *Manchester Guardian* in March 1830:

'As the mass of the middle classes never can have any interests adverse to the happiness and prosperity of those below them in society, the rights of the humblest order would be quite safe from violation under the protection of representatives chosen from a constituency in which that mass had a preponderance'; quoted in N. McCord, 'Some difficulties of parliamentary reform', *Historical Journal*, X:4 (1967), 378. Again we are reminded that Attwood's view was by no means unique or completely idiosyncratic.

41. *Birmingham Journal*, 30 Jan 1830.
42. *Birmingham Independent*, 3 Jan 1828.
43. *Birmingham Journal*, 30 Jan 1830.
44. ibid., 30 Jan 1830.
45. *Poor Man's Guardian*, 3 Dec 1831.
46. *Midland Representative*, 18 Feb 1832. For a similar subsumption of a wider radical programme within agitation for a more limited measure in Coventry, see P. Searby, 'Paternalism, disturbance and parliamentary reform: society and politics in Coventry 1819–1832', *International Review of Social History*, XXII:2 (1977), 210.
47. King to Duke of Wellington, 9 Nov 1831, Papers of 2nd Earl Grey (Political Unions), Department of Palaeography and Diplomatic, Durham University. The events on the continent had been carefully scrutinized at the time. In October 1830 the BPU held a public dinner to celebrate the French Revolution of that year. Local magistrates Thomas Lee and R. Shelton Mackenzie wrote to the Home Secretary on 15 Oct 1830: 'No one can ponder on the marked and loud sympathy of feeling between the English and French on this "Consummation devoutly to be wished" without feeling a moral conviction that unless a speedy change of measures takes place here, we must have something like a revolution – I use the term advisedly'; HO 52/11.
48. H. Ferguson, 'The Birmingham Political Union and the government 1831–1832', *Victorian Studies*, III (1959–60), 268–70; J. Hamburger, *James Mill and the Art of Revolution* (Connecticut 1977), 91–4.
49. M. Brock, *The Great Reform Act* (London 1973), 254; *Poor Man's Guardian*, 8 Oct 1831.
50. Buckley, op. cit., 86.
51. 'Truth' to Home Secretary, 3 Nov 1831, HO 40/29 (i).
52. *Midland Representative*, 12 Nov 1831.
53. ibid., 3 Dec 1831.
54. Broadside, n.d., Attwood Papers.
55. *Midland Representative*, 21 May 1831; *Birmingham Journal*, 26 Feb 1831.
56. *Midland Representative*, 13, 20 Aug 1831.
57. ibid., 17 Mar 1832.
58. Walters to Musgrave, 8 May 1832. *Aris's Gazette*, not an unqualified supporter of Attwood, also calculated the crowd at 200,000. Hamburger, op. cit., 132, calculates that only 90,000 could have stood at Newhall Hill. For details of meeting see also the *Birmingham Journal*, 12 May 1832; *Poor Man's Guardian*, 28 May 1832.

59. *Birmingham Journal*, 5 May 1832.
60. *Aris's Gazette*, 14 May 1832.
61. *Birmingham Journal*, 12 May 1832.
62. ibid., 12 May 1832; *Aris's Gazette*, 14 May 1832. Joseph Sturge was one of this 500.
63. W. H. Ryland (ed.), *Reminiscences of T. H. Ryland* (Birmingham 1904).
64. Arthur Hill to Ellen Hill, 10 May 1832, Hill Family Papers, Bruce Castle, Tottenham.
65. *Birmingham Journal*, 12 May 1832.
66. D. Read, *The English Provinces* (London 1964), 91; Brock, op. cit., 285.
67. British Museum, Add. MSS 27,793 f141; Buckley, op. cit., 101–4; G. Wallas, *Life of Francis Place* (London 1898), 307–18.
68. Wakefield, op. cit., 195 (de Bosco Attwood's narrative).
69. *Birmingham Journal*, 19 May 1832.
70. R. and F. Davenport Hill, *The Recorder of Birmingham: A Memoir of Matthew Davenport Hill* (London 1878), 111.
71. C. Hill (ed.), *Frederick Hill: An Autobiography of 50 Years in Times of Reform* (London 1894), 90.
72. Galton diary, 13 May 1832.
73. Walters to Musgrave, 14 May 1832. The link between the local movement and the soldiers in the town's barracks is a fairly familiar one thanks to Alexander Somerville's *Autobiography of a Working Man* (reprinted London 1967), 155–68; Walters overstated the degree of sympathy, nevertheless it is difficult to disagree with Butler's conclusion that 'Most certainly 150 troops, tinged with disaffection could not have coerced the population of Birmingham'; J. R. M. Butler, *The Passing of the Great Reform Bill* (London 1914), 422; Brock, op. cit., 306–7.
74. Wakefield, op. cit., 195.
75. *Birmingham Journal*, 19 May 1832.
76. E. P. Thompson, *The Making of the English Working Class* (London 1963; all references to 1968 edn), 898; see also E. J. Hobsbawm, *Industry and Empire* (Harmondsworth 1968), 55; Hamburger, op. cit. Rowe deplores this interpretation in his introduction to his selection from the Place papers. Of Hobsbawm's assessment he writes, 'If his were a lone voice one would be less concerned about the impact of this view on the students of history, but it is a much held view'; Rowe, op. cit.
77. Hamburger, op. cit., 51: 'The professional reformer, like the public relations man, dealt in images and in his role as a tactician reality was his concern only in so far as it was necessary to shape it to give plausibility to the image he was trying to create'; see also 252–3. Rowe takes a similar line in his introduction to *London Radicalism*, in which he suggests that Place was attempting to 'hoodwink the authorities'.
78. Hamburger, op. cit., 138.

79. ibid., 74–7.
80. C. Flick, 'Thomas Attwood, Francis Place and the agitation for British parliamentary reform', *Huntington Library Quarterly*, XXXIV:4 (Aug 1971), 361: 'the most immediately important event in the May crisis undoubtedly was the hostile vote of the House of Commons against the formation of a Tory government – a vote which occurred before the Birmingham petition was advertised or delivered'. His later work, *The Birmingham Political Union*, stresses the idea that the Union's assumed role of having pushed through the Bill was based on myth. Ferguson, op. cit., 273, argues 'the threat of insurrection was immaterial because the whole tone of the threat was transparent'. Similar points are made in: D. Fraser, 'The agitation for parliamentary reform', 45–6 in J.T. Ward (ed.), *Popular Movements c.1830–1850* (London 1970); Cannon, op. cit., 240.
81. Buckley, op. cit., 109.
82. *Birmingham Journal*, 28 July 1832.
83. ibid., 22 Sept 1832.
84. *Poor Man's Guardian*, 20 Oct 1832.
85. ibid., 3 Nov 1832.
86. ibid., 3 Nov 1832; *Birmingham Journal*, 3 Nov 1832.
87. *Poor Man's Guardian*, 3 Nov 1832.
88. Tholfsen, op. cit., 478; Flick, op. cit., 128.
89. Cambell to Home Secretary, 26 Oct 1832, HO 40/30 (1).
90. *Birmingham Journal*, 3 Nov 1832.
91. For Wade see T. H. Lloyd, 'Dr. Wade and the working class', *Midland History*, II:2 (1973).
92. *Poor Man's Guardian*, 17 Nov 1832.
93. *Aris's Gazette*, 22 Sept 1834. This disappointment is closely charted in D. J. Moss, 'A study in failure: Thomas Attwood, M.P. for Birmingham 1832–39', *Historical Journal*, XXI:3 (1978).
94. *Birmingham Journal*, 25 May 1833.
95. Hervey to General Charles Grey, May 1833, n.d., Grey Papers. Hervey adds, of the meeting, 'With the exception of Attwood and Daniel O'Connell and one or two more we were the only people dressed like gentlemen.' There has been some dispute as to the size of the meeting: see Thompson, op. cit., 909, 935–6; R. Currie and R. M. Hartwell, 'The making of the English working class?', *Economic History Review*, 2nd ser., XVIII:3 (1965). The *Birmingham Journal* calculated 250,000. Colonel Thorn, who stood by with two troops of Dragoons, estimated only 30,000 (with 20,000 males over 17); Thorn's report, 22 May 1833, HO 40/31. Hervey in his letter says: 'I have no doubt there were 120,000 persons assembled, men, women and children – with thousands of banners floating over their heads.' It was felt by reformers that the meeting was attended by more people than that of 7 May 1832; *Birmingham Journal*, 25 May 1833.
96. *Birmingham Journal*, 3 Nov 1832.
97. ibid., 22 Sept 1832.

98. *Pioneer*, 14 June 1834.
99. *Birmingham Journal*, 20 Sept 1834.
100. ibid., 7 June 1834.

5 THE EARLY CHARTIST EXPERIENCE

1. The clearest exposition of this analysis is to be found in T. R. Tholfsen, 'The Chartist crisis in Birmingham', *International Review of Social History*, III (1958). The groundwork for this approach, with its emphasis on O'Connor and 'physical force' as the major disruptive influence on an otherwise unified BPU, was undoubtedly laid by R. G. Gammage with the publication in 1854 of his *History of the Chartist Movement* (London 1969; reprint of 1894 edn), 83–4, 107–35. Mark Hovell developed this analysis as part of a polemic against O'Connor in *The Chartist Movement*, first published in 1918. See also J. West, *A History of the Chartist Movement* (London 1920), 53–5, 101–3, 135–8; F. F. Rosenblatt, *The Chartist Movement in its Social and Economic Aspects* (Haarlem 1967; reprint of 1916 edn), 153–9; J. T. Ward, *Chartism* (London 1973), 79–82, 109–42; D. Read, *The English Provinces* (London 1964), 113–22; C. Gill, *History of Birmingham* I (Oxford 1952), 240–53; C. Flick, *The Birmingham Political Union and the Movements for Reform in Britain 1830–1839* (Folkestone 1978).
2. D. Fraser, 'The fruits of reform: Leeds in the 1830s', *Northern History*, VII (1972), 89.
3. *Aris's Gazette*, 11 Apr, 11 May 1835.
4. *Birmingham Journal*, 17 Jan 1835.
5. ibid., 21 Feb 1835.
6. *Aris's Gazette*, 12 Jan 1835.
7. C. R. Dod, *Electoral Facts From 1832 to 1853 Impartially Stated* (London 1833; reprinted 1972), 26–7.
8. As in 1835, the Tory candidate on this occasion was Spooner. Joseph Sturge also stood at this election, thus the liberal vote was split along with an absolute increase in Tory votes cast.
9. Foster's work on Oldham demonstrates the wide variety of pressures that electors could be subjected to by non-electors; J. Foster, *Class Struggle and the Industrial Revolution: Early Industrial Capitalism in Three English Towns* (London 1977), 52–9. On the continued importance of popular pressure throughout the period and beyond, see N. Gash, *Politics in the Age of Peel* (London 1969), 137–53; D. Richter, 'The role of mob riot in Victorian elections 1865–1885', *Victorian Studies*, XV:1 (Sept 1971).
10. *Aris's Gazette*, 12 Jan 1835.
11. *BPP, Report from the Select Committee on Bribery at Elections* (547) viii, 1835, Q4108; see also evidence of Joseph Parkes, Q1623.
12. Journal of T. Finigan, 25 July 1837. Finigan adds: 'I also called into a shoemakers, a front house in Litchfield Street, the man was

very busy in his shop, I think electioneering.'
13. *Aris's Gazette*, 12 Jan 1835.
14. *Birmingham Journal*, 22 July 1837.
15. See p. 198.
16. The increase in the Tory vote was all the more remarkable since the candidate was an outsider, Sir Charles Wetherell.
17. *Northern Star*, 25 Jan 1840. Muntz was one of the BPU delegates to the Chartist Convention, who resigned in March 1839.
18. *Birmingham Journal*, 10 July 1841. Voting was as follows: Muntz 2,175; Scholefield 1,963; Spooner 1,825.
19. ibid., 10 July 1841.
20. Voting was as follows: Spooner 2,095; William Scholefield 1,735; Joseph Sturge 346.
21. *Birmingham Journal*, 4 Nov 1837. On the relationship between national and local politics, see N. Edsall, 'Varieties of radicalism: Attwood, Cobden and the local politics of municipal incorporation', *Historical Journal* XVI:1 (1973).
22. *Birmingham Journal*, 11 Mar 1837.
23. ibid., 22 Apr 1837. The Midland Reform Association was formed in February 1835 with a commitment to household suffrage, vote by ballot, and 'shorter parliaments'; ibid., 7 Mar 1835. By 1836 it was clear that such an association with such a programme would never achieve a mass base. At a Reform Association dinner in November 1836, addressed by all the old BPU leaders, William Boultbee said, 'I have spared no pains to establish the Reform Association, I do not expect that its meetings will, at present, be attended by 500 or 600 of the working people, nor do I know that it would be much use were it to happen'; ibid., 12 Nov 1836.
24. ibid., 27 May 1837.
25. ibid., 22 Apr 1837.
26. *Aris's Gazette*, 1 Dec 1834.
27. ibid., 24 Aug 1835.
28. *Birmingham Journal*, 17 June 1837.
29. ibid., 24 June 1837.
30. *Aris's Gazette*, 13 Aug 1837.
31. *Birmingham Journal*, 1 July 1837.
32. ibid., 7 Oct 1837.
33. ibid., 11 Nov 1837.
34. ibid., 11 Nov 1837.
35. ibid., 23 Dec 1837.
36. ibid., 27 Jan 1838.
37. ibid., 4 Nov 1837.
38. Gill, op. cit., 223; J. T. Bunce, *A History of the Corporation of Birmingham* (Birmingham 1878), 131.
39. Gill, op. cit., 224–5; Bunce, op. cit., 131.
40. F. J. Ledsam to Clerk of Privy Council, 6 Feb 1838: 'I would also add that the first petition, although it has 4,394 signatures, contains the names of only 1,349 persons who are assessed to the poor,

leaving 3,045 who pay no rates whatever. On the other hand, that which I had the honour to present, although not so numerously signed contained a larger number assessed to the poor.' Privy Council Papers (PC) 1/1300, Correspondence relating to Incorporation.

41. Bunce, op. cit., 131.
42. PC 1/1300.
43. Dawson to Privy Council, 20 Sept 1838, PC 1/1300.
44. *Birmingham Journal*, 23 Dec 1837.
45. ibid., 20 Jan 1838.
46. ibid., 20 Jan 1838.
47. ibid., 20 Jan 1838.
48. J. Epstein, 'Feargus O'Connor and the English working class radical movement 1832–1841, a study in national Chartist leadership' (unpub. Ph.D. thesis, University of Birmingham 1977), 201–4. The point is developed in J. Epstein, *The Lion of Freedom and the Chartist Movement 1832–1842* (London 1982), 108.
49. ibid.; *Northern Star*, 28 July 1838.
50. Epstein, op. cit., 109; *Northern Star*, 18 Aug 1838.
51. Flick, for example, claims: 'The Birmingham union, nevertheless, had a larger part in the development of Chartism than has been acknowledged. The council of the union were principally instrumental in organizing the movement for democracy in the late 1830s'; Flick, op. cit., 15.
52. *Birmingham Journal*, 23 Dec 1837.
53. ibid., 27 May 1837 (my italics).
54. ibid., 23 Feb 1839. This was a common middle-class position. The *Manchester Guardian*, in November 1837, claimed that the suffrage was not a right, 'it is merely an expedient for obtaining good government; that and not the franchise it is to which the public have a right'; quoted in D. Read, 'Chartism in Manchester', in A. Briggs, *Chartist Studies* (London 1959), 38.
55. See, for example, the analysis of James Mill's view on the applicability of universal suffrage to an hierarchical society as presented in D. C. Moore, 'Political morality in mid-nineteenth century England: concepts, norms, violations', *Victorian Studies*, XIII:1 (Sept 1969).
56. *Birmingham Journal*, 20 Jan 1838.
57. Attwood to wife, 9 June 1837, Attwood Papers.
58. *Birmingham Journal*, 17 July 1841.
59. ibid., 17 July 1841.
60. Hovell, op. cit., 107.
61. The *Star* estimated the crowd at 300,000; *Northern Star*, 11 Aug 1838.
62. *Birmingham Journal*, 11 Aug 1838.
63. ibid., 17 Nov 1838; *Northern Star*, 17 Nov 1838.
64. *Birmingham Journal*, 6 Apr 1839.
65. ibid., 24 Apr 1837.
66. ibid., 11 Aug 1838.
67. ibid., 6 Apr 1839.

68. *Northern Star*, 6 Apr 1839.
69. E. P. Thompson, *The Making of the English Working Class* (London 1963; all references to 1968 edn), 910.
70. Bunce, op. cit., 154–60.
71. Douglas became Registrar of the Mayor's Court, and Edmonds was appointed Clerk of the Peace.
72. See the attack on O'Connor's northern campaign, *Birmingham Journal*, 20 Oct, 3, 10 Nov 1838. On 13 November and 20 November O'Connor confronted the BPU Council and accused them of misrepresentation; ibid., 17, 24 Nov 1838. Salt and O'Connor reached an apparently amicable agreement at a town hall meeting on 26 November; ibid., 1 Dec 1838. In December the *Northern Star* carried an address, from the Manchester Political Union, to the working classes in Birmingham urging them to take matters into their own hands: 'We have no rich men leading or drawing us', it asserted, 'but in the true democratic spirit manage our own affairs'; *Northern Star*, 22 Dec 1838. See also K. Judge, 'Early Chartist organisation and the Convention of 1839', *International Review of Social History*, XX:3 (1975), 371–4.
73. *Birmingham Journal*, 19 Jan 1839.
74. ibid., 1 Dec 1838, 26 Jan 1839.
75. ibid., 23 Feb 1839.
76. ibid., 9 Mar 1839.
77. ibid., 16, 23, 30 Mar 1839.
78. ibid., 23 Mar 1839.
79. ibid., 30 Mar 1839.
80. ibid., 13 Apr, 25 May 1839.
81. ibid., 27 Apr 1839.
82. Tholfsen, op. cit., 465–9; Gill, op. cit., 244–5; Flick, op. cit., 128.
83. British Museum, Add. MSS 34,245.
84. See Chapter 2, p. 90.
85. *Birmingham Journal*, 6 Apr 1839.
86. E. P. Hennock, *Fit and Proper Persons* (London 1973), 10–14.
87. *Northern Star*, 13 Apr 1839; see also the speech of John Powell at Holloway Head, *Birmingham Journal*, 6 Apr 1839.
88. *Birmingham Journal*, 11 May 1839. The three ex-BPU magistrates were William Scholefield, P. H. Muntz, and C. C. Scholefield.
89. ibid., 18 May 1839.
90. ibid., 22, 29 June 1839.
91. *Report of the Committee Appointed by the Town Council, September 3, 1839, to Investigate the Causes of the Late Riots (Birmingham 1840). BPP, Copy of Mr. Dundas Report and the Evidence Taken on the Investigation Held at Birmingham Respecting the Riots on 15 July 1839, and of the Letter of W. C. Alston Esq. (Magistrate) to Lord John Russell, dated 10 July 1839. House of Lords Sessional Papers, Accounts and Papers (xiii), 1840.* Both investigations were reported fully in the local press, where evidence of witnesses was (in the case of the town council's report) given more fully; *Birmingham Journal*, 14, 21, 28 Sept, 5, 12 Oct 1839.

92. Tholfsen, op. cit., 465: 'Birmingham was soon to have its first and last experience with the politics of class struggle'; W. B. Stephens (ed.), *The City of Birmingham* (*A History of the County of Warwick* vol. ii, Victorian County History: London 1964) 'The exceptional pattern of violence of 1839 was never repeated in Birmingham during the 1840s. Instead the more familiar pattern of close association between middle classes and working classes was re-established.'
93. Tholfsen's account, for example, gives detail only on the events of 4 July, arguing that the disturbance of 15 July 'was the work of a mob of boys who had no connection with the Chartist leaders'; Tholfsen, op. cit., 472.
94. 'The Queen against John Collins', in J. MacDonell (ed.), *Reports of State Trials, New Series*, vol. iii, 1831–1840 (London 1891), 1153–4.
95. ibid., 1163 (evidence of George Martin); *Birmingham Journal*, 3 Aug 1839.
96. *Report of Committee Appointed by Town Council*, 16.
97. ibid., 19–20.
98. *Birmingham Journal*, 3 Aug 1839; MacDonell (ed.), *Reports of State Trials*, 1163–5.
99. MacDonell (ed.), *Reports of State Trials*, 1163–5.
100. Evidence of Thomas Lucas to town council investigation, *Birmingham Journal*, 14 Sept 1839.
101. Evidence of J.K. Booth, ibid., 10 Aug 1839; MacDonell (ed.), *Reports of State Trials*, 1159.
102. Fussell to town council investigation, *Birmingham Journal*, 21 Sept 1839.
103. ibid., 6 July 1839; Report of Inspector May to Home Office, 5 July 1839: 'nine prisoners were apprehended last night among whom was Dr. Taylor their principal leader'; HO 40/50. Charged with riotous assembly Taylor was later acquitted.
104. Evidence of William Lovett, 'The Queen against Lovett', in MacDonell (ed.), *Reports of State Trials*, 1182–3; *Birmingham Journal*, 10 Aug 1839.
105. Chance to Home Office, 4 July 1839, HO 40/52; Estimate of cost of London police, HO 45/52; W. Scholefield to Home Office, 5 July 1839, HO 40/50.
106. *Birmingham Journal*, 13 July 1839.
107. ibid., 13 July 1839.
108. ibid., 13 July 1839.
109. List of police duties, Metropolitan Police Papers 2/61.
110. ibid. Inspector May's report to the Home Office for Monday 8 July indicated that the town was quiet up until 8.30 in the evening, when a meeting in the Bull Ring was dispersed, and the streets cleared by the police and the military; HO 40/50. The *Journal* reported of this action: 'The policemen used very little discrimination. Several most orderly and inoffensive inhabitants fell beneath their staffs, with severely bruised heads and bodies, and in some cases,

it is said, with fractured limbs'; *Birmingham Journal*, 13 July 1839.

111. *Birmingham Journal*, 13 July 1839. Harney was subsequently acquitted at Warwickshire Assizes in August. A carpenter from Moor Street, John Wallace Wilson, gave evidence that Harney had referred to a 'biscuit' and not a 'musket'; Treasury Solicitors' Papers 11/142/390. See also A. R. Schoyen, *The Chartist Challenge: A Portrait of George Julian Harney* (London 1958), 73–6.
112. HO 40/50.
113. Evidence of Colonel Chatterton, *Dundas Investigation*, 22–9; *Birmingham Journal*, 21 Sept 1839.
114. 'Statement of Mr. May respecting the riot at Birmingham on Monday evening 15 July 1839'; Metropolitan Police Papers 2/61.
115. Evidence of G. Whateley, special constable, *Dundas Investigation*, 29; *Report of Committee Appointed by Town Council*, 32–3.
116. Evidence of Alfred Webb, 'The Queen against Howell and others', in MacDonell (ed.), *Reports of State Trials*, 1111.
117. Evidence of Thomas Baker, law stationer to town council investigation, *Birmingham Journal*, 14 Sept 1839; *Report of Committee Appointed by Town Council*, 37–9.
118. Evidence of James Osborn, *Dundas Investigation*; *Birmingham Journal*, 21 Sept 1839.
119. The town council's investigation later said of police conduct in the days following 4 July: 'These men, inflamed with resentment at the treatment which they had experienced, seem to have acted as though something like martial law was in force, — all civil rights utterly at an end, - and the persons, almost the lives, of the working people of this town placed at their mercy'; *Report of Committee Appointed by Town Council*, 25–8.
120. Statement of Mr. May, Metropolitan Police Papers 2/61.
121. Evidence of George Redfern, *Dundas Investigation*; *Birmingham Journal*, 21 Sept 1839.
122. Statement of Mr. May, Metropolitan Police Papers 2/61.
123. Evidence of May, *Dundas Investigation*, 75; Metropolitan Police Papers 2/61.
124. Evidence of Thomas Mateley to town council investigation, *Birmingham Journal*, 5 Oct 1839; evidence of Thomas Baker to town council investigation, *Birmingham Journal*, 14 Sept 1839.
125. Evidence of Enos Edwards, 'The Queen against Howell and others', in MacDonell (ed.), *Reports of State Trials*, 1104–7.
126. *Birmingham Journal*, 14 Sept 1839.
127. Evidence of George Redfern, *Dundas Investigation*; *Birmingham Journal*, 21 Sept 1839.
128. Evidence of Chatterton, *Dundas Investigation*, 22–9.
129. Evidence of Captain Moorsam to town council investigation, *Birmingham Journal*, 14, 21 Sept 1839.
130. Scholefield to Home Office, 16 July 1839, HO 40/50.
131. May to Home Office, 16 July 1839, HO 40/50.
132. *Birmingham Journal*, 27 July 1839. P. H. Muntz reported to the

Home Office that 'the fire last night was the work of an incendiary'; Muntz to Home Office, 23 July 1839, HO 40/50. May, perhaps anxious not to extend his sojourn to Birmingham, reported it as an accident; May to Home Office, 23 July 1839, HO 40/50.

133. *Birmingham Journal*, 10 Aug 1839.
134. Tholfsen, op. cit., 471.
135. Ward, op. cit., 126.
136. Tholfsen, op. cit., 471.
137. *Birmingham Journal*, 13 July 1839.
138. *Pilot*, 26 Oct 1844.
139. *Aris's Gazette*, 22 Sept 1834.
140. *Birmingham Journal*, 30 Nov 1839.
141. See p. 90.
142. See, for example, the evidence of Thomas Lucas, surveyor, *Birmingham Journal*, 14 Sept 1839; Thomas Mateley, ibid., 5 Oct 1839. Dundas, as a result of his investigation, acknowledged the essentially peaceful nature of the meetings: 'These meetings, although calculated to alarm the peaceable inhabitants of the place, for the most part passed off quietly'; *Dundas Investigation*, 3.
143. Evidence of Chatterton, *Dundas Investigation*, 22–9; *Birmingham Journal*, 21 Sept 1839.
144. Evidence of Captain Moorsam to town council investigation, *Birmingham Journal*, 14 Sept 1839; Scholefield to Home Office, 11 May 1839, HO 40/50.
145. Moorsam to town council investigation, *Birmingham Journal*, 14 Sept 1839.
146. Fussell to town council investigation, ibid., 21 Sept 1839.
147. May to Home Office, 5 July 1839, HO 40/50. The indictment against John Collins put the figure at an improbable 10,000; MacDonell (ed.), *Reports of State Trials*, 1152.
148. ibid.
149. *Report of Committee Appointed by Town Council*, 18.
150. MacDonell (ed.), *Reports of State Trials*, 1154–5.
151. W. Scholefield to Home Office, 9 May 1839, HO 40/50.
152. *Birmingham Journal*, 11 May 1839.
153. W. Scholefield to Home Office, 11 May 1839, HO 40/50.
154. W. Scholefield to Home Office, 13 May 1839, HO 40/50.
155. J. Scholefield to Home Office, 14 May 1839, HO 40/50.
156. *Birmingham Journal*, 6 July 1839.
157. W. Scholefield to Home Office, 13 May 1839, HO 40/50.
158. *Birmingham Journal*, 30 Nov 1839.
159. Ward, op. cit., 127; Hovell, op. cit., 158.
160. *Birmingham Journal*, 6 July 1839.
161. HO 20/10.
162. MacDonell (ed.), *Reports of State Trials*, 1125.
163. May to Home Office, 7 July 1839, HO 40/50.
164. Evidence of Thomas Mateley to town council investigation, *Birmingham Journal*, 5 Oct 1839.

165. This list has been compiled from the reports of the disturbances and trials as given in the *Birmingham Journal* for July and August 1839, MacDonell (ed.), *Reports of State Trials*, the two official investigations which followed the riots (full references for which may be found on p. 263), the calendar of Warwickshire Summer Assizes 1839 (Warwick Record Office, QS.26/1), and *BPP, Returns From Each Gaol and House of Correction in the United Kingdom of the Name and Designation of Every Person Confined for Charges of Printing and Publishing Seditious or Blasphemous Libels. Accounts and Papers 1840* (600), xxxviii.
166. MacDonell (ed.), *Reports of State Trials*, 1092.
167. British Museum, Add. MSS 34,245.
168. MacDonell (ed.), *Reports of State Trials*, 1093.
169. Earl of Benborough (ed.), *Lady Charlotte Guest, Extracts from her Journal 1833–1852* (London 1950), 94.
170. C. Godfrey, 'The Chartist prisoners 1839–41', *International Review of Social History*, XXIV:2 (1979), 189.
171. *Birmingham Journal*, 17 Aug 1839.
172. James to Home Office, 30 May 1843, HO 45/432.
173. These met regularly at the Association's rooms in Freeman Street and at Bell's Coffee House; Ship Inn, Steelhouse Lane; Domestic Coffee House, Henrietta St; Parkes' Temperance Coffee House, Upper Windsor St; Fox Inn, Swallow St; *Northern Star*, 13 Mar, 2, 23 Oct, 6 Nov. In May 1842 a women's branch was formed and a shoemakers' branch began meeting at the Britannia Inn, Peck Lane. During the first half of 1842 further rooms opened in Aston St, Hill St (Washington Chartists), and at the Black Horse, Prospect Row; ibid., 26 Feb, 7, 14 May, 30 July. The extent of this activity is much underestimated by Tholfsen, who emphasizes the importance of Christian Chartism; Tholfsen, op. cit., 474–80.
174. *Northern Star*, 1 Aug 1840; *Birmingham Journal*, 1 Aug 1840; *Northern Star*, 25 Sept 1841.
175. *Birmingham Journal*, 17 May 1842.
176. HO 40/50; *Birmingham Journal*, 30 Nov 1839; *Northern Star*, 2 Jan 1841.
177. J. Epstein, 'Some organisational and cultural aspects of the Chartist movement in Nottingham', in J. Epstein and D. Thompson, *The Chartist Experience* (London 1982).
178. Journal of W. Jackson, 29 Nov 1844, Carrs Lane Missionary Society.
179. *Northern Star*, 22 Jan 1842. Lindon was a member of the National Chartist Association and elected to the General Council in 1843; ibid., 21 Jan 1843.
180. *Birmingham Journal*, 13 Mar 1841.
181. *Nonconformist*, 6 Oct 1841.
182. *Birmingham Journal*, Mar 1842.
183. Hovell, op. cit., 264; Ward, op. cit., 166.
184. *Birmingham Journal*, 13 May 1841.

185. ibid., 19 Aug 1843.
186. ibid., 17 Oct 1840.
187. 'Address to the People of Birmingham', 8 Aug 1843, Attwood Papers.
188. *Birmingham Journal*, 7 Oct 1843. The movement appears to have dissolved after this.

CONCLUSION

1. *Report of the Commissioner Appointed to Inquire into the Condition of the Framework Knitters*, Appendix to Report, pt 1, Leicestershire, xv (1845).

Index